Windows Vista Cleanup and Maintenance for SENIORS

Studio Visual Steps

Windows Vista
Cleanup and Maintenance
for SENIORS

*Use the built-in cleanup and optimalization
utilities available in Windows Vista*

www.visualsteps.nl

© 2009 Visual Steps

This book has been written using the Visual Steps™ method.

With the assistance of Henk Mol.

Cover design by Studio Willemien Haagsma bNO.

Lay out and editing by Jolanda Ligthart, Rilana Groot and Mara Kok.

Translated by Irene Venditti, *i-write* translation services and
Chris Hollingsworth, *1ˢᵗ Resources*.

Editor in chief: Ria Beentjes.

First printing: May 2009
ISBN 978 90 5905 036 5

Source:
Some of the definitions, descriptions and computer terminology in this book have been derived from the *Windows Help and Support*.

Would you like additional information?
www.visualsteps.com

Do you have any questions or suggestions?
E-mail: info@visualsteps.com

Website accompanying this book:
www.visualsteps.com/vistacleanup

Subscribe to the free Visual Steps Newsletter:
www.visualsteps.com/newsletter

Table of Contents

Foreword

A computer, just like a car, needs regular 'tune ups'. If you do an overall cleanup *Windows Vista* will not only work faster, it will be more stable and efficient as well. More importantly, it will save you a lot of time and eliminate finger-pounding frustration!

So if regular maintenance can enhance the performance of *Windows Vista,* how can you do this systematically? In this hands-on book the maintenance of *Vista* and the hard disk cleanup is thoroughly explained to you step by step. In addition, you will learn about frequently occurring problems that may arise with the hardware and software on your computer.
You will be able to execute all actions directly on your own computer and you will see the results instantly! Your computer will run like clockwork once again.

We wish you good luck and fun too, cleaning up your computer!

Henk Mol
Studio Visual Steps

P.S. Your comments and suggestions are always welcome.
Our e-mail address is: info@visualsteps.com

Newsletter

All Visual Steps books follow the same methodology: clear and concise step by step instructions with screen shots to demonstrate each task.
A complete list of all our books can be found on **www.visualsteps.com**
You can also sign up to receive our **free Visual Steps Newsletter**.

In this Newsletter you will receive periodic information by e-mail regarding:
- the latest titles and previously released books;
- special offers, supplemental chapters, tips and free informative booklets.
Also our Newsletter subscribers may download any of the documents listed on the web pages **www.visualsteps.com/info_downloads** and
www.visualsteps.com/tips

If you subscribe to our newsletter, be assured that we will never use your e-mail address for any purpose other than sending you the information as previously described. We will not share this address with any third-party.
Each newsletter also contains a one-click link to unsubscribe.

Introduction to Visual Steps™

The Visual Steps handbooks and manuals are the best instructional materials available for learning how to work with computers. Nowhere else can you find better support for getting to know the computer, the Internet, *Windows* and related software programs.

Properties of the Visual Steps books:
- **Comprehensible contents**
  Addresses the needs of the beginner or intermediate computer user for a manual written in simple, straight-forward language.
- **Clear structure**
  Precise, easy to follow instructions. The material is broken down into small enough segments to allow for easy absorption.
- **Screen shots of every step**
  Quickly compare what you see on your screen with the screen shots in the book. Pointers and tips guide you when new windows are opened so you always know what to do next.
- **Get started right away**
  All you have to do is turn on your computer, place the book next to your keyboard and begin at once.

In short, I believe these manuals will be excellent guides for you.

Dr. H. van der Meij
Faculty of Applied Education, Department of Instruction Technology, University of Twente, the Netherlands

What You Will Need

In order to work through this book, you will need the following things:

The primary requirement for working with this book is having the US version of *Windows Vista Home Premium*, *Windows Vista Ultimate* or *Windows Vista Home Basic* installed on your computer.

You can check this yourself by switching on your computer and looking at the opening screen.

Network and Internet
View network status and tasks
Set up file sharing

A functioning **Internet connection** is needed for the chapters about the Internet.

How to Use This Book

This book has been written using the Visual Steps™ method. You can work through this book independently at your own pace.

In this Visual Steps™ book you will see various icons. This is what they mean:

Actions
These icons indicate an action to be carried out:

🖱	The mouse icon means you should do something with the mouse.
⌨	The keyboard icon means you should type something on the keyboard.
☞	The hand icon means you should do something else, for example insert a CD-ROM in the computer. It is also used to remind you of something you learned before.

Help

These icons indicate that extra help is available:

 The arrow icon warns you about something.

 The bandage icon will help you if something has gone wrong.

 Have you forgotten how to do something? The number next to the footsteps tells you where to look it up at the end of the book in the appendix *How Do I Do That Again?*

In separate boxes you find tips or additional, background information.

Extra information

Information boxes are denoted by these icons:

 The book icon gives you extra background information that you can read at your convenience. This extra information is not necessary for working through the book.

 The light bulb icon indicates an extra tip for using the program.

How This Book Is Organized

This book is set up in such a way that you do not necessarily have to work through it from beginning to end. We advise you to read the table of contents to see which subjects interest you.

Some chapters deal with specific problems, for instance troubleshooting in the case of hardware problems. If you have not encountered these problems, you can skip the actions and exercises described in these chapters. It is still worthwhile to read each chapter to improve your knowledge about your computer in general and about *Vista* in particular.

Prior Computer Experience

This book has been written for those who have achieved the computer skills covered in the previous volumes of *Windows Vista for Seniors*. If you have worked through these books, you have the basic skills necessary to complete this book successfully:

Windows Vista for SENIORS
Studio Visual Steps
ISBN 978 90 5905 274 1

More Windows Vista for SENIORS
Studio Visual Steps
ISBN 978 90 5905 055 6

The Website That Accompanies This Book

This book is accompanied by a website with current information. The web address is **www.visualsteps.com/vistacleanup**. In the event of corrections or changes to the *Windows Vista* edition described in this book, you will find all the information on this website.

The Screen Shots

The screen shots in this book were made to indicate which button, folder, file or hyperlink on your screen you need to click. In the instruction text (in **bold** letters) you will see a small image of the item you need to click. The black line will point you to the right place on your screen.

The small screen shots that are printed in this book are not meant to be completely legible all the time. This is not necessary, as you will see these images on your own computer screen in real size and fully legible.

Here you see an example of an instruction text and a screen shot. The black line indicates where to find this item on your own computer screen:

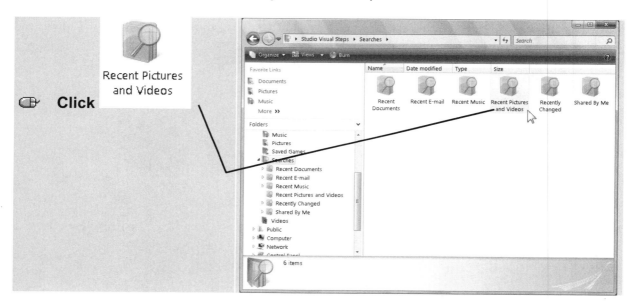

Sometimes the screen shot shows only a portion of a window. Here is an example:

It really will **not be necessary** for you to read all the information in the screen shots in this book. Always use the screen shots in combination with the image you see on your own computer screen.

Test Your Knowledge

When you have finished reading this book, you can test your knowledge by visiting our website **www.ccforseniors.com** and doing one of the free tests.
These multiple choice tests will show you how thorough your knowledge of your computer is.

If you pass the test, you will receive your **free Computer Certificate** by e-mail.
There are **no costs** involved for taking part in these tests. The test website is a free service provided by Visual Steps.

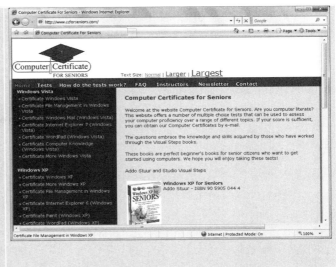

For Teachers

A Visual Steps book is designed as a self-study guide. It is also well suited for use in a group or a classroom setting. For this purpose, we offer some free teacher's manuals containing information about how to prepare for the course (including didactic teaching methods) and testing materials. You can download this teacher's manuals (PDF files) from the website: **www.visualsteps.com/instructor**

The Visual Steps Series for Seniors

The Visual Steps publishing company has issued a complete series of books about *Windows Vista,* especially for seniors.

Would you like to expand and deepen your knowledge? Then you can continue with the other books of Visual Steps:

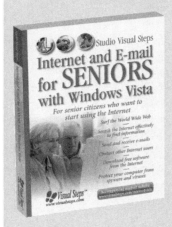  

Internet and E-mail for SENIORS with Windows Vista
Studio Visual Steps
ISBN 978 90 5905 284 0

Photos, Video and Music with Windows Vista for SENIORS
Studio Visual Steps
ISBN 978 90 5905 065 5

Interesting Online Applications for SENIORS
Studio Visual Steps
ISBN 978 90 5905 285 7

Visual Steps has also published books on various other computer topics, such as photo editing.

More information about other Visual Steps books, including the complete table of contents and sample chapters, can be found on the website **www.visualsteps.com**.

Do you have a question regarding a certain subject or book, or would you like additional information?
Then send an e-mail to info@visualsteps.com

1. Getting to Know Your Computer

Why are computers so different from one another? Some seem better suited for heavy duty applications while others are good at 3D gaming or video editing. Even if two computers use exactly the same processor, they may be more suited for different kinds of programs. The difference is determined by the number of components inside the computer. In this chapter you will learn more about the inner workings of your computer. You will discover which components make up your computer, and how fast these components can perform. Based on this information you can find out whether your computer is suitable for the programs you want to use and what sort of problems may arise.

If necessary, you may want to modify your computer, for example by adding internal memory, changing the graphics card or installing a faster hard disk, also called a hard disk drive or hard drive. You can even install a speedier processor. If you do this, however, bear in mind that some of the other components of your computer may not be able to keep up with a faster processor.

You will also learn how to check your computer's *performance score* and discover that the overall speed of your computer is determined by its slowest component.

In this chapter you will learn how to:

- view basic information about your computer system;
- find out what the *System* and *Task Manager* windows are all about;
- check which programs, processes and services are running on your computer;
- get information about the network usage of your computer;
- check the performance of your computer's processor and memory;
- use the reliability and performance monitor;
- find out your computer's performance score;
- use the performance score to decide whether your computer is suitable for the tasks you want to perform;
- find out how the processor allocates its time;
- find out how large the paging file is.

⇨ **Please note:**

The screen shots have been made on a computer using *Windows Vista Home Premium*. If you are using a different edition of *Vista,* the windows that appear on your own computer may be slightly different.

1.1 Basic Information about Your Computer System

Your computer's performance is determined by several different elements. The processor and the computer's *internal memory* or *RAM* (*Random Access Memory*) are very important components. This is how you can view these components:

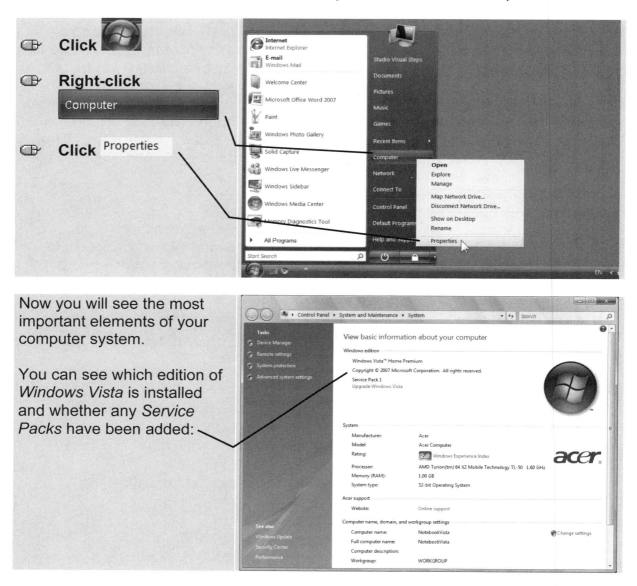

Now you will see the most important elements of your computer system.

You can see which edition of *Windows Vista* is installed and whether any *Service Packs* have been added:

Once *Windows Vista* was installed on your computer, additional software programs and several enhancements of the *Vista* program may have been added. These programs are all issued by *Microsoft* and are called *updates*. If you have an Internet connection and have activated the feature *Install updates automatically*, these updates will be installed automatically. Major updates are called *Service Packs*.

Here you see the make and model of your computer:

This is the speed score:

Read more about this in *paragraph 1.6 The Performance Index*.

The make and model of the processor:

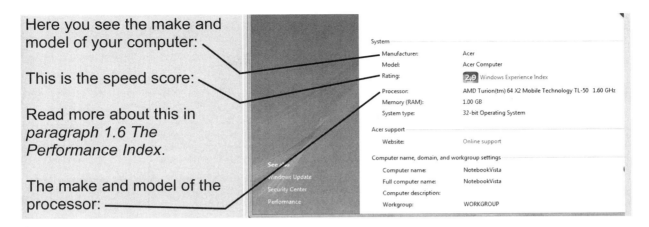

The processor is the heart of your computer. Every task you perform on your computer is routed through the processor. State-of-the-art processors today are capable of enormous speeds: millions of actions per second can be performed. This speed is measured in megahertz (MHz) or gigahertz (GHz). The higher the number, the faster the processor is, and so the computer.

The RAM memory:

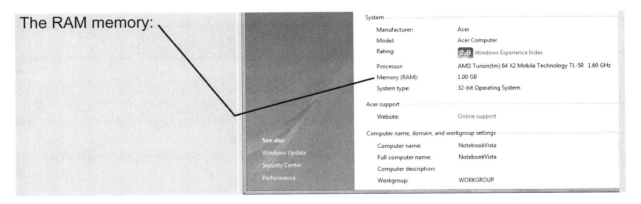

The RAM memory of the computer is the internal memory, also called the system memory. While you are using *Windows Vista,* the programs you use and the documents you work with are stored in this RAM memory. This memory is much faster than your hard disk. Before you switch off or restart your computer, you need to save your work first, because the RAM memory only stores data while the computer is switched on. The size of the RAM memory is measured in megabytes (MB) or gigabytes (GB).

 Tip

Work faster with a larger RAM memory
If you have a larger RAM memory, the computer will not have to retrieve data from the hard disk as often. Your computer will perform its tasks faster. Enlarging the RAM memory is a simple and inexpensive way of enhancing your computer's performance.

In *Windows Vista* System type: you will see a 32-bit or a 64-bit operating system:

In the *Background Information* at the end of this chapter you can read more about the different operating systems.

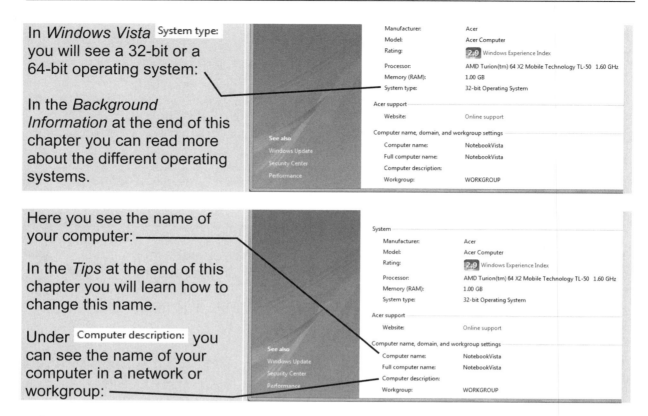

Here you see the name of your computer:

In the *Tips* at the end of this chapter you will learn how to change this name.

Under Computer description: you can see the name of your computer in a network or workgroup:

⇨ **Please note:**

A *Windows Vista Home Basic* computer cannot be a member of a workgroup.

🖱 **Drag the scroll bar down**

Here you can see whether your copy of *Windows Vista* has been activated by *Microsoft*:

A copy that has not yet been activated can only be used for a short period of time.

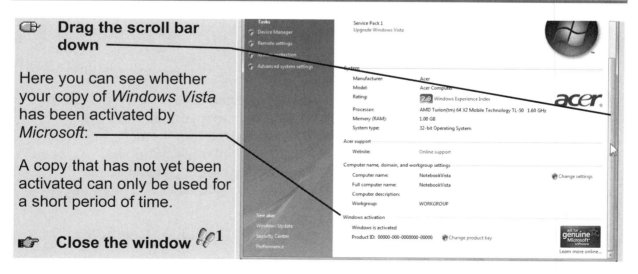

☞ **Close the window** 🖐1

⇨ **Please note:**

Never change the product ID number yourself. A different product ID number will have to be activated all over again and if you do not have the correct activation code *Windows Vista* will no longer function properly.

1.2 System Information

A computer is comprised of a large number of different components. In the *System Information* window you can find all the relevant information about your computer system. In this section you will just take a look at the information. In the following chapters you will learn how to change several settings. This is how you open the *System Information* window:

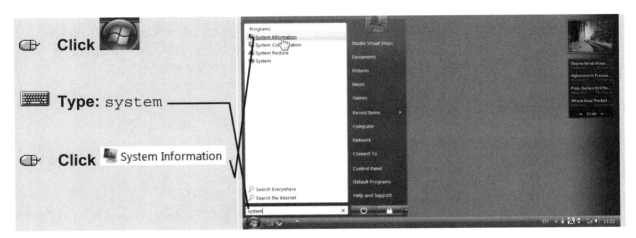

Click

Type: system

Click System Information

➡ **Please note:**

In the following screen shots you will see several windows which contain a lot of technical information. Most of it will be very clear and understandable to technicians, but the average computer user will have some difficulty with it. That is not a problem. Just take a look at the information, you do not need to understand everything. But if you are ever in the situation where you need to explain your computer problems to someone, for example, a help desk technician, it will be useful to know where to find this information.

Here you see a lot of information about your computer:

You already viewed some of this information in the previous section.

Click ⊞ next to Hardware Resources

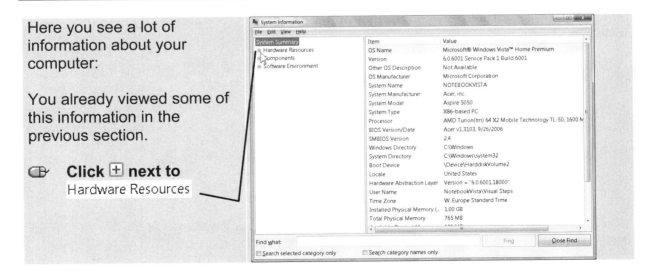

The *System Information* window contains detailed information about your hardware configuration, your computer components, software programs and the operating system.

In the left pane of the window you see the different categories and in the right pane you see the details of each category. The categories are:
- *System Summary*: general information about the computer and its operating system, such as the name and manufacturer of the computer, the BIOS type (Basic Input/Output System) and the amount of memory installed.
- *Hardware Resources*: advanced details about the computer hardware. This information is important to IT professionals.
- *Components*: information about disk drives, sound devices, modems and other components installed on your computer.
- *Software Environment*: information on operating systems, network connections and other details about the software.

If you are looking for specific information in the *System Information* window, you can type a keyword in the *Find what* Search box at the bottom of the window. For example, if you are looking for the *IP address* (Internet Protocol) of your computer, you type *IP address* in the box next to Find what: and then click Find .

Source: Windows Help and Support

For example, let us take a look at the *IRQs* (*Interrupt Request*). These are the alarm sounds a device uses when it needs attention from the processor. This could be a printer that has run out of paper, for example. It is important that two similar devices do not use the same IRQ, because then the processor will not be able to tell which device needs its attention. This may lead to devices malfunctioning. This is how you view the IRQs:

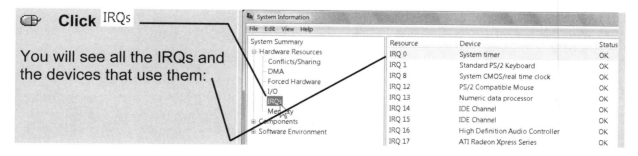

☞ **Click** IRQs

You will see all the IRQs and the devices that use them:

Usually, IRQs are set up during the installation of the hardware devices. Do not change an IRQ, unless the device does not work properly.

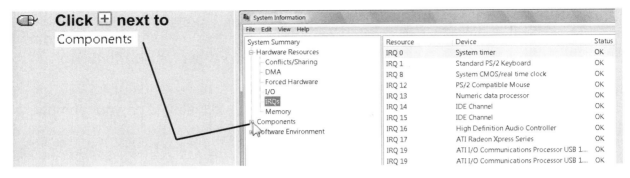

Click ⊞ **next to** `Components`

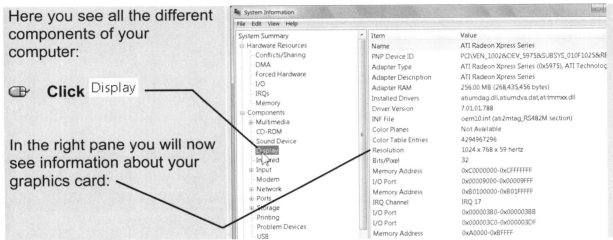

Here you see all the different components of your computer:

Click `Display`

In the right pane you will now see information about your graphics card:

 Tip

Troubleshooting

Are you having problems with a particular device? Then click `Problem Devices` in the `Components` section. You will be able to see if the device has a problem with *Windows Vista*, or if you should look elsewhere for a solution.

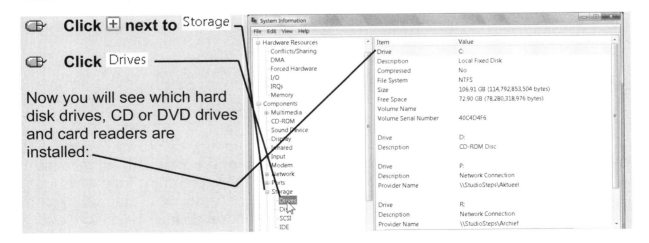

Click ⊞ **next to** `Storage`

Click `Drives`

Now you will see which hard disk drives, CD or DVD drives and card readers are installed:

For each storage device you can see the type of device, the designated drive letter and the file system for which it was formatted. You can read more about file systems in this chapter's *Background Information*. In the *Tips* at the end of this chapter you can read how to change the name of a drive.

In this window you will see information about the software installed on your computer:

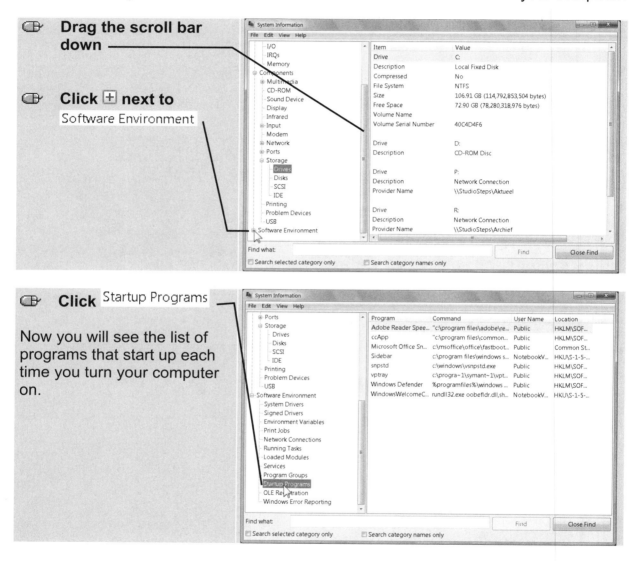

Drag the scroll bar down

Click ⊞ next to Software Environment

Click Startup Programs

Now you will see the list of programs that start up each time you turn your computer on.

You may not recognize several of these programs. There may be programs that execute background tasks, such as operating a mouse or a webcam. If you recognize any well-known programs, you can decide to exclude these programs from the automatic startup list. This is one of the ways to get your computer to start up a bit faster. In *Chapter 2 Speeding Up Vista* you will learn how to do this. In this window you also see some very important programs, such as your antivirus program and your firewall. It is best not to disable these programs.

Please note:

If you click 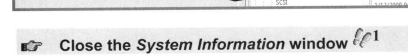 , you will get a summary of *Windows Vista* system errors, or errors from other programs you use. It may take a while to generate the list and the information in the list may not seem relevant to you. Meanwhile you will see the text **Refreshing System Information...**

An example of the *Windows Error Report*:

Close the *System Information* window ⨖¹

1.3 Windows Task Manager

Along with the programs that you start up yourself, additional processes and sometimes even other programs are executed in the background. Normally you do not notice this because you will not see this on your screen. The *Windows Task Manager* gives you a better picture of what is actually going on.

 Tip

Close all programs
If you really want to see which background tasks your computer is executing, then close all programs before continuing.

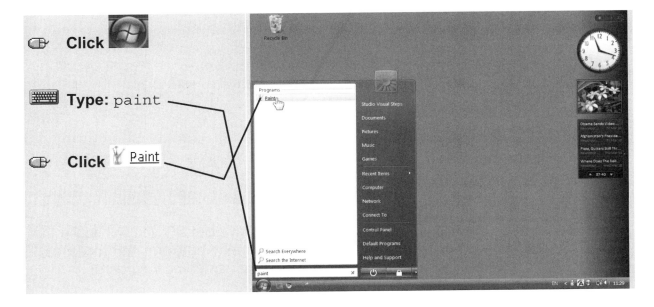

Click

Type: paint

Click Paint

On your desktop you will see the *Paint* window:

The size of the *Paint* window may be different on your screen.

☞ **Right-click the taskbar**

☞ **Click** Task Manager

Now you will see the programs that you have opened:

☞ **If necessary, click the** Applications **tab**

☞ **Click** Untitled - Paint

☞ **Click** End Task

Now *Paint* will be closed.

You can also see the processor (CPU) usage:
CPU Usage: 4%

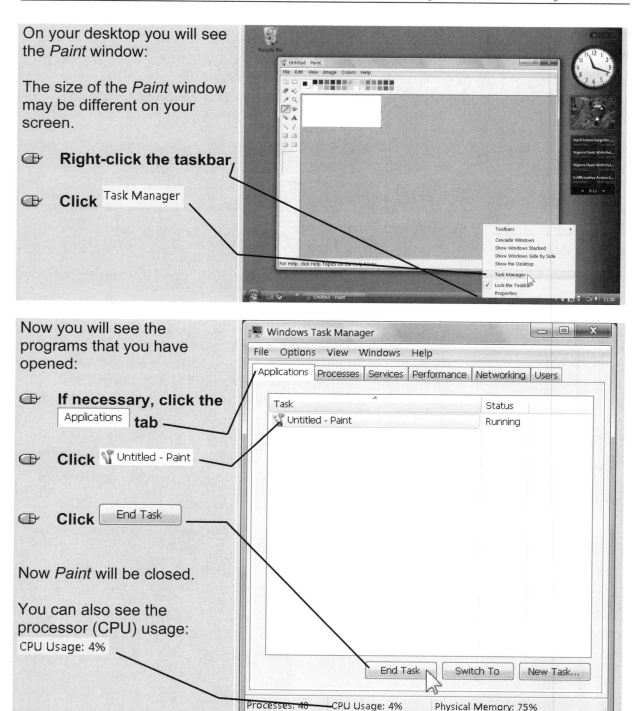

When all programs are closed, the CPU usage will be low. But still you will notice that the CPU usage changes every now and then. This is due to background processes or caused by movements you make with your mouse or use of the keyboard.

Tip

Viewing the processor usage
When you have minimized the *Windows Task Manager* window, you will see a small

green square on the taskbar: 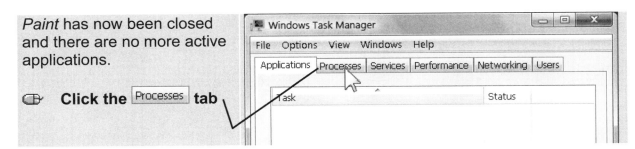.

If you point the mouse arrow to the green square, you will see the actual CPU usage. If you double-click the square, the *Windows Task Manager* window will open again.

Paint has now been closed and there are no more active applications.

☞ **Click the** Processes **tab**

You will see all the programs and processes your computer is executing at this moment:

Your own screen will show different processes.

If other users have logged on to your computer as well, you can view all processes by clicking
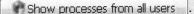.

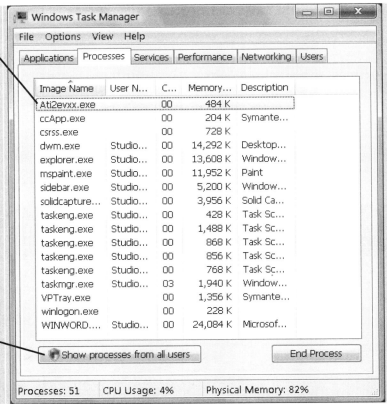

HELP! What are processes?

Processes are small computer programs that run in the background. Regular programs run in a window, but processes do not have their own window. You cannot see a process on your desktop or on the taskbar. That is why they are called background processes. Usually several processes are started at the same time you open a program.

In the *Windows Task Manager* window you can also close programs or processes. For example, you can close the *Windows Sidebar* on the right side of your desktop.

⇨ Please note:

Do not close processes unless you are sure no harm can be done. Do not close processes that do not have a user name.

Click sidebar.exe

Click End Process

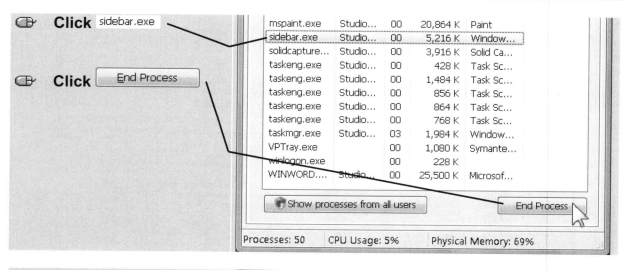

You will see a warning:

Click End Process

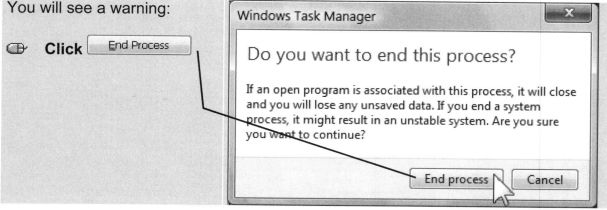

The `sidebar.exe` process has been removed from this list and the *Windows Sidebar* has been removed from your desktop:

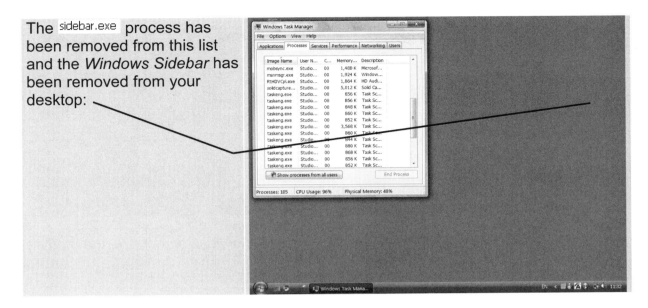

⇒ **Please note:**

Normally, you will not use the *Task Manager* to close a program or process. The program may not close properly or data may be lost if you close applications in this manner. This is why you should always close your programs the normal way. You should only try the *Task Manager* if you cannot close a program in the regular way.

Now you can open the *Windows Sidebar* again. This is how you do that:

Click

Type: side

Click Windows Sidebar

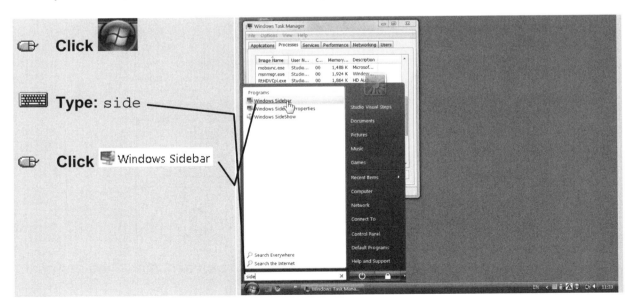

The *Windows Sidebar* is back on your desktop and sidebar.exe is back in the list of processes.

dwm.exe	Studio...	04	14,304 K
explorer.exe	Studio...	00	12,768 K
sidebar.exe	Studio...	48	12,596 K
solidcapture...	Studio...	00	3,716 K

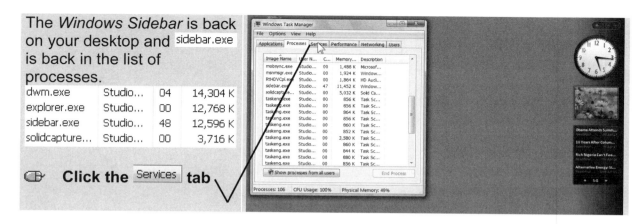

☞ **Click the** Services **tab**

Like processes, services also run in the background. Services do not operate on their own. They are used to support other programs.

Now you will see the services:

☞ **Click** Services...

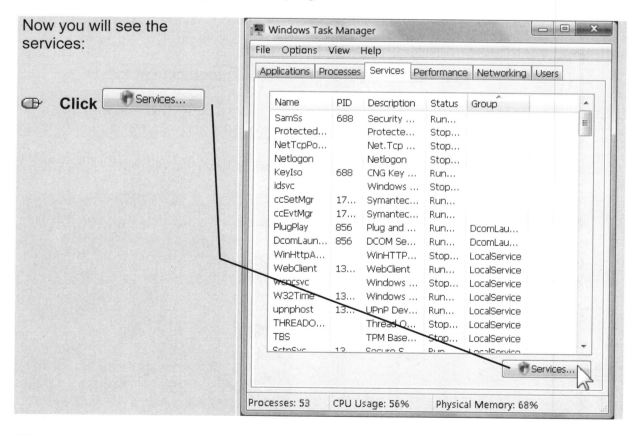

Your screen goes dark and you will need to give permission to continue the program:

☞ **Click** Continue

The *Services* window will be opened behind the *Task Manager* window. You can minimize the *Task Manager* window for the moment.

👉 **Click** ⬜

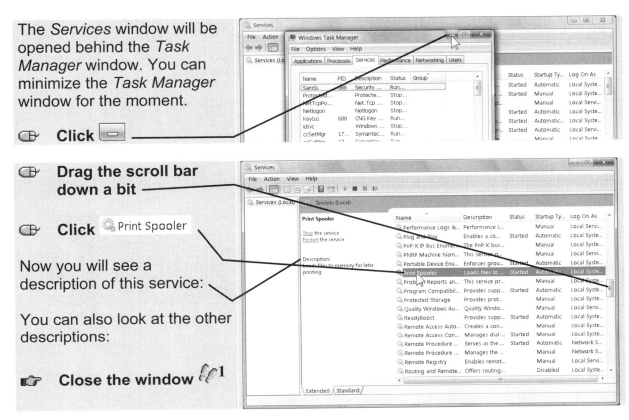

👉 **Drag the scroll bar down a bit** ——

👉 **Click** 🔧 Print Spooler

Now you will see a description of this service:

You can also look at the other descriptions:

☞ **Close the window** 👣¹

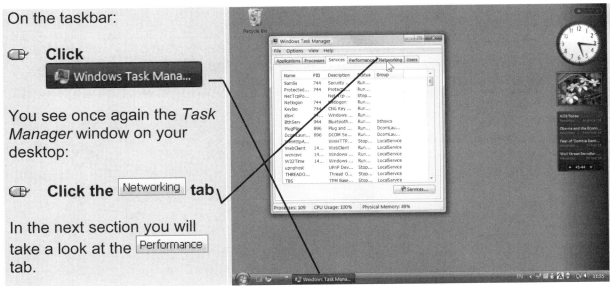

On the taskbar:

👉 **Click**

🖳 Windows Task Mana...

You see once again the *Task Manager* window on your desktop:

👉 **Click the** ⬚Networking⬚ **tab**

In the next section you will take a look at the ⬚Performance⬚ tab.

If your computer is connected to a network, or to the Internet, you can see if this connection is in use, and check the intensity of the usage.

Here you will see a graph of the Internet connection via a local area connection (LAN):

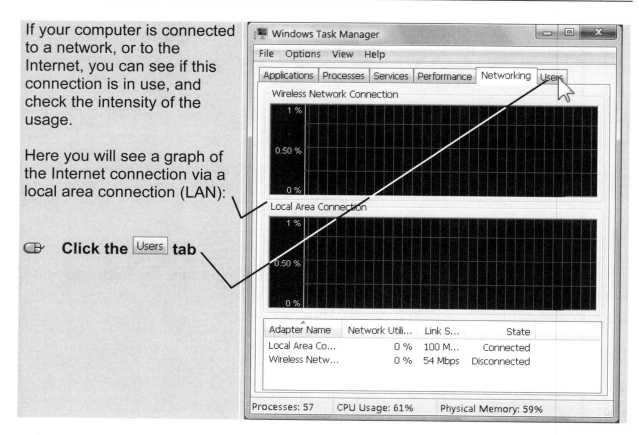

 Click the Users **tab**

⇨ **Please note:**

Do you see a large amount of Internet traffic (wireless or via your LAN), even when you are not using your computer? This could indicate that your computer is being used for sending spam.

If there are more users logged on to your computer, you will see all the active users.

In this example there is only one active user.

 Click the Performance **tab**

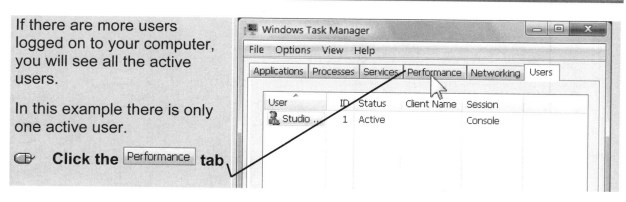

💡 **Tip**

Log off the users who are not active
Every user who is logged on will take up memory space and increase processor usage. Make sure that users who do not want to use the computer are logged off.

1.4 CPU Usage and Use of Resources

The speed of your computer is determined by various components. If one of these components is too busy, the other components will not be able to work at full speed and the computer will slow down. The *Windows Task Manager* monitors the use of a number of important components.

You will see the CPU usage in percentages and in a graph:

Here you will see two graphs indicating the CPU usage, because this computer has a dual-core processor. This means that the processor consists of two cores, which divide the work between them. You can read more about processors in the *Background Information* at the end of this chapter.

You will also see the memory (RAM) usage:

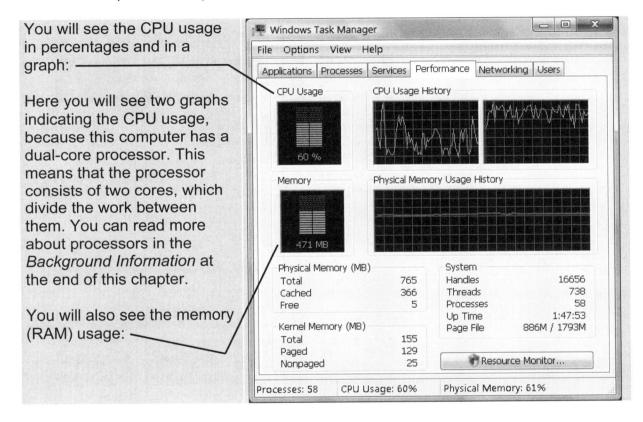

In the *Resource Monitor* window you can get even more detailed information:

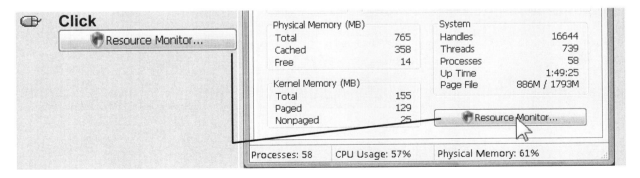

Your screen goes dark and you will need to give permission to continue:

☞ **Click** `Continue`

☞ **Minimize the *Windows Task Manager* window** ⏳**11**

Here you see the activity of the various components of your network connection:

☞ **Click** `CPU`

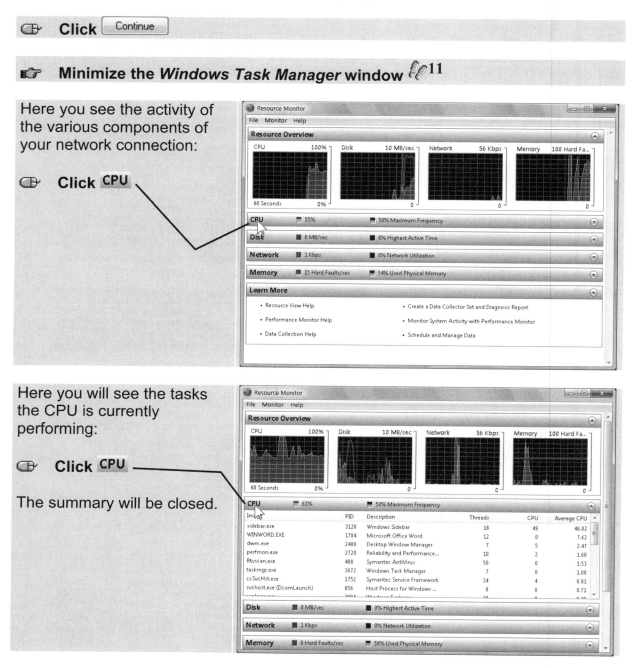

Here you will see the tasks the CPU is currently performing:

☞ **Click** `CPU`

The summary will be closed.

Click Disk

Now you will see all the disk activity:

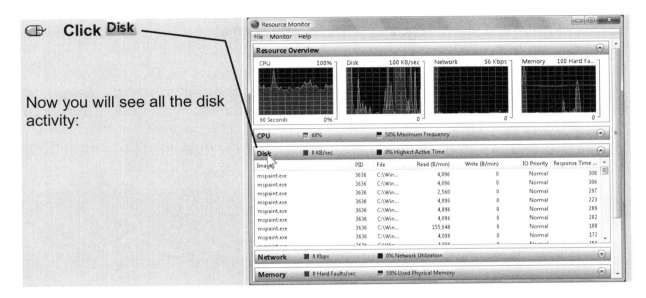

In the same way you can view the network activity and the memory usage. This data may not make much sense to you right now. But you can use this monitor to check whether one or more of the components are showing higher usage. This may indicate that you should modify and expand your computer with new components. You might want to add for example, extra memory, or a faster network connection or even a faster hard disk.

If you hardly touch your computer and the monitor still shows a lot of activity, then this could be caused by a computer virus.

☞ **Close the *Resource Monitor* and *Task Manager* windows** 1

1.5 Reliability and Performance Control

If all of the components of your computer are in sync with one another you can achieve high performance and great reliability. Sadly, this is not always the case, and sometimes you find yourself trying to solve some strange and inexplicable errors. The reliability and performance monitor measures the *performance* of your computer. In other words how quickly it completes application and system tasks. You can open the monitor like this:

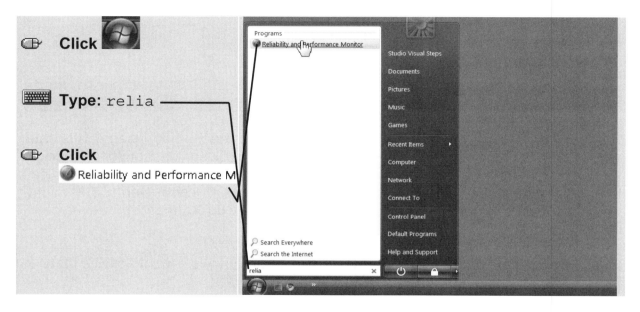

Your screen goes dark and you will need to give permission to continue:

☞ Click Continue

Now you will see the *Resource Overview* in the *Reliability and Performance Monitor* window:

☞ Click
Performance Monitor

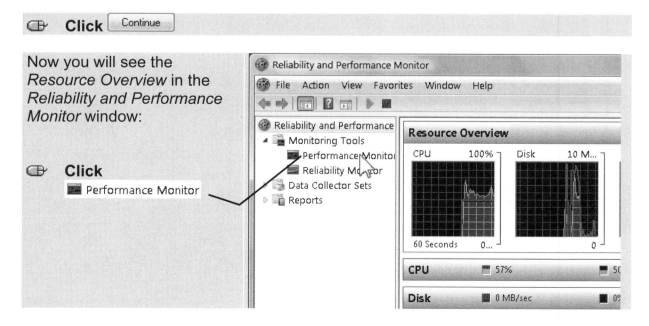

You will see a graph showing recent CPU activity:

This will range from 0% (no activity) to 100% (maximum capacity).

You can expand this graph to view other performance statistics.

Click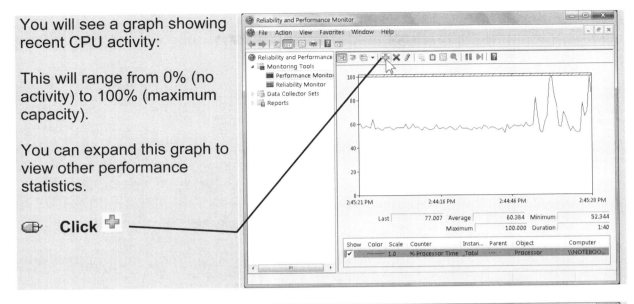

Drag the scroll bar down until you see System

Click System

Click Add >>

Click OK

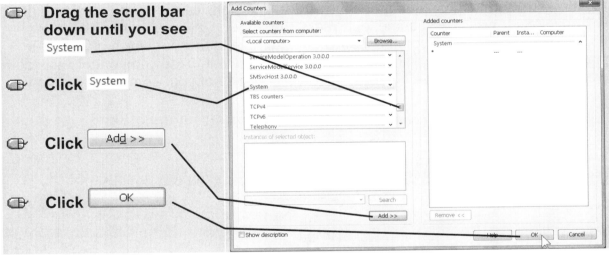

Now you will see various colored lines in the graph:

Under the graph you will see the explanation for these colors.

By checking the box ☑ next to an item, you can remove the corresponding line from the graph. In this way you can view different items more clearly:

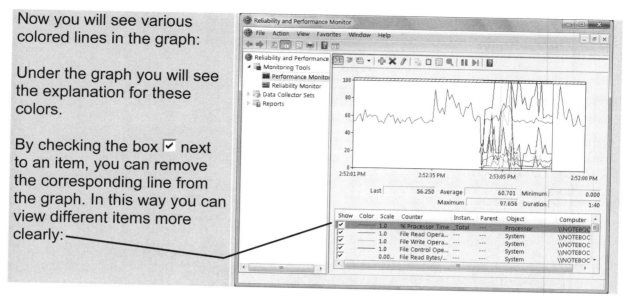

Most of the information in this graph may have little significance to you right now. It will be useful to users with some technical knowledge of their computer. Still, this information may one day come in handy, for example to monitor which graph lines show regular bursts of high activity. This could mean that these components are too weak or too slow, which will influence the overall speed of your computer and slow it down.

💡 Tip

Which component do the lines indicate?
Click a line in the graph, and you will see the corresponding component.

👉 **Click a line**

Here you will see the name of the component that goes with the line:

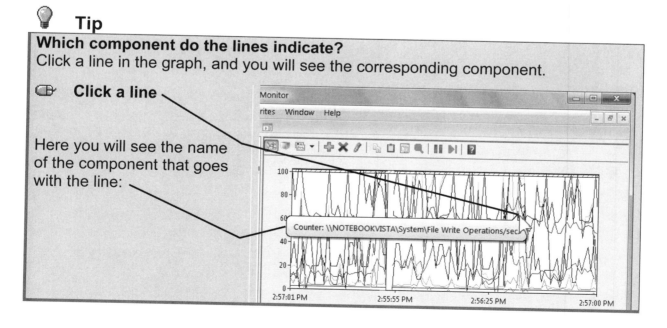

Click ▬ Reliability Monitor

Now you will see the average reliability of your system, on a scale of 1 (unreliable) to 10 (fully reliable):

If there are any particularities, you will see a ⬇ symbol on the related line:

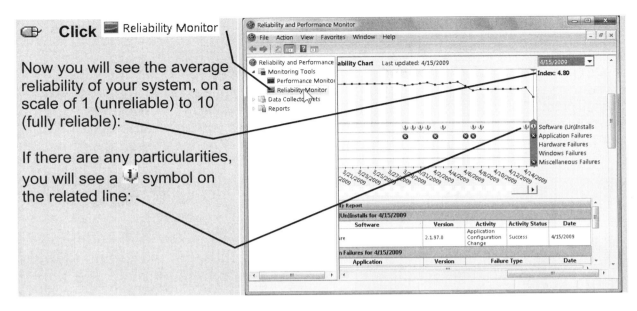

HELP! The reliability chart shows a dotted line.

It takes at least 28 days before the reliability monitor is able to draw an accurate picture of your system. If *Windows Vista* has been installed within the last 28 days, you will see a dotted line. The reliability data will be saved for a year.

Click a ⬇ symbol

If you do not see a ⬇ symbol, then you need to drag the scroll bar to the left or to the right, or try again in a few days time:

At the bottom of the window you will see information regarding the point you have chosen:

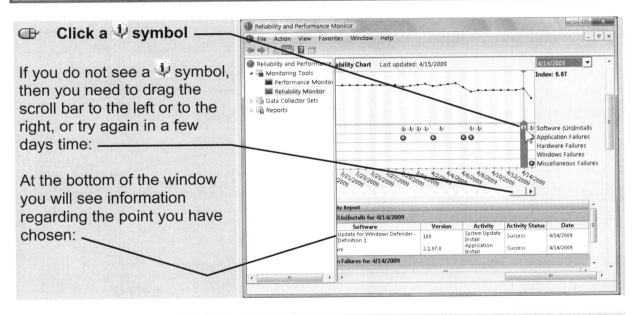

Close the *Reliability and Performance Monitor* window 👆1

1.6 The Performance Index

Your computer's performance depends heavily on the way you use it. If you play a lot of 3D games or use the computer to edit videos, you will need a much more powerful system than if you only use the computer for sending e-mails. The *Windows Performance Index* (*Windows Experience Index*) will tell you how suitable your computer is for certain tasks. This is how you view the *Windows Performance Index*:

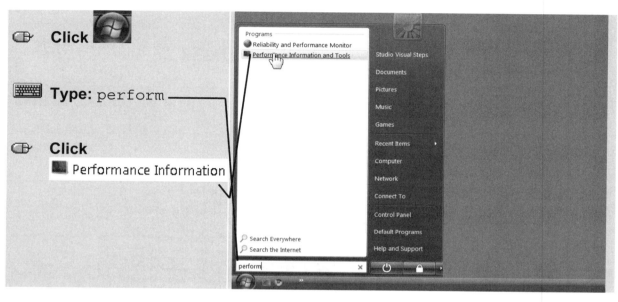

Now you will see your computer's score. It ranges from 1.0 (slow) to 5.9 (fast):

The score is based on the present status of your computer. If the computer is modified, the score will be computed again.

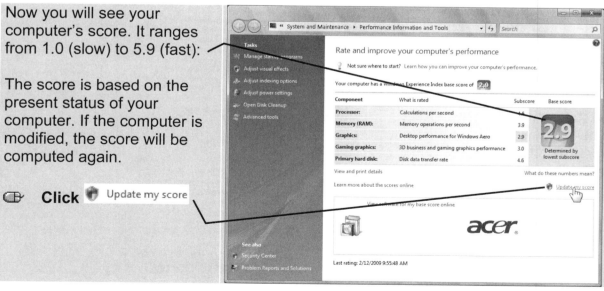

Your screen goes dark and you will need to give permission to continue:

👆 **Click** [Continue]

Now the various components of your computer will be tested.

During this task you will see this window:

Here you will see the new score:

The score is determined by the lowest score of one of the components. In this case the graphics perform badly:

So this computer is less suitable for gaming and business applications that require large amounts of graphic processing.

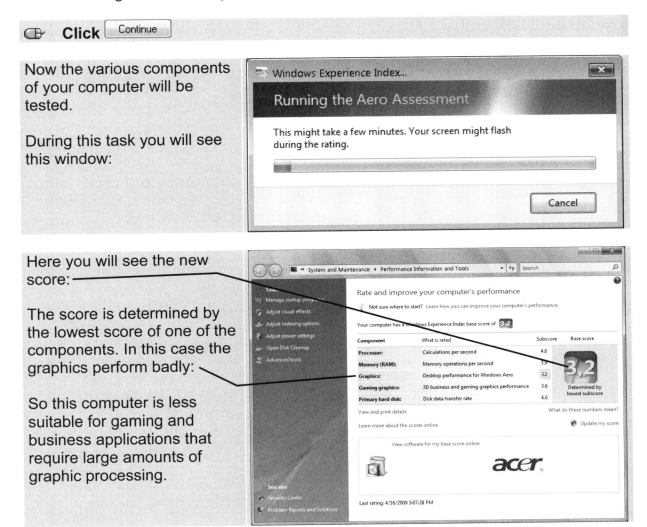

👉 **Close the window** 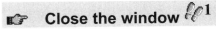[1]

What is the base score?

The base score measures the performance of your computer system as a whole, based on various components, such as the RAM memory, processor, hard disk, overall graphic performance and 3D graphics capability.

Here are general descriptions of the kind of experience you can expect from a computer that receives the following base scores:

- A computer with a base score of 1 or 2 generally has sufficient performance for the majority of the tasks, including regular office applications and searching the Internet. However, it will be very difficult to run *Windows Aero* on such a system, as well as using the advanced multimedia options in *Windows Vista*.
- A computer with a base score of 3 will be able to execute *Windows Aero* and a large number of *Windows Vista* options at a basic level. It is possible that some of the newest *Windows Vista* features will not be fully functional. A computer with a base score of 3 can display the *Windows Vista* theme at a screen resolution of 1280 x 1024, but will have difficulty running this theme on multiple monitors. Another example: this computer will be able to play digital TV content, but will experience problems with HDTV (High Definition Television) content.
- A computer with a base score of 4 or 5 will be fully functional regarding *Windows Vista* and will run all new features. This computer can be used for advanced high end graphics, like multiplayer gaming, 3D gaming and the recording or playback of HDTV content. When *Windows Vista* was released, computers with a base score of 5 were the highest performing computers available.

The *Windows Performance Index* has been designed with an eye to future developments in computer technology. Faster hardware components and higher overall performance will lead to higher base scores. However, the standards for each level of the index stay the same. So the base score of your computer will remain the same, unless you upgrade the hardware of the computer. This could be the case if you need a higher base score to run a certain program or to fully use *Windows Vista*.

If you have installed new hardware and you want to check if your base score has changed, click 🛡 Update my score . If you want to view detailed information about your hardware, click View and print details .

Source: Windows Help and Support

1.7 Priorities and the Paging File

Your computer's processor is continually running programs and background tasks. Sometimes several tasks have to be run simultaneously. The processor must then decide which task to execute first. Usually the programs you are currently working with have priority, while other tasks, such as printing, are executed a bit later on. This should not be a problem, however, because a print command is usually one of the last things you want to do.

An action such as typing something on the keyboard, or moving the mouse arrow will always get top priority. In general, you want to see immediate results from these actions. The same goes for the programs you use.
You can see for yourself in the following windows:

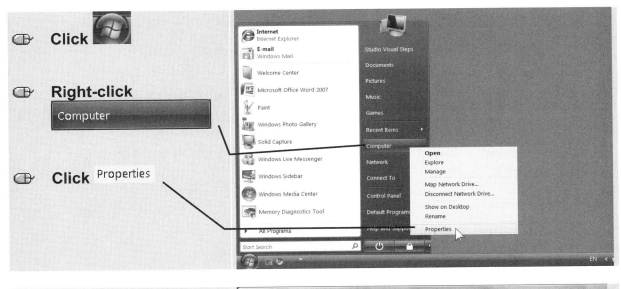

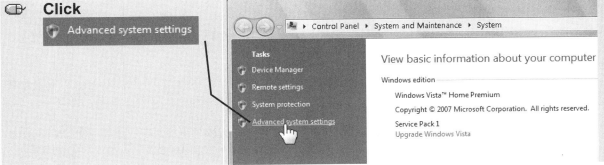

Your screen goes dark and you will need to give permission to continue:

Under Performance :

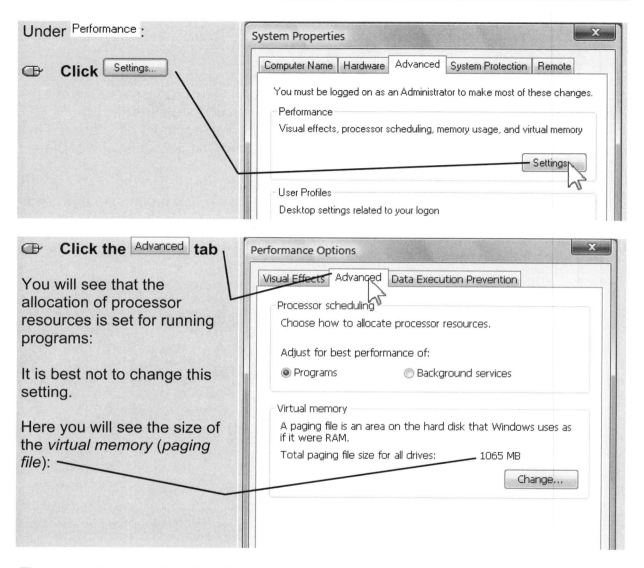

☞   **Click** Settings...

☞   **Click the** Advanced **tab**

You will see that the allocation of processor resources is set for running programs:

It is best not to change this setting.

Here you will see the size of the *virtual memory* (*paging file*):

The computer uses the virtual memory in case there is not enough space in the RAM memory. In the next chapter you will learn how to adjust this setting and you can read about the consequences of this adjustment.

☞   **Close all windows** ₰₰¹

After this introduction to your computer, in *Chapter 2 Speeding Up Vista* you will learn how to work faster using *Windows Vista*. You will learn how to do this by applying changes to some of the settings you have read about in this chapter.

1.8 Background Information

Dictionary

Base score	The base score represents the overall performance of your system as a whole, based on the capabilities of different parts of your computer. A higher base score means that the computer performs better and faster than a computer with a lower base score, especially in cases where advanced tasks are executed which include extensive use of resources.
Paging file	A hidden file or files on the hard disk that *Windows* uses to hold parts of programs and data files that do not fit in RAM memory.
Performance index	The *Windows Performance Index* measures the capability of your computer's hardware and software configuration and expresses this measurement as a number called a base score.
Process	A process is a (small) computer program that runs in the background. Programs run inside a window, whereas processes do not have their own window. Therefore you cannot view a process on your desktop or in the taskbar. That is why they are called background processes. Usually, when you run a program, several processes are started simultaneously.
Processor	The main circuit chip in your computer. The processor (or CPU) performs most of the calculations necessary to run the computer.
RAM memory	The main internal storage area the computer uses to run programs and store data. Information stored in RAM is temporary and is designed to clear when the computer is turned off. The RAM (Random Access Memory) is also called the internal memory.
Service	A computer program or process that runs in the background and provides support to other programs.
Service Pack	A software update that combines new security and performance enhancements with existing updates. Unlike update rollups, *Service Packs* can contain new features or design changes for a product.

- Continue reading on the next page -

System information	This contains detailed technical information about the configuration, components and software running on your computer, including the operating system.
Windows Task Manager	In *Windows Task Manager* you can see which programs, processes and services run on your computer. You can use *Windows Task Manager* to monitor the computer's performance, or to close a program that does not respond anymore.

Source: Windows Help and Support

NTFS or FAT file system

A file system is the underlying structure a computer uses to organize data on a hard disk. If you are installing a new hard disk, you need to partition and format it using a file system before you can begin storing data or programs. In *Windows Vista*, there are three file system options to choose from: NTFS, FAT32, and the older and rarely-used FAT (also known as FAT16).

NTFS

NTFS is the preferred file system for this version of *Windows Vista*. It has many benefits over the earlier FAT32 file system, including:

- The capability to recover from some disk-related errors automatically, which FAT32 cannot.
- Improved support for larger hard disks.
- Better security because you can use permissions and encryption to restrict access to specific files to approved users.

FAT32

FAT32, and the lesser-used FAT, were used in earlier versions of *Windows* operating systems. FAT32 does not have the security that NTFS provides, so if you have a FAT32 partition or volume on your computer, any user who has access to your computer can read any file on it. You cannot create a FAT32 partition greater than 32 GB in this version of *Windows*, and you cannot store a file larger than 4 GB on a FAT32 partition.

Any additional partitions you will need to access when using other (earlier) versions of *Windows* must also be formatted with FAT32.

Source: Windows Help and Support

Processor

The processor is the heart of your computer. Every action you undertake on your computer will run through the processor. Even when you are typing a text in a word processing program, the processor will be busy computing the actions.
Modern processors can do computations at lightning speed. The speed of a processor is measured in megahertz or gigahertz, for example 800 MHz or 3 GHz. The higher the number, the faster the processor will be.

The overall speed of your computer, however, is also determined by the speed of other computer components. If the processor is fast, but other components are not, the computer as a whole will experience delays and will work slower.

In the past years many different processors have been built by various manufacturers. These are some of the most well-known:
- *Intel 8088/8086/80286*:
  These were the processors used in the first computers. They could process 8 to 16 bits at once. That is why they were called 8 or 16 bits processors. A bit is one computer signal, for example on/off, yes/no, or 0 and 1. Computers are able to function only by using bits.
- *Intel 80386/80486*:
  This processor could process 32 bits at once. It was faster and capable of processing large quantities of data.
- *Intel Pentium/Celeron*:
  These are the newest 32 bits processors, best suited to *Windows Vista*. The *Pentium M* is a special type, built for use in notebooks ('M' stands for mobile) and using less power.
  There exist also 64 bits Pentium processors, but they are still not used very often (for this, see 32 or 64 bits *Vista*).

Similar types of processors are made by other manufacturers, such as AMD and Cyrix.

Modern processors are built as multi core processors. These processors have multiple cores (for example, dual core uses two cores), which perform independently from one another. This shortens the waiting period.
To use these types of processors, you will need to have an operating system and programs that can work with the multi core technology. *Windows XP* and *Windows Vista* use this technology, as well as many modern programs.

1.9 Tips

 Tip

Changing the computer name
When *Windows Vista* is first installed on your computer, the installation process asks for a computer name. This name appears in a variety of different windows. Usually, the manufacturer of the computer has assigned a computer name to your computer. If you would like to change this name, here is how to do that:

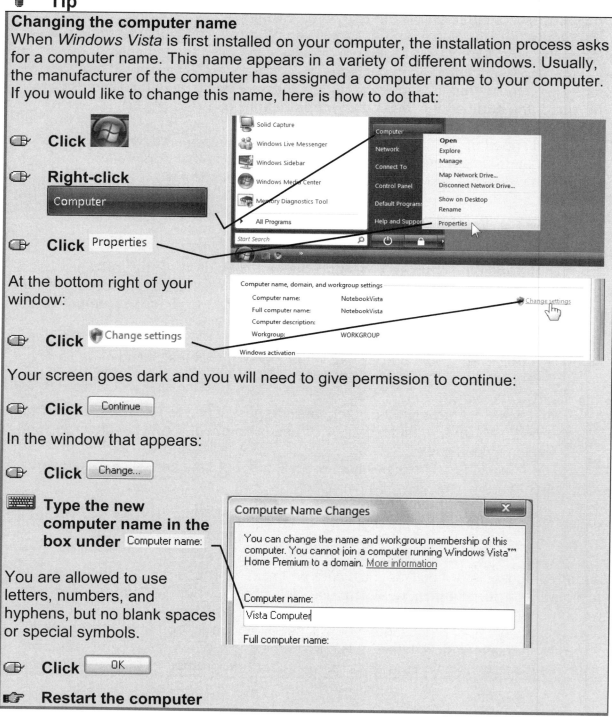

Click

Right-click Computer

Click Properties

At the bottom right of your window:

Click Change settings

Your screen goes dark and you will need to give permission to continue:

Click Continue

In the window that appears:

Click Change...

⌨ **Type the new computer name in the box under** Computer name:

You are allowed to use letters, numbers, and hyphens, but no blank spaces or special symbols.

Click OK

☞ **Restart the computer**

Tip

Changing the name of a disk drive
You can also change the names of the disk drives in your computer. This may help you to remember what kind of data you have stored in this drive, or whose drive it is. For example, by calling a drive 'Data', 'Hank' or 'Video', it will make more logical sense to you especially when you do not work at your computer every day.
This is how to change the name:

☞ **Open the window *Computer* ℓℓ21**

Now you will see all the disk drives:

☝ **Right-click the drive**

☝ **Click** Rename

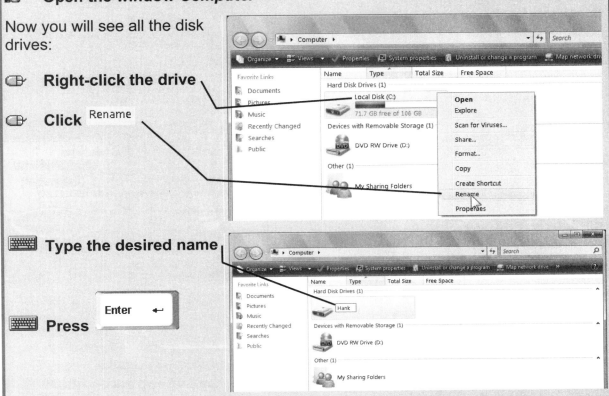

⌨ **Type the desired name**

⌨ **Press** Enter ←

Your screen goes dark and you will need to give permission to continue:

☝ **Click** Continue

Now you will see the new disk drive name. You cannot change all of the disk drive names. If you are not allowed to change the name, you will not be able to click

Tip

Opening windows by using the Control Panel
In this chapter you have opened several windows by typing a keyword in the Search box. But you can also open these windows by using the *Control Panel*:

☞ **Open the *Control Panel* ℰℰ14**

👆 **Click** System and Maintenance

👆 **Drag the scroll bar down**

👆 **Click**
Performance Information and Tools

👆 **Click** Advanced tools

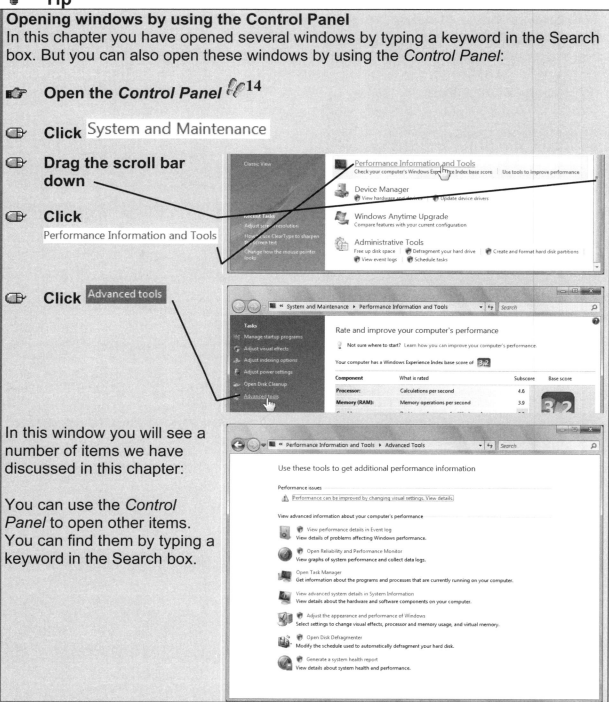

In this window you will see a number of items we have discussed in this chapter:

You can use the *Control Panel* to open other items. You can find them by typing a keyword in the Search box.

2. Speeding Up Vista

You may have noticed that after working on your computer for a while, it starts to get slower. This may have occurred after new software was installed, for example an upgrade from *Windows Vista,* or other new, larger software programs. A new edition of *Microsoft Office* or *Pinnacle Studio*, for example, requires an increased amount of processor capacity. These programs have great new features and wonderful graphics but your computer's resources become more strained. If your computer is relatively new, this need not be a problem. But if you own an older computer, you will most likely be looking for ways to increase the speed of its processing.

Even if you use earlier editions of familiar software programs, you will notice that the computer starts getting slower. Opening, loading and even closing a program seems to take longer and longer. This can be caused by several different issues.

This is why it is important to check the settings of your computer regularly. In this chapter you will learn different methods to check these settings and change them, if necessary.

In this chapter you will learn how to:

- search for programs that start up automatically and remove them from the startup procedure;
- choose between visual effects or enhanced performance;
- search faster by using indexes;
- control performance by using the power plan;
- clean up your hard disk;
- speed up your hard disk by using the disk defragmenter;
- create a status report of your system;
- check your hard disk for wear marks;
- understand the paging file and the virtual memory;
- set the paging file.

⇨ Please note:

The screen shots have been made on a computer using *Windows Vista Home Premium*. If you are using a different edition of *Vista,* the windows that appear on your own computer may be slightly different.

2.1 Managing Startup Programs

When you switch on your computer, not only does *Windows Vista* start up, but several other programs as well. Some of these programs are important, such as an antivirus program. But sometimes other, less important programs will also start automatically, for example *Internet Explorer*, or a calendar program. These programs may have been added to the startup list during installation, or maybe you added them yourself later on. These additional programs may slow down the computer when it starts up and may also affect some of the programs you regularly work with.

To demonstrate how you can add a program to the startup list yourself, we will start by showing you how to add the program *Paint* to the *Startup* folder:

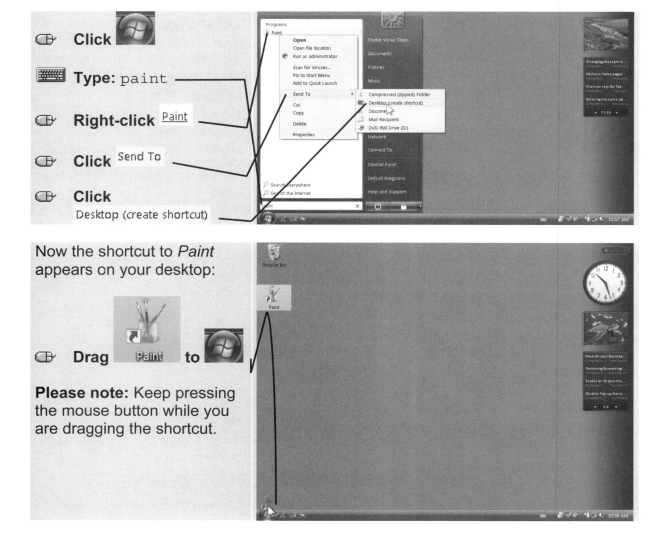

Now the *Start menu* will open:

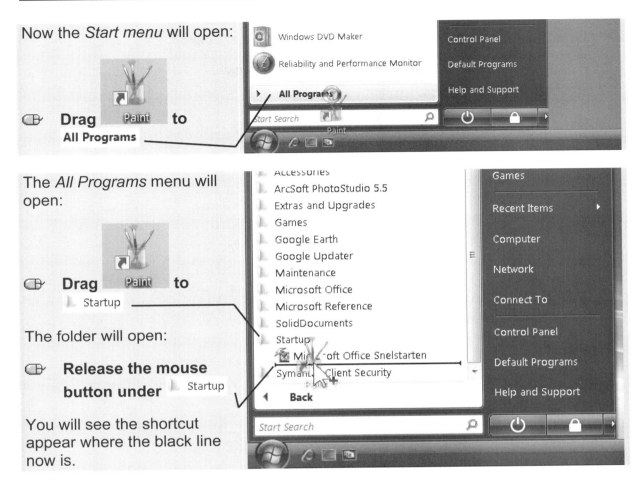

⊕ **Drag** Paint **to**
All Programs

The *All Programs* menu will open:

⊕ **Drag** Paint **to**
Startup

The folder will open:

⊕ **Release the mouse button under** Startup

You will see the shortcut appear where the black line now is.

The next time you log on, *Paint* will open automatically.

☞ **Log off and then log on again**

After *Windows Vista* has started up, you will see the *Paint* program opened on your desktop.

You can close this window:

⊕ **Click** ✕

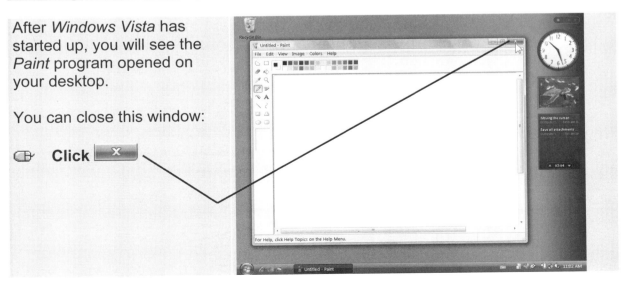

☞ **Open the window *Performance Information and Tools***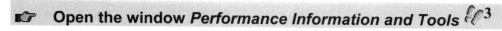

Click

Manage startup programs

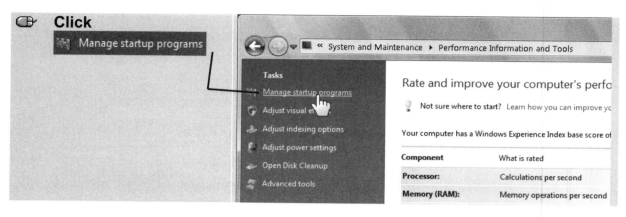

Now you will see all the programs that start up when *Windows Vista* is started:

Click Microsoft Paint

Next to Microsoft Paint you will see the *Paint* icon :

On the right side of the window you see
File Name: mspaint.exe.

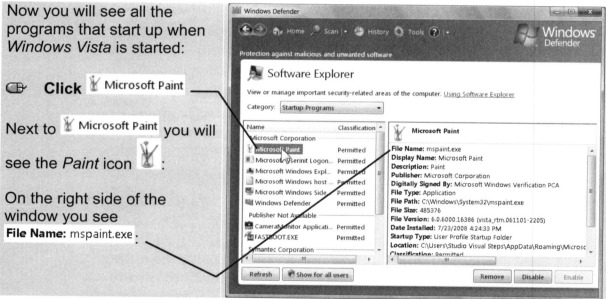

At the bottom of the window:

Click Remove

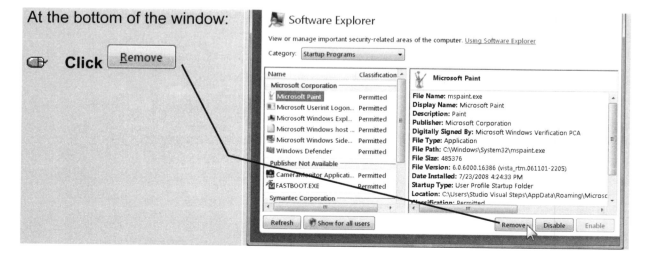

Please note:

Removing antivirus programs, programs from the operating system, or communication programs from the *Startup* folder can result in computer failure. Only remove programs from this list if you are sure of their importance. If in doubt, then do not remove the program, but disable it by using the Disable button. When you start up your computer again, the program will be loaded as usual.

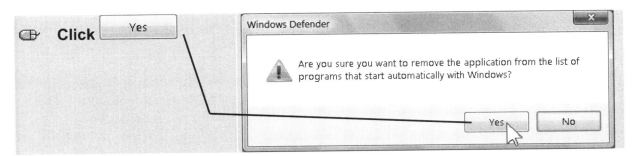

Click Yes

Windows Defender

Are you sure you want to remove the application from the list of programs that start automatically with Windows?

Yes   No

 Tip

Every user has their own startup programs
Each user can identify what programs are running at startup. If multiple users are logged on to the computer, these startup programs may slow the computer down. To view the startup programs of the other users, you click the button

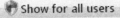 Show for all users

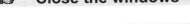 **Close the windows** 🕮1

 Log off and then log on again

Paint will no longer be opened.

In the *Software Explorer* window you can also view all the programs that have been loaded. But the *Windows Task Manager* window, which you read about in *Chapter 1 Getting to Know Your Computer*, gives you a better view of these startup programs.

 Tip

Removing hidden startup programs
In this exercise you have added *Paint* to the *Startup* folder in the *Start menu* yourself. You could also have removed the program in the usual way. However, you will not see all of the programs in the *Startup* folder, even though they are loaded automatically when the computer starts up. By checking *Windows Defender* once in a while, you can see which hidden programs start up automatically and then remove them from the list, if you want to. This may help to speed up your computer.

2.2 Visual Effects

Windows Vista uses many graphic effects, such as translucent windows, shadows and color schemes. These graphics are processor intensive and demand a lot from your graphics card. The computer will perform faster if you disable these effects. This is especially noticeable when your computer barely meets the requirements for running *Windows Vista*. If you run *Windows Vista Home Basic* on your computer, these effects are not available. This is how to switch off the visual effects:

 Tip

Windows Vista warns us sometimes
When the color scheme uses most of the available memory, or when the computer is getting too slow, *Windows Vista* will display a warning message. In these cases it will be hard to execute routine tasks, such as moving a window. You can either disable the graphic effects, which you will learn how to do in this chapter, or you can choose a different color scheme $\ell\ell^2$.

☞ **Open the window *Performance Information and Tools* $\ell\ell^3$**

Notice the transparency of the windows: —

Here you see the base score. In this score, the graphics score is lowest: —

This is why you may want to disable the visual effects.

⌨ **Click** Adjust visual effects

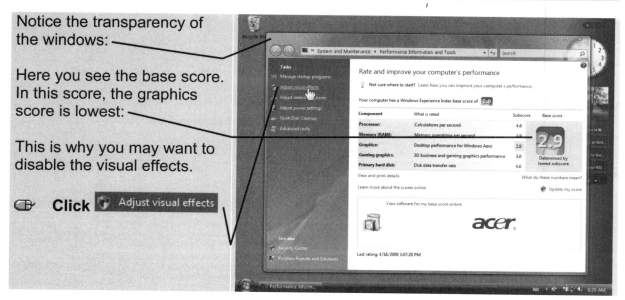

Your screen goes dark and you will need to give permission to continue:

⌨ **Click** Continue

⇨ **Please note:**

When you adjust the visual effects, the scores will not change. You have not changed anything in your computer hardware. This is why the scores do not change.

The current setting is
◉ Let Windows choose what's best for my

In the list you will see which visual effects are enabled:

⊕ **Click the box ☑ next to** Enable transparent glass

Is this feature already disabled on your computer? Then you do not need to do anything.

At the bottom of the window:

⊕ **Click** Apply

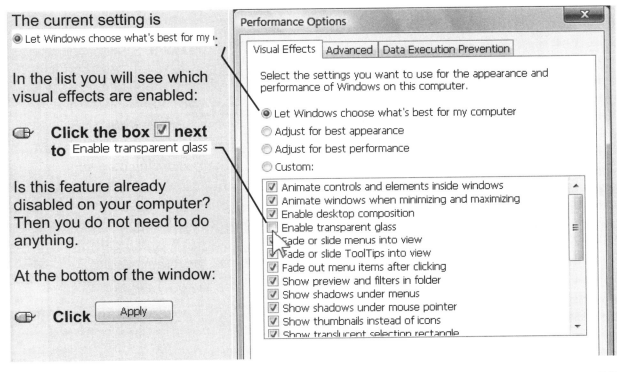

The windows are no longer transparent:

In this way you can enable or disable visual effects, and view the results.

⊕ **Click the box ☑ next to** Enable transparent glass

⊕ **Click** Apply

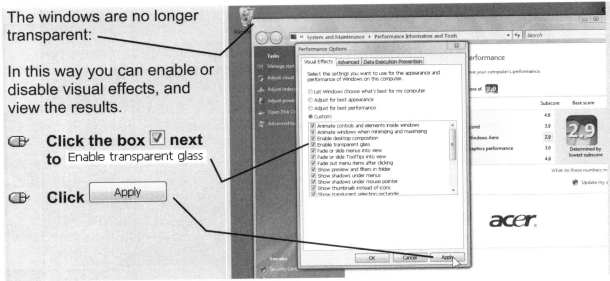

⇨ **Please note:**

If you have changed a visual effect setting, the main setting will remain the ◉ Custom:
setting. Even if you changed it back again later. If you want, you can reselect the
◉ Let Windows choose what's best for my computer setting. Then you can be assured that all the
settings are restored to the standard setting.

Usually, the ◉ Let Windows choose what's best for my computer setting will be the best option.
Windows Vista will take into account your computer's graphic capabilities. That is
why most programs will perform well with this setting. However, sometimes the
graphic effects can cause delays while working with your computer, even though you
do not really need these effects. If this occurs, you can choose a simpler graphics
setting:

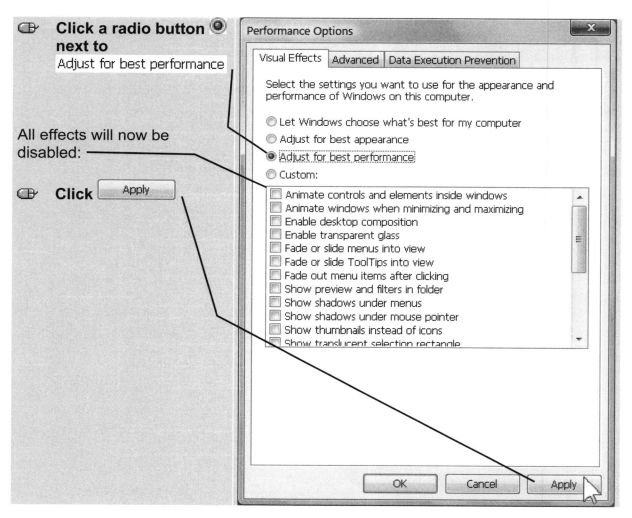

☞ **Click a radio button** ◉
   next to
   Adjust for best performance

All effects will now be
disabled:

☞ **Click** Apply

Now you will see a very simple rendering of windows and buttons:

The computer will work faster this way.

⊕ **Click a radio button** ◉ **next to**
    `Adjust for best appearance`

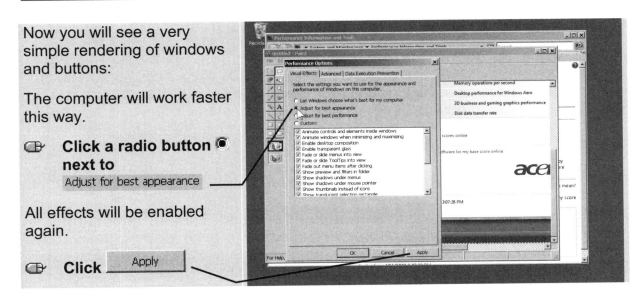

All effects will be enabled again.

⊕ **Click** `Apply`

Do you work with graphics software or do you really like the *Windows Vista* graphics? Then you can choose the best graphic appearance. It still is better, however, to let *Windows Vista* decide what the best balance is between graphic appearance and computer speed, based on the capabilities of your computer.

⊕ **Click**
    `Let Windows choose what's b`

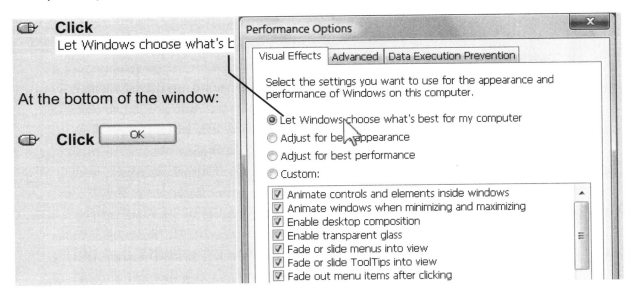

At the bottom of the window:

⊕ **Click** `OK`

2.3 Indexing

In order to quickly locate files on your hard disk, *Windows Vista* automatically creates search tables. These are called *indexes. Windows* uses these indexes while searching for files or programs, for example, in the Search box at the bottom of the *Start menu*, or in *Windows Explorer*. In the *Background Information* of this chapter you can learn more about indexes.

Indexing all the disks and folders where the user files are located, takes quite a lot of time. For example, the *Users* folder can be quite large. Folders such as *Windows* or *Program files* will not be indexed. You can view the folders that are indexed in the following way:

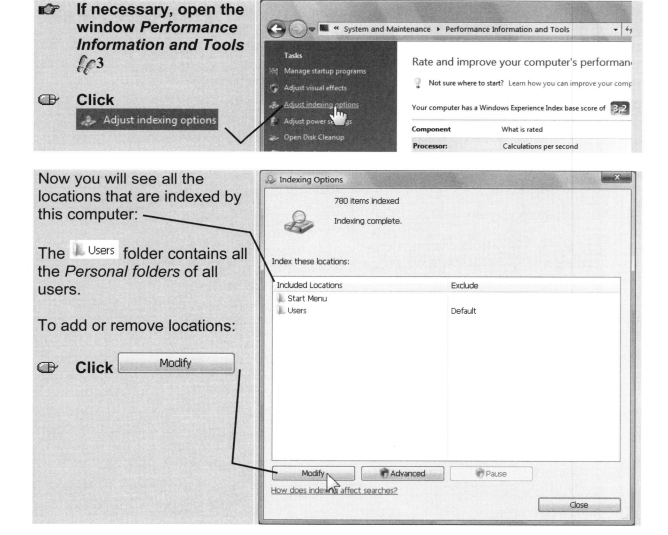

☞ **If necessary, open the window *Performance Information and Tools*** 𝓁𝓅3

☞ **Click**

  Adjust indexing options

Now you will see all the locations that are indexed by this computer:

The Users folder contains all the *Personal folders* of all users.

To add or remove locations:

☞ **Click** Modify

Now you will not see the Users and Start Menu folders any longer, because these folders are indexed by default.

Here you will only see the folders you have added yourself.

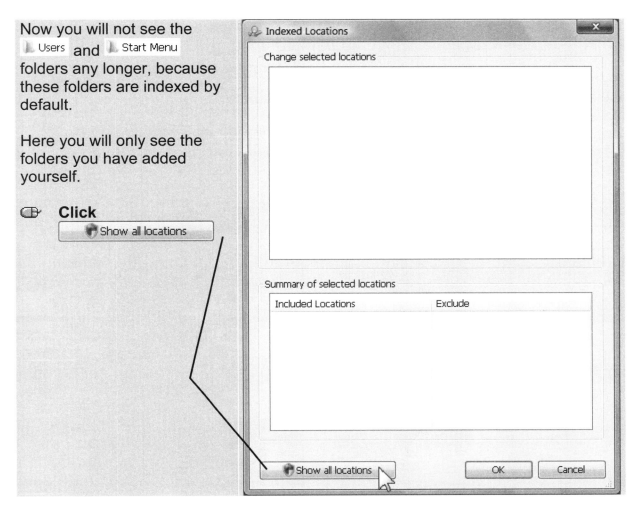

Now your screen goes dark and you will need to give permission to continue:

As an exercise, you will now add your *Personal folder*:

In this example this folder is called Studio Visual Steps. On your computer you will see your own user name.

☞ **Click ▷ next to**
   🗀 Local Disk (C:)

☞ **If necessary, click ▷**
   next to 🗀 Users

☞ **Click the box ☑ next to your *Personal folder***

Now the folder has been added:

At the bottom of the window:

☞ **Click** [OK]

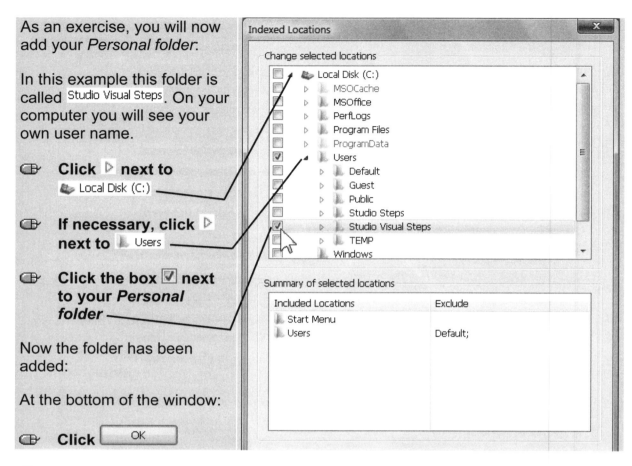

💡 Tip

Remove redundant folders from the index
Indexing takes time. If you see folders that do not contain important information, then switch off the indexing option.

Your *Personal folder* has now been added:

Meanwhile, this folder will be indexed. You will see the number of items increase, until the entire folder has been indexed:

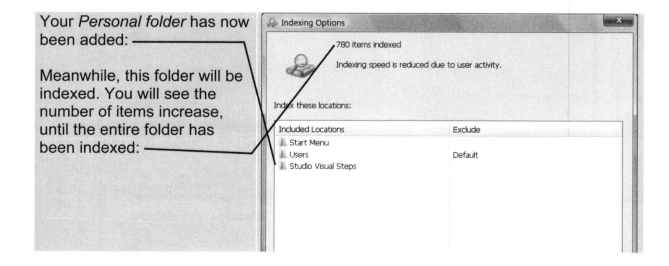

When all of the folders have been indexed, you will see this message:

You do not have to wait until the indexing has finished. The indexing process will continue, even if you close the window.

At the bottom of the window:

☞ **Click** [Close]

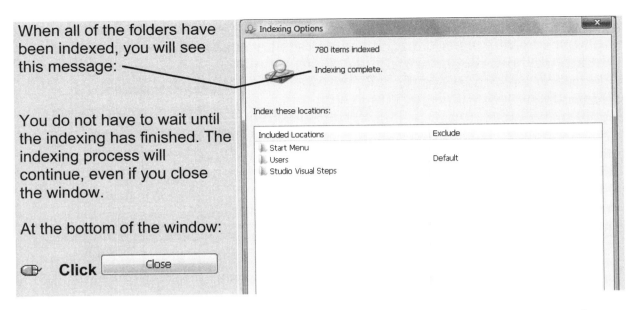

From now on, the files in your *Personal folder* will immediately be found, every time you type a keyword in the *Start menu* Search box.

⇨ **Please note:**

If you add too many folders or disks to the indexing feature, your computer will perform slower, rather than faster. Only switch on the indexing option for important folders.

2.4 Power Management

To save energy, the *Power management* feature on your computer will automatically disable certain programs or components that have not been used for a while. This feature is especially useful for notebook computers that have a limited battery life, but it can also be used for desktop computers. Saving energy usually affects the speed of the computer, so if you want to speed up the computer you should partially disable the power settings. This is how you choose a power plan:

☞ **If necessary, open the** *Performance Information and Tools* **window** ℰℓ3

☞ **Click** [Adjust power settings]

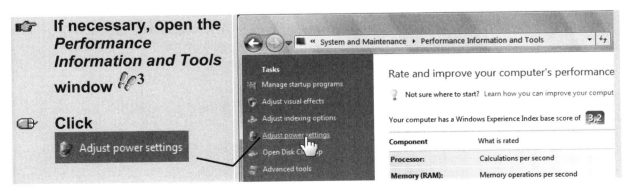

There are three power plans:
- *Balanced*: average performance and average battery life;
- *Power saver*: lower performance and slower computer;
- *High performance*: a desktop computer will perform faster while a notebook computer will have a shorter battery life.

You can also change the settings yourself. For example, if you want to save a lot of energy, but you do not want your display to switch off so quickly, you can change the settings as follows:

⇒ **Please note:**

The following screen shots are made with a notebook computer. This is why you will also see the settings for working while using a battery. If you have a desktop computer, you will not see these settings. In that case, you can change the settings for your desktop computer.

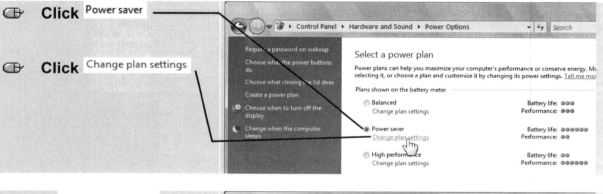

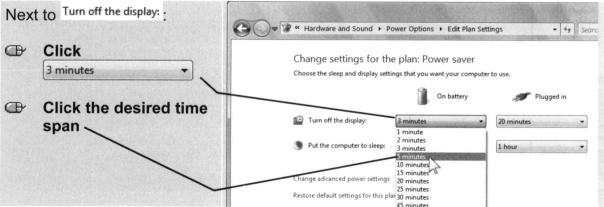

The screen display uses a lot of energy. If you choose a long period of time, you will save less power and will only be able to use your notebook computer for a short time before the battery will need recharging.

Tip

Not switching off the computer while using an AC power outlet
If your computer uses an AC power outlet, you can work at your computer as long as you wish. In that case you may be more concerned about keeping the energy bill as low as possible. You might choose a longer period to turn off the display, or disable this setting altogether, which will let you work faster.

Apart from these options, you can also set the time periods for switching off several separate components. If the computer goes to sleep too quickly, you will often have to wait until the computer 'wakes up' again, which can be annoying. This is how you can set a longer time period before the computer goes to sleep:

Click
Change advanced power settings

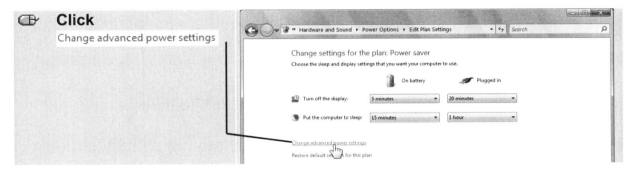

Now you will see all the components you can customize:

Click ⊞ **next to** Hard disk

⊞ changes to ⊟:

Click ⊞ **next to** Turn off hard disk after

Click 20 Minutes **next to** Plugged in:

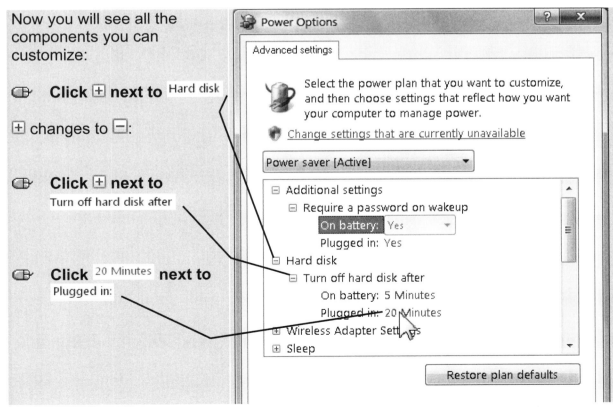

Tip

Extra options

If you are not logged on as an administrator, you will see this message in the window: 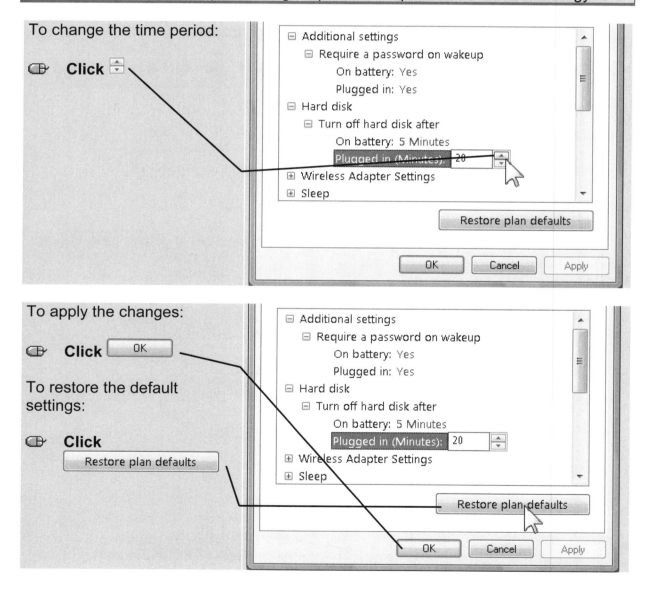 Change settings that are currently unavailable.

If you click this message, and then click the button Continue, you might see some additional options. This depends on the capabilities of your computer.

Some computers will allow you to change the processor speed using the Processor power management option. A higher processor speed will cost more energy.

To change the time period:

☞ **Click** ⬍.

To apply the changes:

☞ **Click** OK

To restore the default settings:

☞ **Click**
Restore plan defaults

If you have chosen to restore the default settings:

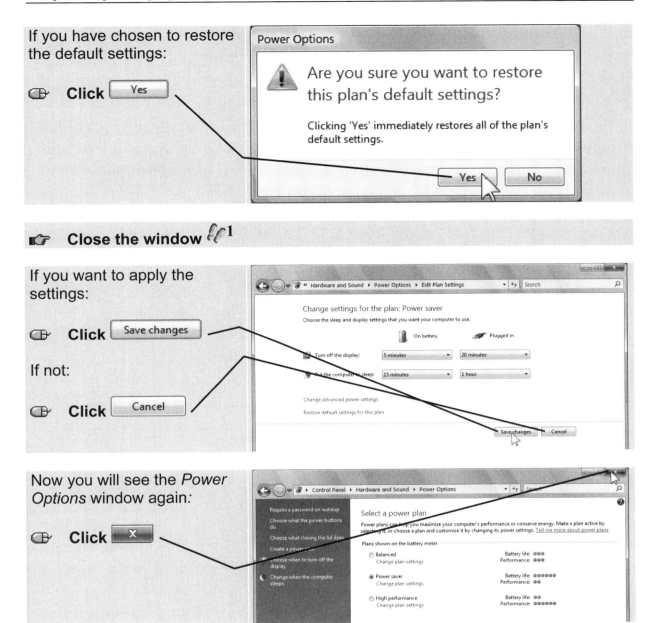

Click **Yes**

☞ **Close the window** ✍1

If you want to apply the settings:

Click **Save changes**

If not:

Click **Cancel**

Now you will see the *Power Options* window again:

Click **X**

2.5 Cleaning Up the Hard Disk

A large amount of data is temporarily stored on your hard disk. This data can slow down your computer. These temporary files might include the web pages you have visited, temporary files created by several programs, safety backups, etcetera.
By regularly cleaning up your hard disk you will speed up your computer.

☞ **If necessary, open the**
 Performance
 Information and Tools
 window 𝓵𝓸³

⌨ **Click** Open Disk Cleanup

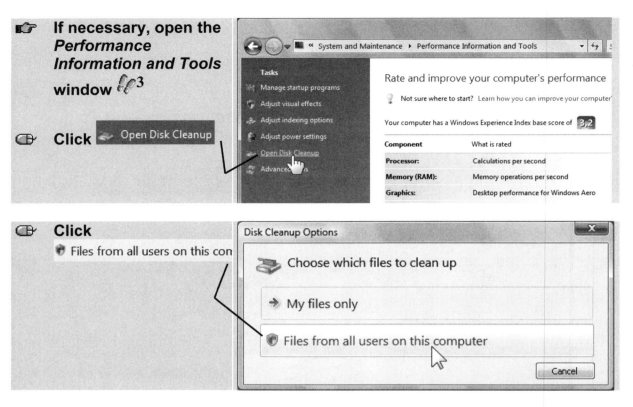

⌨ **Click**
 ⛏ Files from all users on this com

Please note:

If your computer is used by other users, then choose ➔ My files only . Otherwise there is a chance that you will delete other users' files. In this case the computer will not perform much faster.

Now your screen goes dark and you will need to give permission to continue:

⌨ **Click** Continue

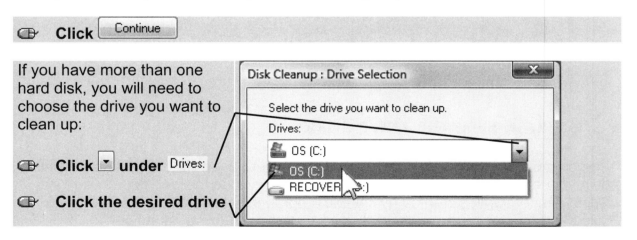

If you have more than one
hard disk, you will need to
choose the drive you want to
clean up:

⌨ **Click** ▾ **under** Drives:

⌨ **Click the desired drive**

☞ **Click** [OK]

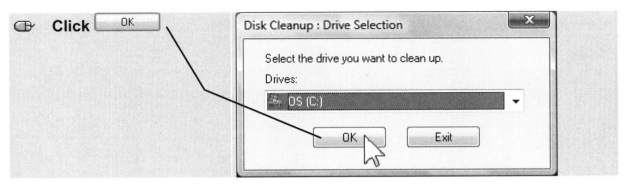

Disk Cleanup is now checking the C drive:

Here you will see which types of files can be deleted. When you check a box, you can see a description of the file type at the bottom of the window: —

Usually it is safe to delete all of these files. If you do not want to do that, clear the checkbox ☑ next to the file types you want to keep.

On this disk a total of 21.8 MB can be cleared: —

☞ **Click the tab** [More Options]

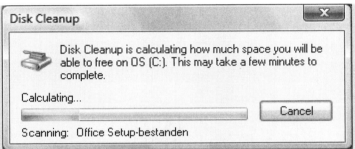

HELP! I do not see the More Options **tab.**

If you have chosen the → My files only option, you will not see the More Options tab. If this is the case, continue reading on page 72.

Sometimes you can delete other program files and system files as well. This is how you do that:

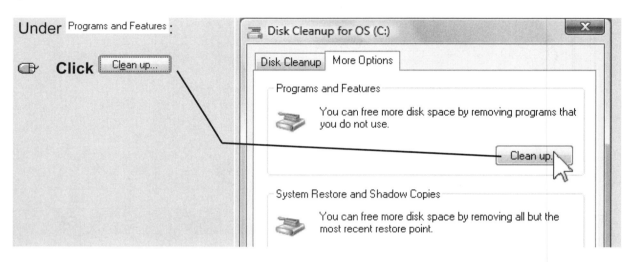

Under Programs and Features :

☞ **Click** Clean up...

Now you will see all of the programs that have been installed on your computer:

You can read more about deleting programs in *Chapter 3 Installing and Removing Programs*.

☞ **Click** ✕

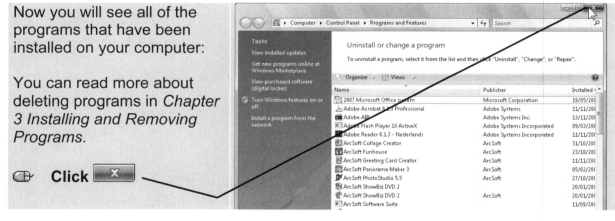

⇨ **Please note:**

In this list of programs you will also find additional auxiliary programs that are used to help other programs function correctly. Most likely you will not recognize the names of these auxiliary programs. That is why you should only remove known programs. If you are not sure, check the publisher's name. You may recognize this name if you have installed other programs from the same publisher.

Under System Restore and Shadow Copies.

👆 **Click** Clean up...

This is how you remove old backups and restore points.

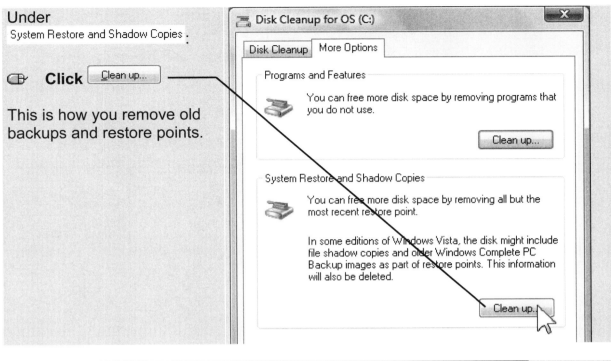

👆 **Click** Delete

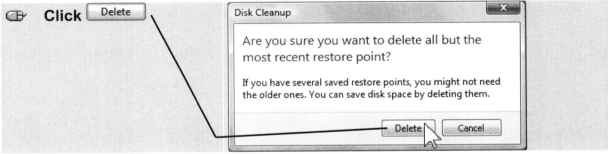

At the bottom of the window:

👆 **Click** OK

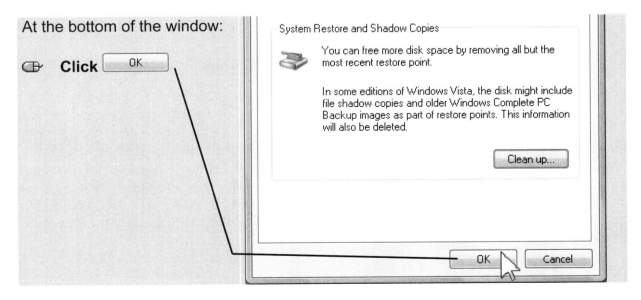

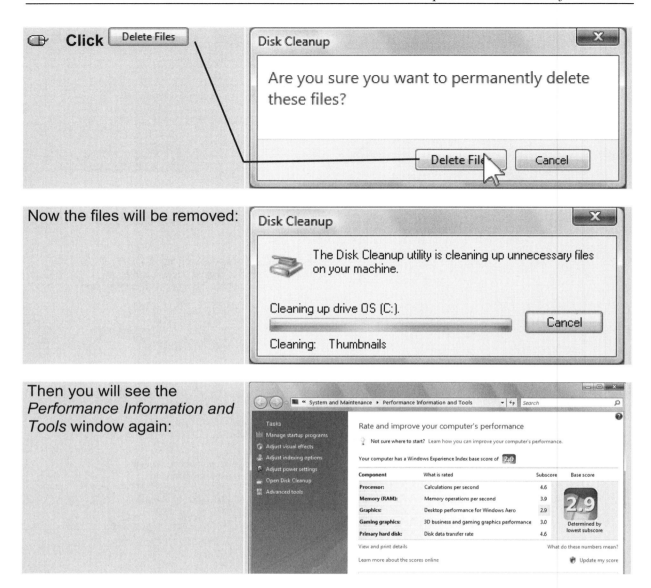

Click `Delete Files`

Now the files will be removed:

Then you will see the *Performance Information and Tools* window again:

2.6 Disk Defragmentation

When you have cleaned up your hard disk, you may be surprised to learn that a few empty spaces still remain on the disk. This is because you have deleted several files during the cleanup. The empty spaces will be filled over time when you save files or install new programs. However, to be able to work faster now, you can first re-arrange the existing data by using *Disk Defragmenter*. The files will then be stored on the hard disk in a more efficient manner. This will allow you to open your files in the quickest possible way.

This is how you do disk defragmentation:

⇨ **Please note:**

If you want to use *Disk Defragmenter* you need to have at least 15% free space on your hard disk.

☞ If necessary, open the *Performance Information and Tools* window **3**

👆 Click Advanced tools

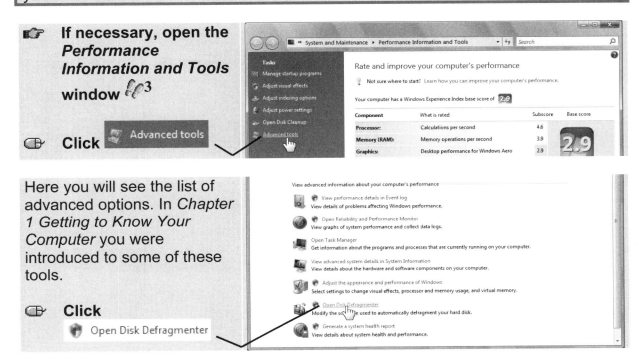

Here you will see the list of advanced options. In *Chapter 1 Getting to Know Your Computer* you were introduced to some of these tools.

👆 Click 🛡 Open Disk Defragmenter

Your screen goes dark and you will need to give permission to continue:

👆 Click Continue

The hard disk(s) will be analyzed:

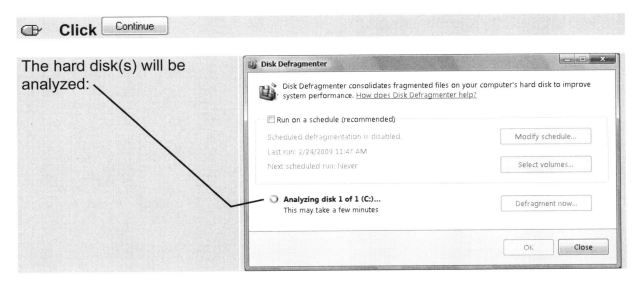

Now you will see an advice about whether to use disk defragmentation or not: ───

To defragment the hard disk:

☞ **Click**

[Defragment now...]

If defragmenting is not necessary, or if you want to execute this task later on:

☞ **Click** [Close]

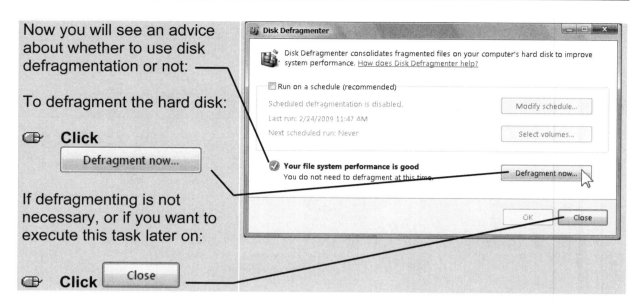

In the following steps you will see what happens when you start the disk defragmentation:

☞ **Select the disk or disks** ───

At the bottom of the window:

☞ **Click** [OK]

Which disk is most important to defragment depends on the way you use your computer. You can read more about this topic in the *Background Information* at the end of this chapter.

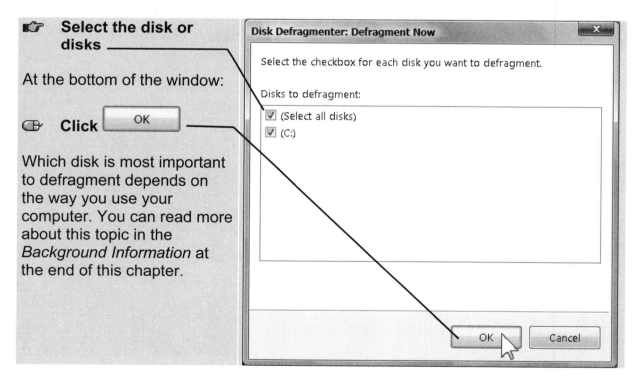

The defragmentation will start and you will see the message *This may take from a few minutes.*

While the defragmentation task runs you should not switch off the computer, but you can continue working as usual.

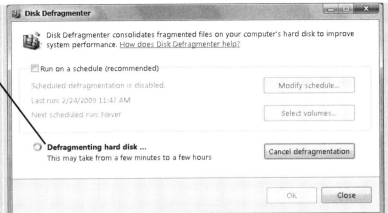

After defragmentation the disk will be analyzed again:

If the defragmentation task was completed succesfully, you will see the message *You do not need to defragment at t.*

Click [Close]

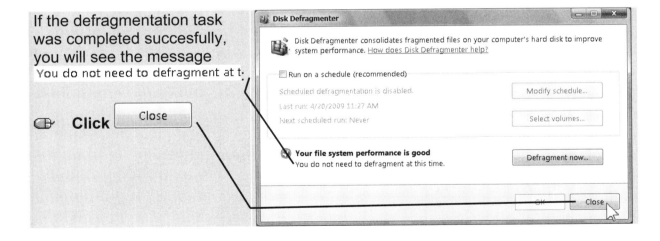

💡 **Tip**

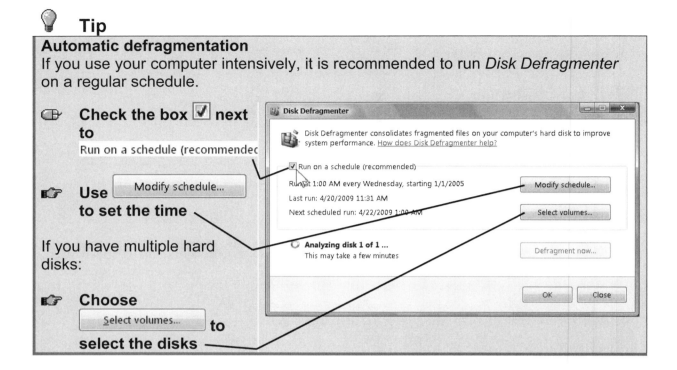

Automatic defragmentation

If you use your computer intensively, it is recommended to run *Disk Defragmenter* on a regular schedule.

☞ **Check the box ☑ next to**

Run on a schedule (recommended)

☞ **Use** [Modify schedule...] **to set the time**

If you have multiple hard disks:

☞ **Choose** [Select volumes...] **to select the disks**

2.7 System Health Report

Problems with your hardware, or with the programs you have installed, will often result in loss of computer speed. The System Health Report will help you analyze your system and find out what the problems are.

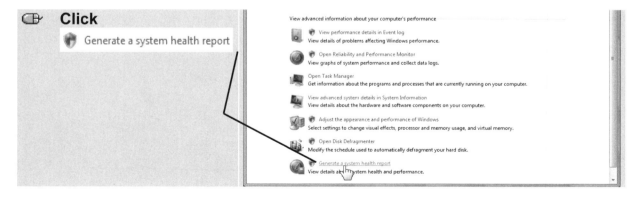

☞ **Click**

Generate a system health report

Your screen goes dark and you will need to give permission to continue:

☞ **Click** [Continue]

Now System Diagnostics will analyze your system:

After this, a report will be made and you will see this message:

Generating report...

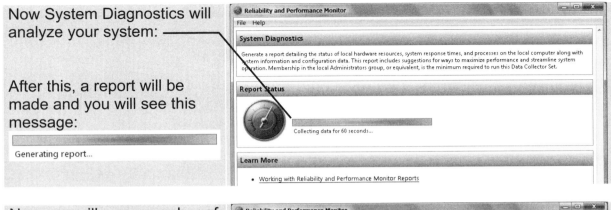

Now you will see a number of diagnostic results:

☞ **Click ⊞ next to** Disk Checks

You will see the tests and their results:

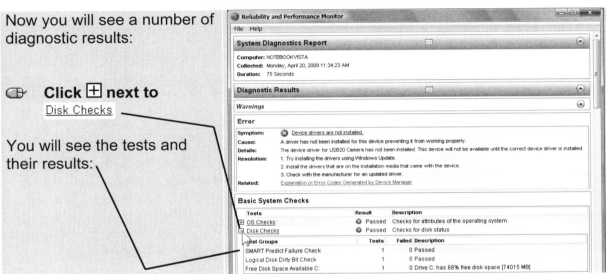

☞ **Drag the scroll bar down**

Here you will see other components that have been analyzed:

☞ **Click ⊙ next to CPU**

You will see some of the tests that were performed on the CPU (the processor):

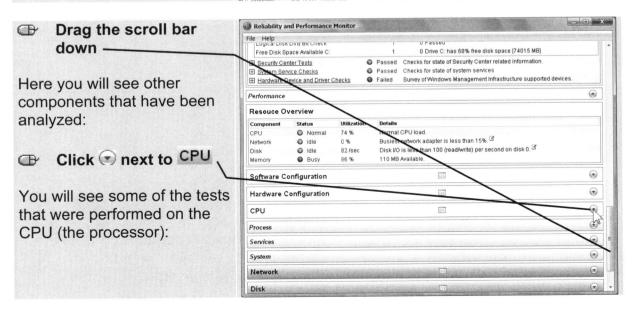

Sometimes you can click for further details:

To view the details:

 Click ⊙ next to *Process*

 Drag the scroll bar down

Now you will see the technical information about the processes:

☞ **Close all windows** ✐1

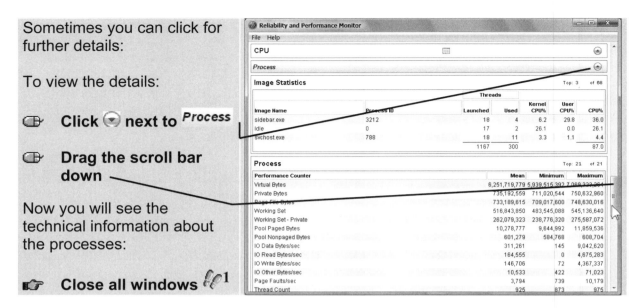

⚒ HELP! I do not understand what this information means.

You do not need to understand all the details of this information. It is important to notice any warnings the System Diagnostics Report might give you. On the Internet you can look up these warnings, read a description about it and perhaps find a solution. You can also contact your hardware supplier for support. You can find the warnings at the top of the report window:

Diagnostic Results		
Warnings		
Error		
Symptom:	⊗ Device drivers are not installed.	
Cause:	A driver has not been installed for this device preventing it from working properly.	
Details:	The device driver for USB20 Camera has not been installed. This device will not be available until the correct device driver is installed.	
Resolution:	1. Try installing the drivers using Windows Update.	
	2. Install the drivers that are on the installation media that came with the device.	
	3. Check with the manufacturer for an updated driver.	
Related:	Explanation of Error Codes Generated by Device Manager	

2.8 Checking Your Disk

The hard disk is one of the few moving mechanical parts of your computer. Mechanical components can wear out, that is why you should check your disk regularly. *Windows Vista* uses the *Disk Check Tool* to check the surface of the disk and mark sections that may be damaged. These sections will not be used anymore. If these sections contain data, the *Disk Check Tool* will try to save this data by storing it in a safe place. This will result in a higher speed, as well as in higher reliability, because data that is stored on damaged parts of a disk often cannot be retrieved quickly. It may take several attempts before the information can be retrieved.

It is best to check the disk before starting the disk defragmentation. *Windows Vista* will then be able to tell which sections of the disk are unreliable, and will skip these parts while storing data.

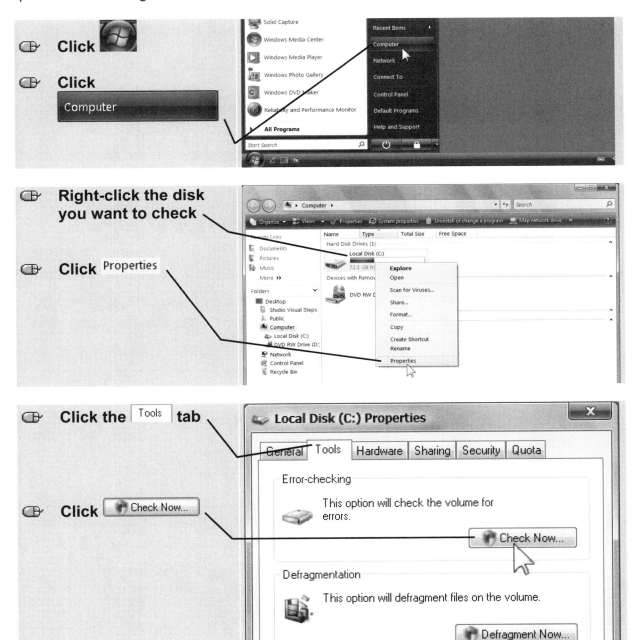

Your screen goes dark and you will need to give permission to continue:

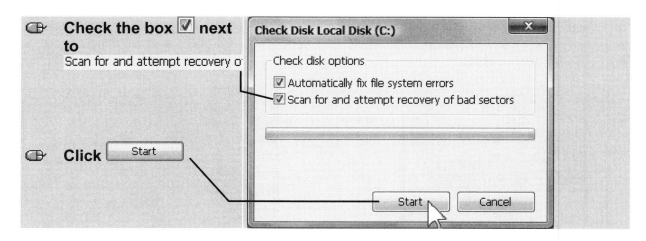

The Automatically fix file system errors option will only check if all data on the hard disk is still stored in the right place. This check will be performed quite quickly. The Scan for and attempt recovery of bad sectors option will check the disk itself for technical integrity. This takes much longer.

⇒ **Please note:**

Checking the disk can take up to several hours, particularly if you have a large hard disk. Do you want to postpone the check? Then click the Cancel button in the next window.

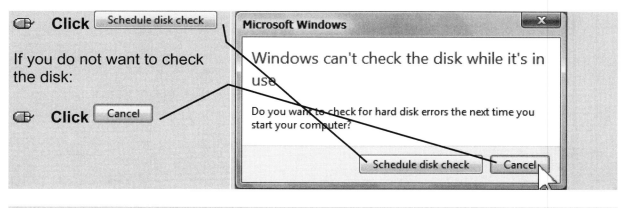

☞ **Close all windows** ℓℓ¹

☞ **Restart the computer**

⇒ **Please note:**

Do you want to postpone the *Disk Check* again after restarting your computer? Then press a key, when prompted. If you do not undertake any action after restarting the computer, the *Disk Check* will start automatically. You will not be able to cancel this task anymore.

The *Disk Check* will check the following items:

- are the files stored in the correct place on the hard disk, that is the place they should be stored according to the disk content list;
- are the indexes correct;
- are the 'security descriptions' correct; these descriptions indicate who the owner of a file is, who has access to the file, and which actions are allowed for this file;
- the content of the files; the content will be compared to the control information in the file itself;
- the free disk space and the reliability of this space.

If any errors are found, you will see error messages appear during the check. After having completed the check, *Windows Vista* will restart.

 HELP! My hard disk contains errors.

Usually you do not have to worry when *Disk Check* has found any errors on your hard disk. In due time most hard disks will show some wear and there will appear small lesions on the magnetic surface of the disk.
By regularly checking your disk using *Disk Check*, most data stored in damaged areas can be saved. If you postpone these checks for too long, the number of errors will increase and the disk will get slower and slower. Also, there is a bigger chance of losing data.
Does the number of errors increase with every check? Then this might be a signal that your hard disk should be replaced.

2.9 Paging File

In *paragraph 1.7 Priorities and the Paging File* you read about the size of the *paging file* (*virtual memory*) of your computer. The correct size of this paging file is important to the performance of your computer.

What is virtual memory?
If the computer cannot dispose of sufficient RAM memory to run a program or execute a task, *Windows* uses virtual memory.
This means that the RAM memory of the computer will be combined with a temporary memory space on the hard disk. When RAM is insufficient, data will be moved from the RAM to this space on your hard disk. This space is called the paging file. By swapping data to and from the paging file, RAM memory will be freed for tasks that still have to be executed.

- Continue reading on the next page -

A larger RAM will let you run programs much faster. If your computer's performance is deteriorating due to insufficient RAM, you would think that expanding the virtual memory would be a good idea. However, your computer can read data from RAM much more quickly than from a hard disk, so adding RAM is a better solution.

If you receive error messages that warn of low virtual memory, you need to either add more RAM or increase the size of your paging file so that you can run the programs on your computer. *Windows* usually manages the size automatically, but you can manually change the size of virtual memory if the default size is not enough for your needs.

Source: Windows Help and Support

☞ **Open the *System* window** ℓℓ⁴

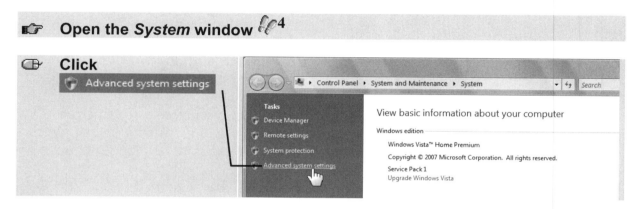

Your screen goes dark and you will need to give permission to continue:

Click [Continue]

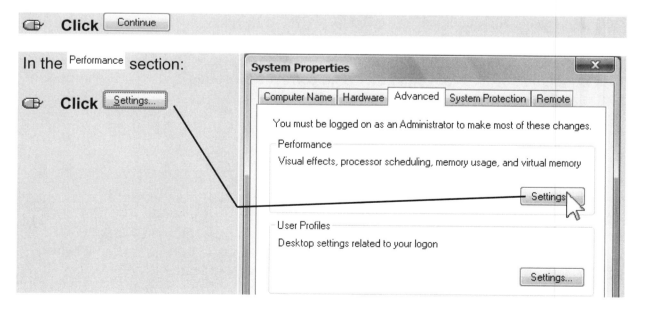

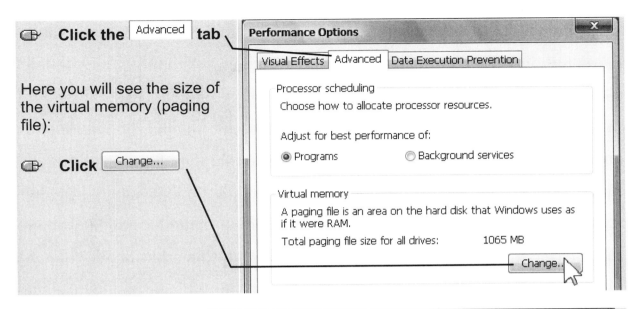

Click the `Advanced` **tab**

Here you will see the size of the virtual memory (paging file):

Click `Change...`

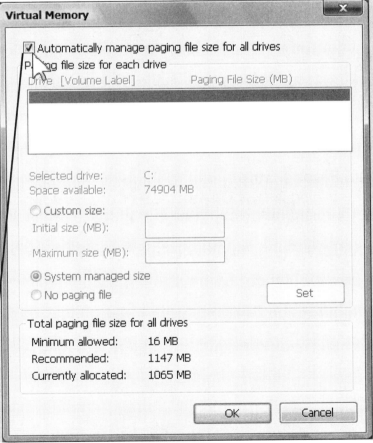

If your system functions properly, it is best to let *Windows Vista* manage the size of the paging file. Here you see the current settings:

The paging file can be located on one or more hard disks. In this window the paging file is located on the C drive.

If you want to change the size:

Click a check box ☑️ **next to**
Automatically manage paging file si

Now the paging file will no longer be managed automatically, but you can manage it yourself.

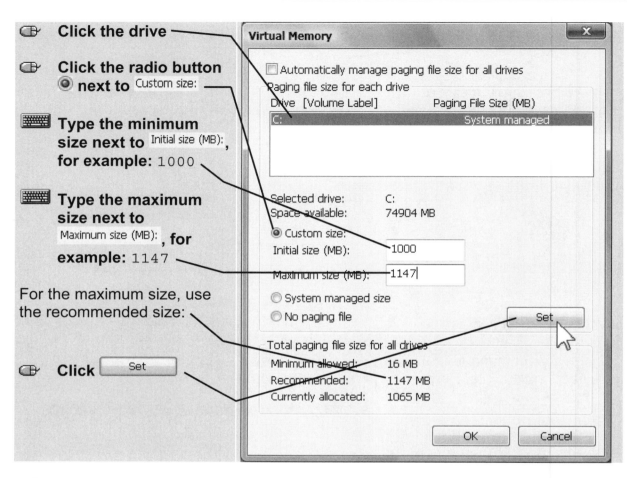

Click the drive

Click the radio button next to Custom size:

Type the minimum size next to Initial size (MB):, **for example:** 1000

Type the maximum size next to Maximum size (MB): , **for example:** 1147

For the maximum size, use the recommended size:

Click [Set]

⇨ **Please note:**

If the paging file is too large, the extra space will hardly be used, but will be set aside on your hard disk. You will have less space left for your own data.

If the paging file is too small, you will see a message:

Only click the button [Yes] if you do not have enough space on your hard disk and therefore cannot choose a larger paging file.

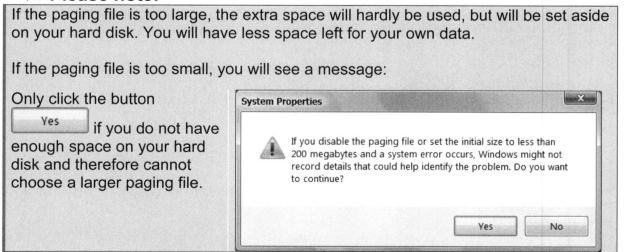

If you have little RAM memory, but enough space on your hard disk, you can choose a large paging file. If you have a lot of RAM memory, you can use a smaller paging file and save space on your hard disk. How you define a large or a small RAM memory depends on the way you use your computer. Video editing programs, for example, will use a lot of RAM memory and will often need to use the paging file.

Now you will see the new settings:

To apply these settings:

☞ **Click** OK

If you do not want to change anything:

☞ **Click** Cancel

If your system performs slower afterwards, you can go back to letting the system manage your paging file automatically.

☞ **Close all windows** ℓℓ¹

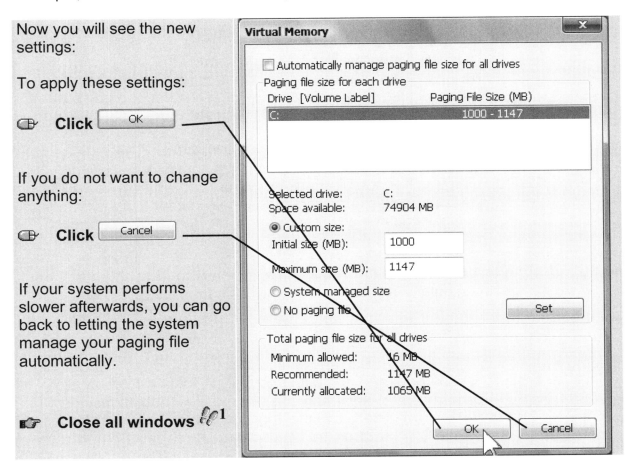

2.10 Background Information

Dictionary	
Disk cleanup	To free up space on your hard disk, *Disk Cleanup* finds and then removes temporary files on your computer that you decide you no longer need. Disk space will be freed up and your computer will run faster. Also, the *Recycle Bin* will be emptied and several unnecessary system files will be removed.
Disk defragmentation	Fragmentation happens to a hard disk over time as you save, change or delete files. As a result, the hard disk has to work harder to find your files and programs, and will slow down. *Disk Defragmenter* is a tool that rearranges your hard disk and reunites fragmented files so your computer can run more efficiently.
Index	A collection of detailed information about the files on your computer. The index allows you to perform fast, accurate searches by using information about the files to help you find them.
Paging file	A hidden file or files on the hard disk that *Windows* uses to hold parts of programs and data files that do not fit in memory. The paging file and physical memory, or random access memory (RAM), comprise virtual memory. *Windows* moves data from the paging file to memory as needed and moves data from memory to the paging file to make room for new data. Also known as a swap file.
Power management	Automatically enabling or disabling computer components if they are not used within a set period of time. This will save computer energy.
Startup program	Program that will automatically start after *Windows Vista* has been loaded.
Visual effects	Graphics that enhance your screen image, such as color schemes, shadow windows and transparent windows.

Source: Windows Help and Support

Indexes

An index will allow *Windows Vista* to find files on your computer faster, the same way you look up a topic in the index of a book. The index contains information about files, such as the file name, the date when it was last modified, and other properties, for example the author, labels and classification. The index is never displayed, but will be used by *Windows Vista* to execute quick searches for most common files on your computer.

When you search for a file name or file property, *Windows* will not search the complete hard disk but only the *Windows* index, which will usually produce much quicker results than searching without using the index.

If you cannot find what you are looking for, you can use other search tools, such as *Windows Explorer*, to search through all the data. This will take much longer.

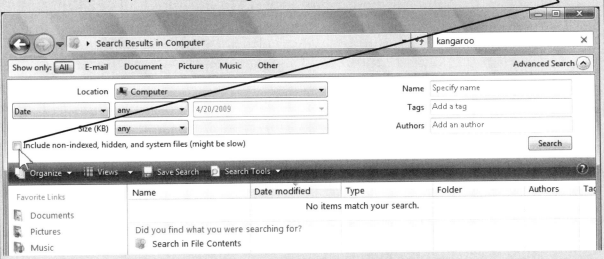

If you add too many folders or drives to the index, your computer will run much slower instead of faster. Only add the folders to the index that you use to store your data in. Remove unused folders from the index.

You can only add locations to the index from your local computer. Network locations or external disks cannot be indexed, that is why searches executed on these external locations will always be slower than searches on the computer itself.

Disk defragmentation

When you save a file to the computer, this file will not be stored in one single location. Depending on the size of the file, the file will be stored in several pieces (fragmented) that are located in different places on the hard disk. The original file consists of all these fragments put together. The reason for this is faster access and storage of files. A hard disk usually consists of multiple disks, assembled in one storage unit. Each side of these disks has its own read/write head. You will not notice any of this, because *Windows* regards this as one disk and has assigned the drive letter C or D to the disk. If you save or open a file, and this file would be stored in a single location, one read/write head would be very busy while the others would be idle. Instead, the tasks are divided between the various heads. *Windows* uses tables to keep track of all the file locations and fragments.

Fragmentation happens to a hard disk over time as you save, change, or delete files. The changes that you save to a file are often stored at a location on the hard disk that's different from the original file. Additional changes are saved to even more locations. Over time, both the file and the hard disk itself become fragmented, and your computer slows down as it has to look in many different places to open a file.

Disk Defragmenter is a tool that rearranges the data on your hard disk and reunites fragmented files so your computer can run more efficiently. In *Windows Vista*, *Disk Defragmenter* runs on a schedule so you don't have to remember to run it, although you can still run it manually or change the schedule it uses (see the *Tip* at the end of *paragraph 2.6 Disk Defragmentation*).

Defragmenting your disk with *Disk Defragmenter* may take minutes or even several hours, depending on the size and free space of your hard disk. If you want to use this tool you need at least 15% free space on your hard disk. If you do not have enough free space, you need to delete files or move them to another location first.

While the disk is being defragmented you can keep using your computer.

Do you have more than one disk or partition? Then you can defragment each disk or partition separately. The disk which is used most, usually the disk which contains your data, will be defragmented most often.

Source: Windows Help and Support

Different types of memory
Besides hard disks, CD-ROMs and DVDs the computer uses various types of electronic (digital) memory. Digital memory is much faster than the mechanical memory mentioned above.

RAM   *Random Access Memory* also called built-in or internal memory. The main internal storage area the computer uses to run programs and store data. Information stored in RAM is temporary and is designed to clear when the computer is turned off.
The RAM consists of several cards which contain memory chips. You can often expand this type of memory by inserting extra cards. Because these chips are very fast, the size of RAM memory is very important and decisive for the overall speed of your computer. Please note that different types and speeds of RAM memory exist. A memory card with the wrong speed can result in errors and computer failure.

ROM   *Read Only Memory*. This memory can only be accessed to read. Built-in computer memory that can be read by a computer but cannot be modified. Unlike random access memory (RAM), the information stored in ROM is not cleared when the computer is turned off. Among other things, the ROM contains the instructions for the computer to start up, once it is switched on.

Flash   A small device used to store data, for example a USB stick. USB sticks can be inserted into the USB port of a computer and you can use them to transport data between various computers. After removing the stick from the USB port, the data will remain stored on the USB stick. The memory can be cleared and the data on the flash device can be overwritten. Memory cards in digital cameras and mobile phones also use flash memory.

Virtual   Temporary storage space on a hard disk or USB stick, used to run programs that need more RAM memory than the computer contains.

- Continue reading on the next page -

| Cache | Cache memory is extremely fast but expensive memory, built-in in the processor or hard disk. This memory is used to temporarily store much-used data, so the computer does not have to look up these data every time. Furthermore, the indexing tables are often stored in the cache memory. A large cache memory can really increase the speed of your computer. Because the cache memory is built-in, you cannot expand this type of memory yourself. |

Of all these types of memory, the RAM influences your computer speed the most. Keep in mind that the 32 bits edition of *Windows Vista* can address a maximum of 4 GB directly. If the RAM is larger, the speed will decrease somewhat.

Checking and maintaining your disk
In this chapter you have learned how to check and maintain your hard disk. It is best to do this in the following order:

- *Disk Cleanup*
  First delete the temporary files with *Disk Cleanup*. Do this regularly, for example once a week.
- *Disk Defragmentation*
  If you use your hard disk frequently to save, modify or delete files, you should use *Disk Defragmenter* quite often. It is not necessary to use this tool after every disk cleanup, but once a month would be a good idea.
- *Disk Check*
  Also use the *Disk Checker Tool* regularly. If your computer is fairly new, once every three months should be enough. If you have an older computer, or if you often experience read or write failures while working, then you need to perform this check more often.

Run these checks separately for each disk. You can also set a schedule for each disk. A disk which contains your personal data will have to be defragmented more often than a disk which contains only software programs, because these programs do not change much.

In addition to this, it is very important to make an extra backup copy of your data before you start defragmenting the disk. If the defragmentation task goes wrong, you might lose data.

2.11 Tips

 Tip

Check your computer for viruses and spyware
Does your computer run much slower all at once? Run a full scan of your hard disk and check for viruses and spyware by using your antivirus program and *Windows Defender*.

 Tip

Use a single antivirus program and a single firewall
It may seem very safe to use more than one antivirus program or firewall, but it is better not to do so. Usually these programs do not work well together and they may even work against each other.
At any rate your computer will often run much slower. So disable your old antivirus program or firewall first, before installing a new program.

 Tip

Keep your desktop simple
Desktops with large amounts of animated pictures will slow down the computer. Removing all unnecessary icons from your desktop will speed up the computer.

 Tip

Close programs you do not use
Many users start up programs they use for just a minute, and do not close them until they switch off the computer. Because these programs will remain stored in the internal memory they will slow down the other programs, even when you do not use them. That is why you should close the programs you do not use for a longer period of time.

 Tip

Paging file and index on the fastest disk drive
A hard disk is much slower than RAM memory. If you have more than one hard disk, then store your paging file and indexes on the fastest disk drive. This will cause the least amount of delay. These files cannot be stored on external disks.

Tip

Speed up your computer by expanding your hardware
Even if you choose the best possible settings, your computer will slow down in due time. By adding new hardware you might be able to get the computer to perform a bit faster again. Here are some possibilities for expanding your computer effectively:

Faster hard disk	A faster internal hard disk can add quite a bit more speed. Pay attention to the speed of the hard disk, usually expressed in rpm (rotations per minute). A disk with 5400 rpm is clearly slower than a disk with 7200 rpm. Besides this, hard disks contain a cache memory, a very fast memory that is used to temporarily store frequently used data, so they do not have to be retrieved from the (slower) hard disk every time. It is not easy to expand cache memory, so if you value speed you need to choose a hard disk with a large cache memory. External hard disks always experience a certain delay because they use a USB or firewire connection. When you purchase a hard disk, you should also note the speed of these connections.
More RAM memory	RAM memory is cheap and can really increase speed. But keep in mind that the 32 bit edition of *Windows Vista* can address a maximum of 4 GB RAM directly. If the RAM memory is larger, the speed will decrease again. In the *Background Information* at the end of this chapter you can read more about the different kinds of memory.
Faster graphics card	*Windows Vista* along with other programs is graphic intensive. A faster graphics card will allow the computer to display windows much quicker and will save processor capacity. A graphics card which uses *shared memory* (a part of your RAM memory), will perform much slower than a card which uses its own memory.
Faster processor	This may seem a logical solution, but is quite expensive and the results will depend on the overall configuration of your computer. And remember that not every motherboard is suited to a faster processor.

Which expansion is best suited to speed up your computer, will depend on the way you use your computer. If you pay attention and note exactly when the computer experiences delays, you will probably be able to determine the components that cause the delays yourself.

Tip

...uding certain file types from the indexes

...des choosing the location that needs to be indexed, you can also define which ...ypes will be indexed. If you have stored thousands of photos on your hard disk, ...ave them neatly arranged in folders, you do not need to index these photos. ...means you can disable the index option for the .JPG and .JPEG file types. If ...lecide to do this, then keep in mind that all files of this type will no longer be ...ced.

Open the *Performance Information and Tools* window $\ell\ell^3$

Click
☐ Adjust indexing options

... bottom of the window:

Click ☐ Advanced

...creen goes dark and you will need to give permission to continue:

...lick Continue

...lick the File Types tab

...ou will see all the file ...extensions). By ...g a box ☑ or ...cking a box ☐ you can ... or disable the indexing

...an choose to have the ...ties or the content ...d. Indexing the ...nts will take longer and ...ly be useful if the files ...n readable text.

Click OK

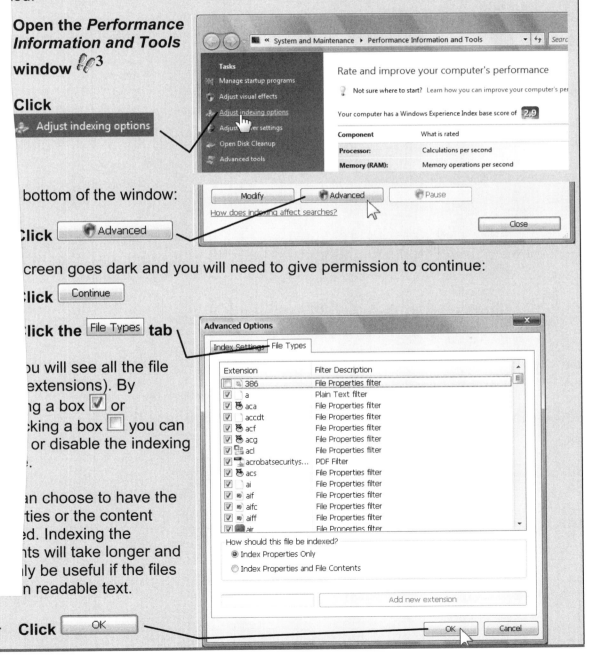

Tip

Per user disk quota
If your computer is being used by multiple users, you can restrict the space these users can occupy on the hard disk. For each hard disk you can set certain quota, to prevent users from filling the fastest hard disk. You can only set these quota for new users, not for existing users:

☞ **Open the *Properties* window of the hard disk where you want to set quota** 📖5

☞ **Click the** `Quota` **tab**

☞ **Click**
`Show Quota Settings`

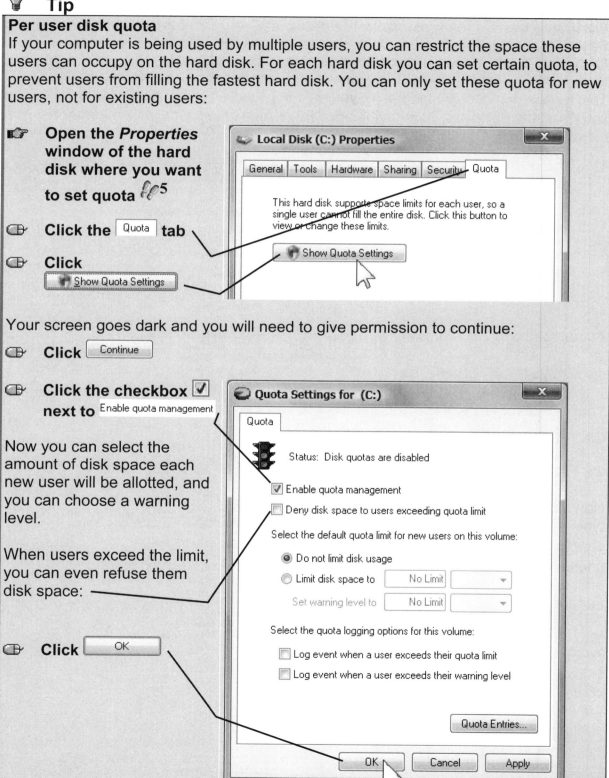

Your screen goes dark and you will need to give permission to continue:

☞ **Click** `Continue`

☞ **Click the checkbox** ☑
next to `Enable quota management`

Now you can select the amount of disk space each new user will be allotted, and you can choose a warning level.

When users exceed the limit, you can even refuse them disk space:

☞ **Click** `OK`

Tip

Windows ReadyBoost

With *Windows ReadyBoost* you can use storage space on external, removable media (such as a USB stick), in order to make your computer perform faster. When you attach such a device to your computer, you will see an option at the bottom of the *AutoPlay* window. This enables you to speed up your computer using *Windows ReadyBoost*.

☞ **Click**

    Speed up my system
    using Windows ReadyBoost

If you do not see this option in this window, the USB stick is not suitable for *Windows ReadyBoost*.

> Play videos
> using Windows Media Center
>
> General options
>
> Open folder to view files
> using Windows Explorer
>
> Speed up my system
> using Windows ReadyBoost
>
> Set AutoPlay defaults in Control Panel

Now you will see the *Properties* window:

☞ **Click the radio button**
   ◉ **next to** Use this device.

Here you can choose how much memory space you want to reserve:

> **UDISK (E:) Properties**
>
> General | Tools | Hardware | Sharing | ReadyBoost | Customize
>
> Speed up your system by utilizing the available space on this device.
>
> ○ Do not use this device.
>
> ◉ Use this device.
>
> Space to reserve for system speed:
>
> 1800 ▲▼ MB
>
> While the device is being used for system speed the reserved space will not be available for file storage.
>
> Windows recommends reserving 1800 MB for optimal performance.
>
> Please read our privacy statement (online)
>
> OK | Cancel | Apply

- Continue reading on the next page -

The recommended amount of memory for *Windows ReadyBoost* is about one to three times as large as the RAM memory of your computer. For example: if the computer has a 512 MB RAM memory and you attach a USB stick of 4 GB, you will achieve the best results if you reserve from 512 MB up to 1,5 GB of this USB stick for the *Windows ReadyBoost* enhancement.

There might be situations where you will not be able to use all the available memory on the storage device to speed up your computer. USB sticks can contain slow flash memory, as well as fast flash memory, and *Windows Vista* can only use fast flash memory to enhance the computer speed. If your storage device uses slow flash memory and also fast flash memory, you can only use the fast memory for *Windows ReadyBoost*.

Windows ReadyBoost memory is faster than the virtual memory of your paging file, but slower than normal RAM memory. You can only use *Windows ReadyBoost* while the USB stick is inserted into your computer. If you are looking for a more permanent solution, you would be better off expanding your RAM memory. You can ask your hardware supplier to expand the RAM memory for you.

Please note: not all USB sticks are suitable for *Windows ReadyBoost*. If you want to buy a USB stick for use with *Windows ReadyBoost*, then first check the specifications carefully before buying.

3. Installing and Removing Programs

Installing new software programs is a task that can be done in different ways, depending on the program and your computer. The instructions in this chapter are based on the most common installation procedures. Some software may require a different set of instructions. Computers are not alike. They use different programs and the hardware attached can vary greatly. Before you start an installation you need to read the instructions carefully. It is also important to pay attention to what you see in the various windows, to read the text carefully and to follow the instructions you see on the screen.

In this chapter you will see a few examples of standard installation procedures. However, you should always follow the instructions in the installation manual of your specific program.

In this chapter you will learn how to:

- install programs;
- use the compatibility settings;
- repair programs;
- remove programs.

⇨ **Please note:**

In this chapter you will learn how to start an installation program for installing or removing software. To install the program itself you need to follow the instructions applicable to the specific program.

3.1 Installing Programs in Vista

Installing programs in *Windows Vista* is quite simple. After inserting the CD or DVD, or after starting the installation program, you can proceed by following the instructions on the screen.

⇨ **Please note:**

If you want to install full programs you usually need to be logged in as an administrator. If you are logged in as a standard user, *Windows* will not always allow you to modify the computer settings and as a result, the program will not work well.

There are three common installation methods:

Method 1: installing from an autorun CD or DVD.

If the program you want to install is stored on a CD or a DVD, it will often start up automatically:

☞ **Insert the CD/DVD in the CD/DVD drive**

After a while you will see the *AutoPlay* window:

☞ **Click**

The name of the program and its manufacturer will be different on your own computer.

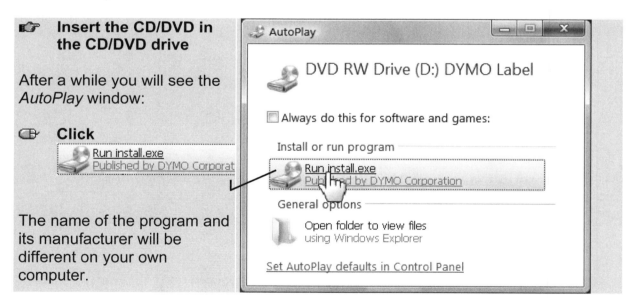

Your screen goes dark and you will need to give permission to continue:

☞ **Click** Continue

After this you need to follow the instructions in each consecutive window or as shown in the installation manual. Usually you will need to accept the license agreement first. If you do not accept this, you will not be allowed to install the program.

Method 2: installing from a CD or DVD that does not start automatically.

Whether a CD or DVD will start automatically, depends on the settings on your computer. If the *Autorun* option is disabled, you will need to start the installation program manually:

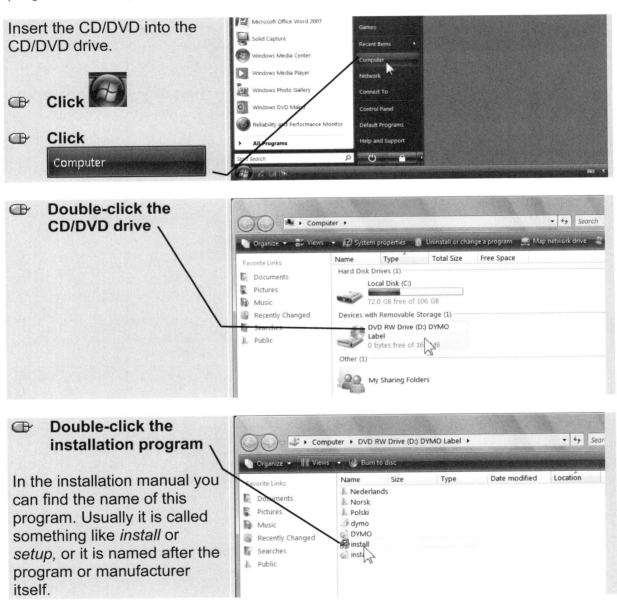

Insert the CD/DVD into the CD/DVD drive.

☞ **Click**

☞ **Click** Computer

☞ **Double-click the CD/DVD drive**

☞ **Double-click the installation program**

In the installation manual you can find the name of this program. Usually it is called something like *install* or *setup,* or it is named after the program or manufacturer itself.

Your screen goes dark and you will need to give permission to continue:

☞ **Click** Continue

In most cases, just follow the instructions in each consecutive window or as shown in the installation manual. You will also need to accept the license agreement. If you do not accept this, you will not be allowed to install the program.

Method 3: downloading and installing a program.

If you download a program, you will be able to start the installation program right after you have finished downloading. This is how you can download and install a program:

In this example the photo editing program *Picasa* will be downloaded:

☞ **Read the download instructions for this program on the *Picasa* website**

☞ **Click the button to start downloading**

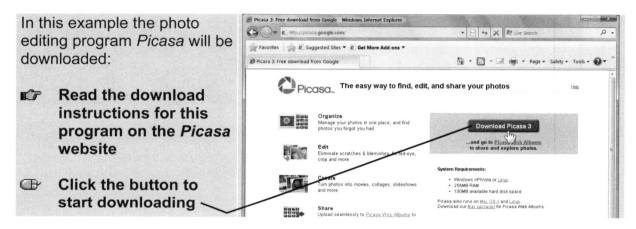

While you are downloading programs you may also bring in unwanted viruses. That is why *Internet Explorer* often blocks downloads. This is how you can solve this issue:

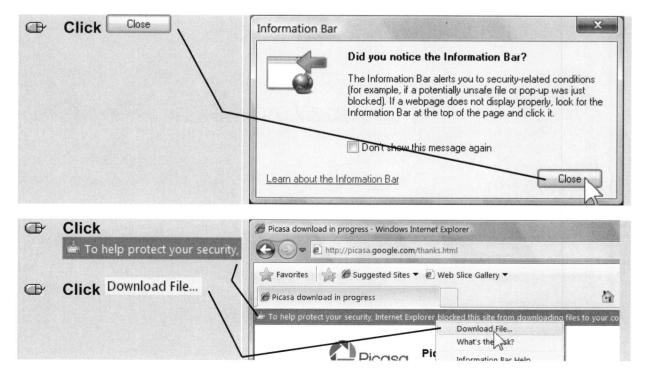

HELP! The download does not start.

It may often take a while before the downloading begins. If this takes too long, then click the link that will start the download immediately:

If necessary, click the download button click here **to start downloading right away**

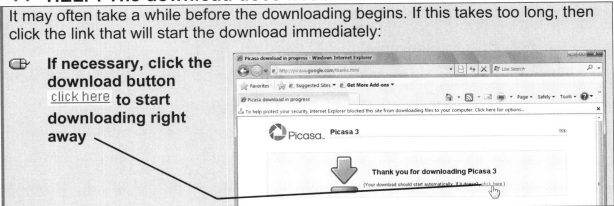

You can open the installation program right away, or you can save the program to your computer first. If you choose to save the program first, you will be able to use it later on to install the program again, in case the program no longer works. If your Internet connection is slow, it is better to save the program first.

In this example the program is saved first:

Click Save

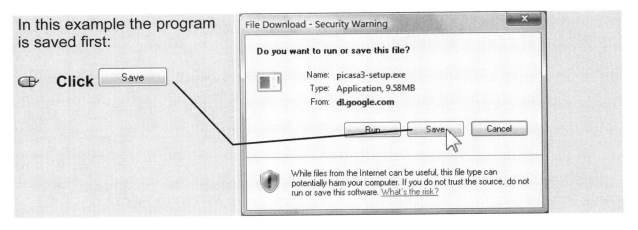

⇨ Please note:

The files you have saved will take up space on your hard disk. If you want to, you can delete them again after you have installed the program.

The file will be saved in the Downloads **folder:**

If you want to choose another location, click Browse Folders .

Click Save

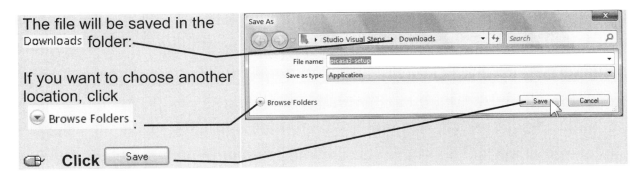

After the download is complete, you can open the installation program:

Click Run

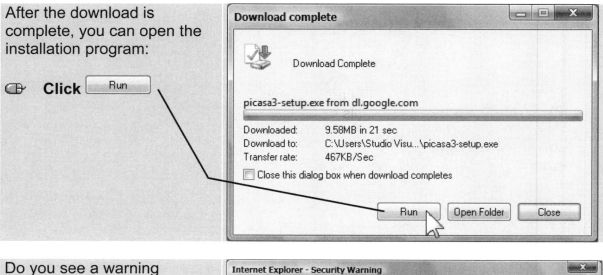

Do you see a warning message?

☞ **Check if the name of the program is correct**

Click Run

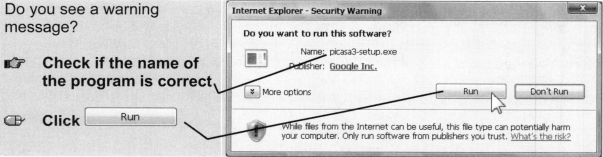

Your screen goes dark and you will need to give permission to continue:

Click Continue

After this the installation program will start and the installation will continue in the same way as described for an installation procedure from a CD or a DVD.

 Tip

Many programs, websites or manufacturers provide registration numbers and user names via e-mail. Create a separate folder for this data in your e-mail program, or in your *Personal folder*, so you will be able to retrieve this information quickly. Keep in mind that your computer may one day crash or be stolen. This is why it is essential that you store important passwords and user names separately, and make regular backups. You can also print a list of these important items and store them in the same way you store other important documents.

3.2 Program Compatibility Assistant

Most of the time, you can install older programs on a *Windows Vista* computer without any trouble. Sometimes this will work in the same way as described in the previous section, but other times the actual program or the installation process does not fit well with *Windows Vista*. In this case you can use the *Program Compatibility Assistant*. This is how you use it:

🖝 **Open the program**

Windows Vista detects a problem:

If you have installed the program correctly and have not experienced any problems during the installation, you can do this:

🖰 **Click**

→ This program installed correctly

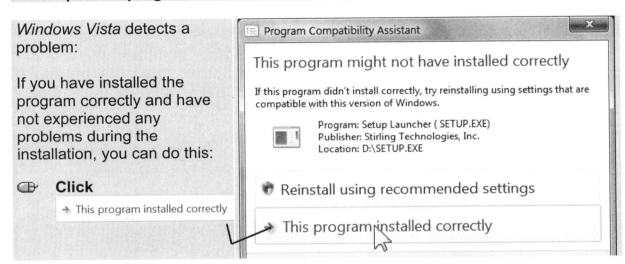

If you choose Reinstall using recommended settings the program will be installed again. Since the files previously installed are going to be overwritten, you will need to click *Yes* quite a few times, in order to give permission to overwrite these files. This can be very annoying, especially if it is a large program with lots of files. It is better to start the program first, by clicking This program installed correctly . If necessary, you can adjust the settings manually later on. In the next section you will read how to do this.

Program Compatibility Assistant or Wizard?
If you open a program that was created for an older edition of *Windows*, the *Program Compatibility Assistant* will check if the program is compatible with *Windows Vista*. If a problem is detected, you will see the message above. If the problem is serious, you will see a warning message, or the program is actually blocked. In this case you will be able to search for an online solution.

- Continue reading on the next page -

The *Program Compatibility Assistant* is a *Windows* program that will automatically start when compatibility problems are detected, due to an older program. You cannot open this program yourself.
The *Program Compatibility Wizard* on the other hand, is a tool that you can open yourself. You can use this tool to solve compatibility problems manually. Later on in this chapter you will read how to use the *Wizard*.

If a program is not suitable for *Windows Vista*, an error message will be displayed:

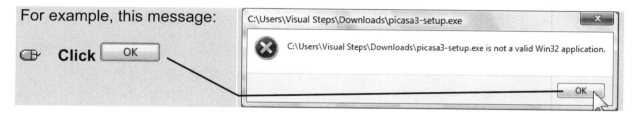

⇨ **Please note:**

Depending on the specific problem, other types of error messages may appear. These messages may show up when installing or opening a particular program.

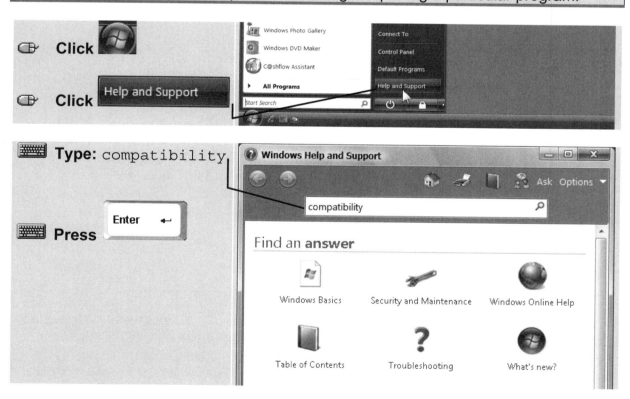

Click
Make older programs ru

On your screen, this hyperlink
might occupy a different
position when the list is
shown.

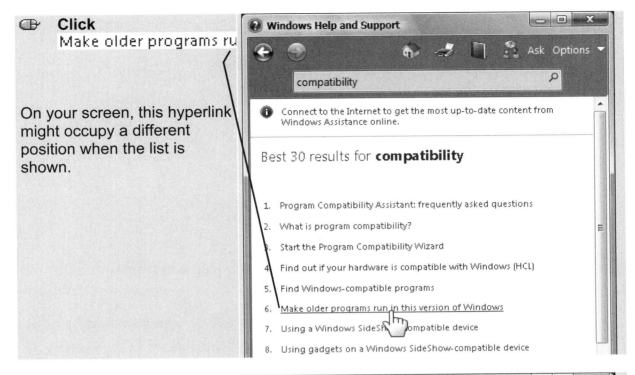

Read the information

Click
→ Click to open the Progran

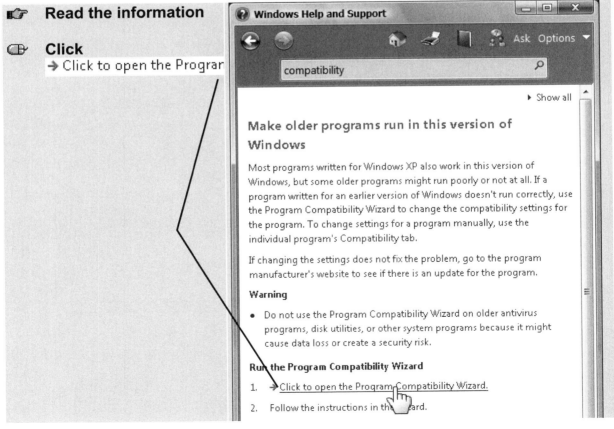

Note the warning:

In the *Background Information* at the end of this chapter you will find more information about this topic:

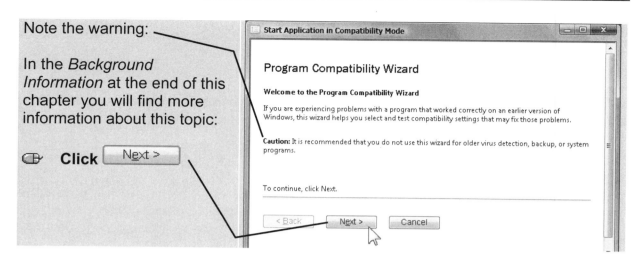

There are three options. Choose the option that best fits your situation:

Situation 1: the program has already been installed, but will not start.

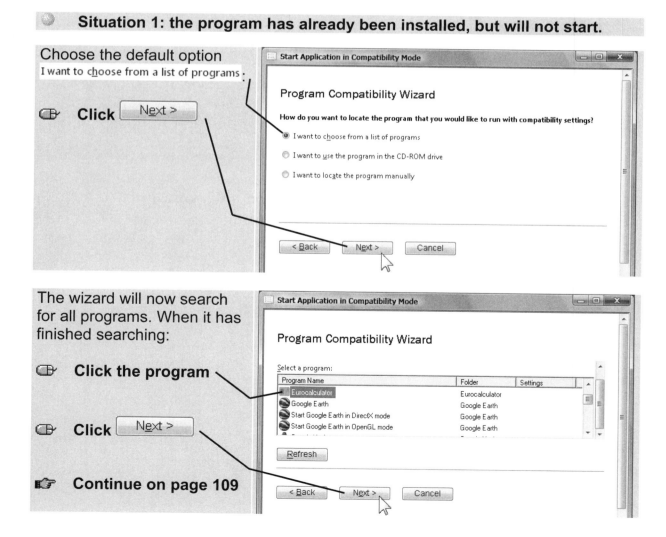

Choose the default option
I want to choose from a list of programs

The wizard will now search for all programs. When it has finished searching:

Click the program

Click Next >

☞ **Continue on page 109**

Situation 2: the program is still stored on a CD or DVD.

☞ **Insert the installation CD/DVD**

☞ **If necessary, close the *AutoPlay* window** 📖¹

🖱 **Click the radio button ◉ next to**
I want to use the program in the CI

🖱 **Click** [N<u>e</u>xt >]

☞ **Continue on page 109**

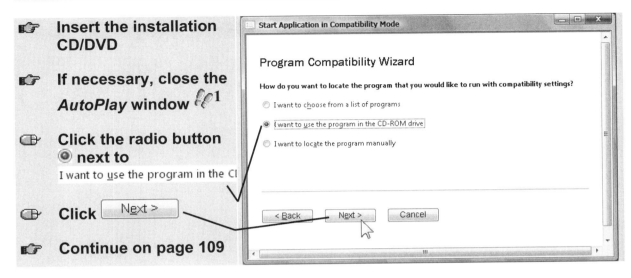

Situation 3: the program has not yet been installed, or cannot be found.

🖱 **Click the radio button ◉ next to**
I want to loc<u>a</u>te the program man<u>u</u>

🖱 **Click** [N<u>e</u>xt >]

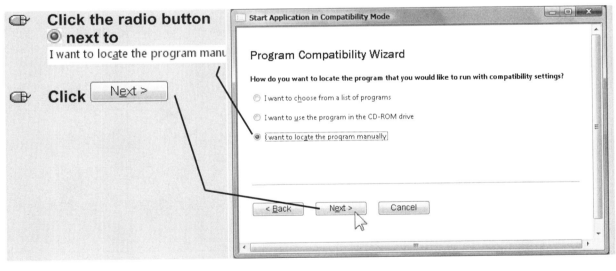

🖱 **Click** [Bro<u>w</u>se]

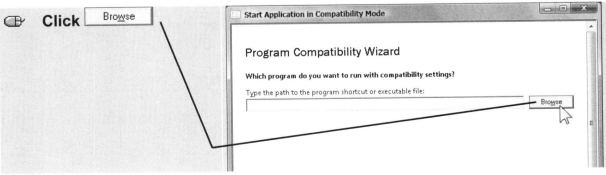

☞ **Browse to the folder that contains the installation program**

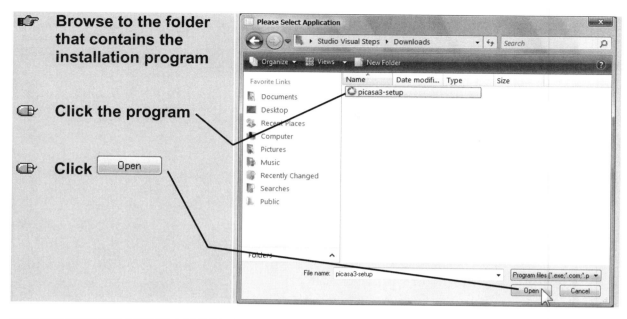

🖱 **Click the program**

🖱 **Click** [Open]

Now the program's location information has been filled in:

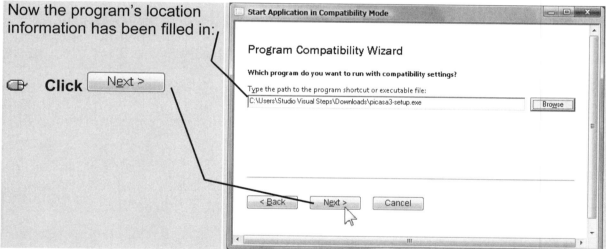

🖱 **Click** [Ne_xt >]

⇨ **Please note:**

When *Windows* closes a program due to compatibility problems, this will be because there is a chance that running this program will damage *Windows*. If *Windows* detects an incompatible program that might damage your computer (for example, by damaging important system files), the program will be closed and you will see a warning message.

You can always ask the manufacturer if an updated version of this program exists.

By choosing compatibility settings, you can determine how *Windows Vista* should behave while running older programs, for example *Windows 95* or *Windows XP*.

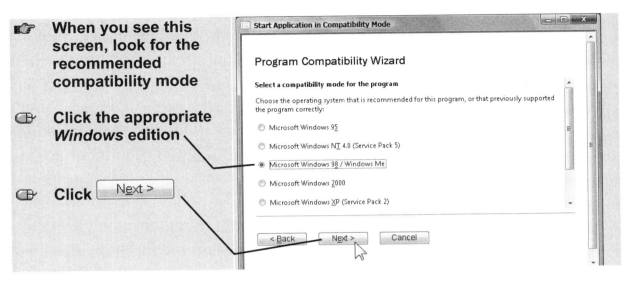

☞ **When you see this screen, look for the recommended compatibility mode**

🖱 **Click the appropriate *Windows* edition**

🖱 **Click** [N<u>e</u>xt >]

✺ HELP! For which Windows edition is my program best suited?

If there are no specifications available for your program, then try the most recent edition of *Windows* first, that is *Windows XP*. If this does not work, try *Windows 98* and after that, *Windows 95*. By selecting *Windows 95* first when the program is also suitable for *Windows XP* or *98*, there is a chance you will not be able to use all of the features of the particular program.

The other editions of *Windows* listed above are special editions. If you do not succeed with *Windows XP*, *98* or *95*, then you can always try one of the other editions, but there is only a small chance that your program will run with these editions.

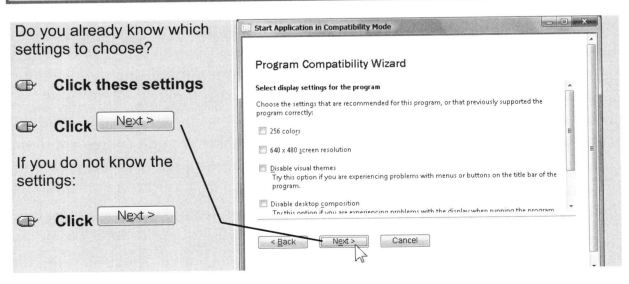

Do you already know which settings to choose?

🖱 **Click these settings**

🖱 **Click** [N<u>e</u>xt >]

If you do not know the settings:

🖱 **Click** [N<u>e</u>xt >]

An installation program will often need to adjust certain system settings, and that is only possible when you are logged in as an administrator.

If the program needs to run with *Windows 98* or an earlier edition:

☞ **Check the checkbox ☑ next to**

Run this program as an administrator

☞ **Click** Next >

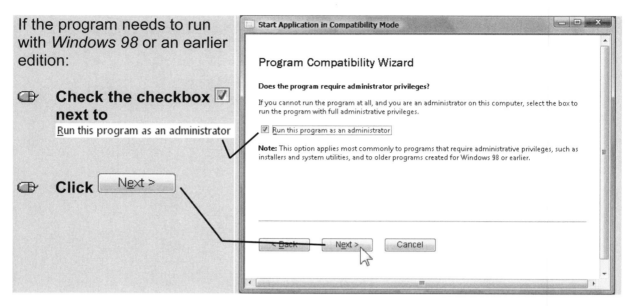

Now you will see the settings you have chosen:

☞ **Click** Next >

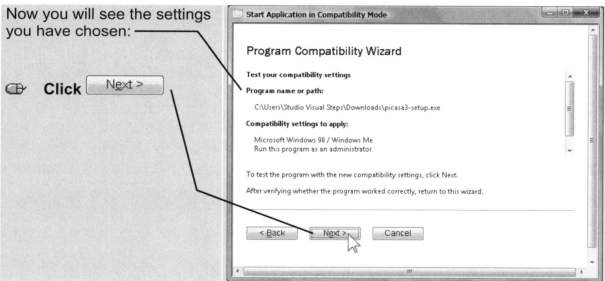

Your screen goes dark and you will need to give permission to continue:

☞ **Click** Continue

After this, the program for which you have chosen these settings will start. Follow the instructions you see in the next consecutive windows, or the instructions in the installation manual.

Then you will see the *Program Compatibility Wizard* again:

If the program functions correctly, you can now choose *Yes*. If the program does not work well, you choose *No*.

☞ **Make your choice**

🖰 **Click** Next >

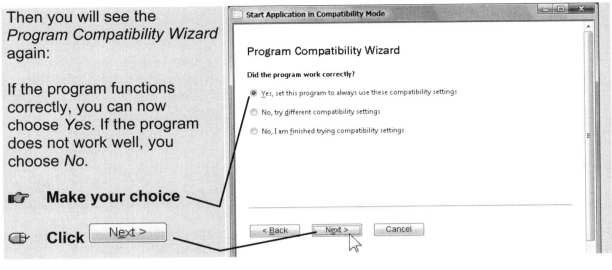

You can decide whether or not to tell *Microsoft* about this program.

☞ **Make your choice**

🖰 **Click** Next >

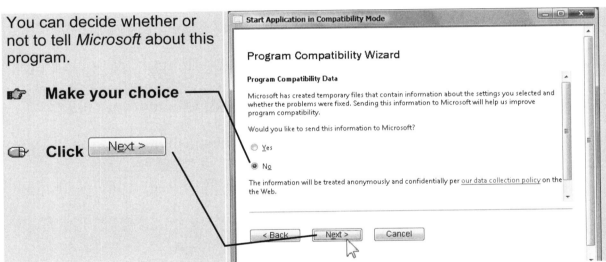

🖰 **Click** Finish

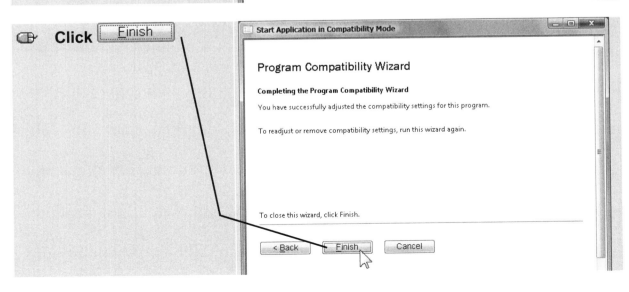

Close the *Windows Help and Support* window 1

Depending on the options you have chosen, you will now see one of the previous windows of the *Program Compatibility Wizard*, or you will close this program. If the installed program is running well and you want to keep the settings, you can start the *Program Compatibility Wizard* again and verify the settings you have chosen.

💡 **Tip**

> If the program does not run as it should, you can disable the compatibility settings. Open the *Program Compatibility Wizard* again and try different settings.

If the program still does not run after you have tried to install it several times, then it is time to remove the program from your computer (see *paragraph 3.4 Removing Programs and Windows Features*).

 HELP! The program looks different.

> In spite of the compatibility settings, your program may look or perform different from your *Vista* programs. This is inevitable, because the program was not written to be used with *Vista*. The purpose of the *Program Compatibility Assistant* and the *Program Compatibility Wizard* is to enable you to work with the program. The program will not be fully adapted to *Vista*. That is something the manufacturer should do. Unfortunately, some older programs will not be adapted to *Vista*.

💡 **Tip**

> **The program will help you**
> If a program requires specific screen settings or other settings, an alert screen will appear upon startup. You can then change your settings accordingly.
> But you need to keep in mind that the instructions for earlier editions of *Windows* may be different from the instructions for *Windows Vista*.

◊ Tip

Changing compatibility settings without the wizard
You do not have to use the *Program Compatibility Wizard* to change the settings for older programs. You can also change the settings in the following way:

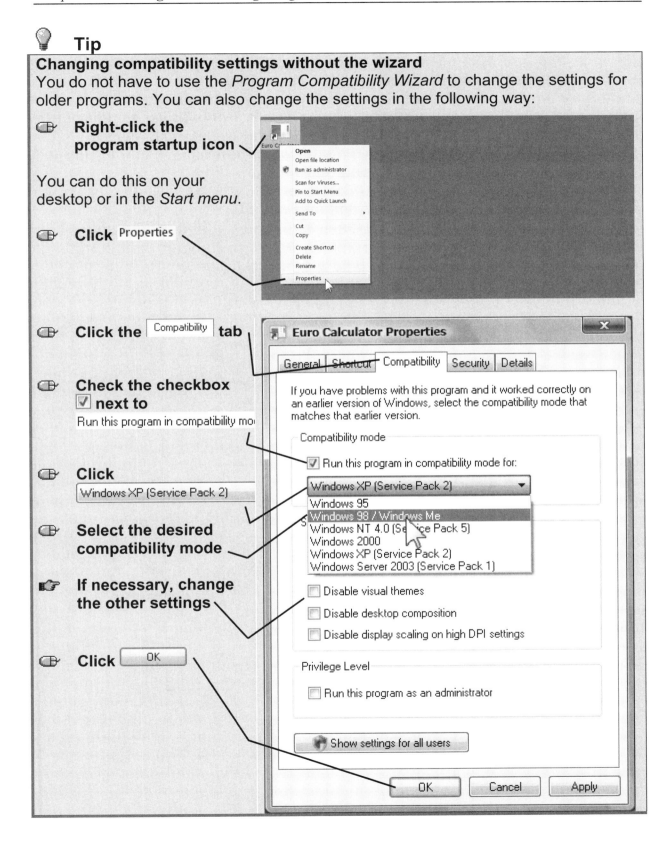

☞ **Right-click the program startup icon**

You can do this on your desktop or in the *Start menu*.

☞ **Click** Properties

☞ **Click the** Compatibility **tab**

☞ **Check the checkbox** ☑ **next to**
Run this program in compatibility mo

☞ **Click**
Windows XP (Service Pack 2)

☞ **Select the desired compatibility mode**

☞ **If necessary, change the other settings**

☞ **Click** OK

3.3 Repairing Programs

Even when a program has been correctly installed and has performed satisfactorily, there is always a chance that you may suddenly experience problems running the program. Usually these problems occur with the installation of another program, or with a *Windows Vista* update. Another source of problems may occur with the cleaning up of files by your antispyware or antivirus programs, which may tend to get overzealous at times.

⇨ **Please note:**

If you want to repair a program, you will often need to use the original installation CD or DVD that came with the program, as well as the license codes.
Repairing a program you have downloaded is usually only possible if you have stored the installation files onto your hard disk.

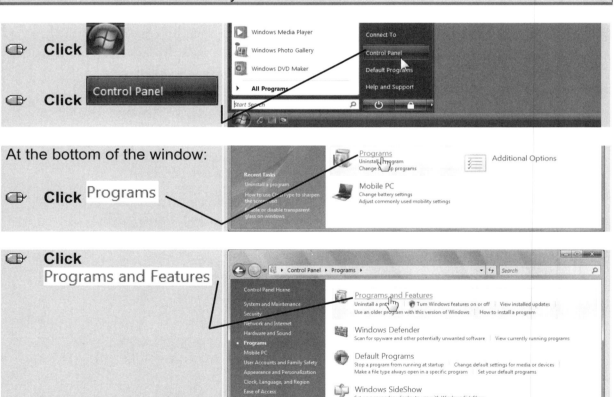

Now you will see the list of installed programs.

👉 **Click on different programs**

Watch the bar above the programs:

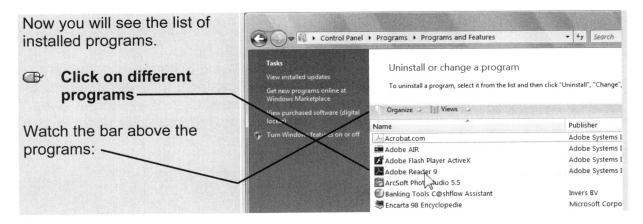

You will see that this menu bar can contain various options, depending on the program you have selected:

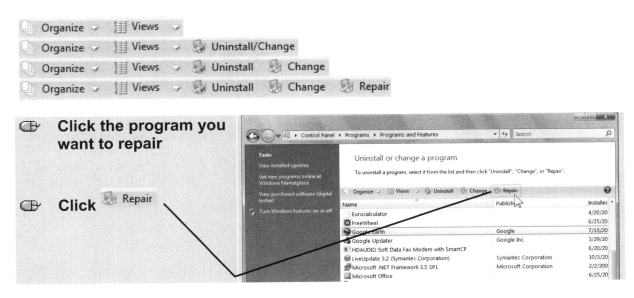

👉 **Click the program you want to repair**

👉 **Click** 🔧 Repair

✖ **HELP! I do not see a** 🔧 Repair **button.**

Is there no 🔧 Repair button for the program you have selected? Then you will need to remove the program first and install it again, in order to solve the problem. Only do this when you have the original CD or DVD and the license codes. If you can find the 🔧 Change button on the menu bar, you can try to solve the problem by clicking this button.

What happens next will depend on the program. Just follow the instructions that appear in the next few windows on your screen.

👉 **Close all windows**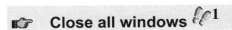

3.4 Removing Programs and Windows Features

Removing or uninstalling programs should be done by using the specific software removal or uninstall procedures. These procedures will not only remove the selected program from your hard disk, but will also delete all references to the program in the *Windows* registry. Some programs have their own uninstall program, which you can find in the *Start menu*:

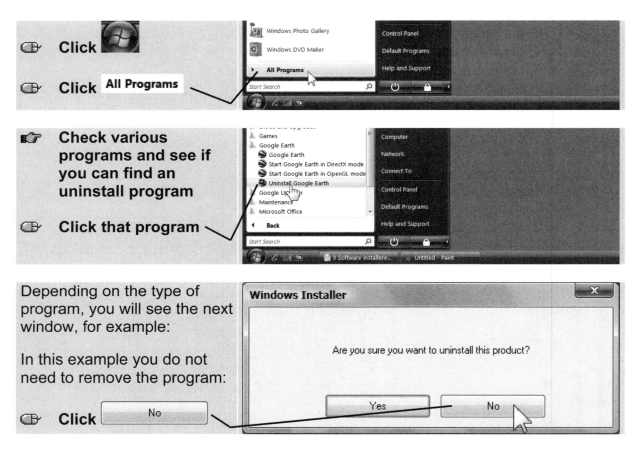

➪ **Click [windows icon]**

➪ **Click All Programs**

☞ **Check various programs and see if you can find an uninstall program**

➪ **Click that program**

Depending on the type of program, you will see the next window, for example:

In this example you do not need to remove the program:

➪ **Click No**

Windows Installer

Are you sure you want to uninstall this product?

Yes   No

➪ Please note:

If you have created your own shortcuts to a program or a *Windows* feature, and have added them to your desktop, for example, then these shortcuts will not be removed automatically. You need to delete these shortcuts manually, to prevent you from getting error messages when you click them after the program has been deleted.

If a program does not have its own uninstall program, you can uninstall the *Windows* program by using the *Control Panel*:

☞ **Open the *Control Panel* ℰℰ¹⁴**

At the bottom of the window:

☞ **Click** Uninstall a program

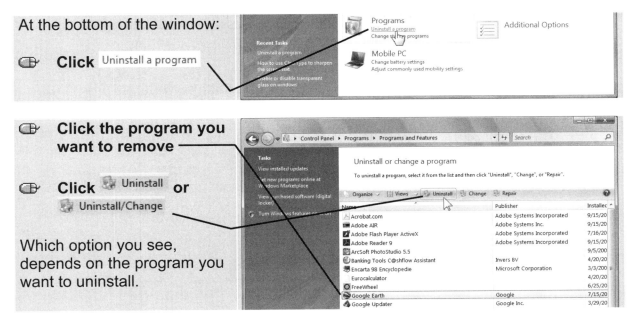

☞ **Click the program you want to remove**

☞ **Click** 🔧 Uninstall **or**
🔧 Uninstall/Change

Which option you see, depends on the program you want to uninstall.

Your screen goes dark and you will need to give permission to continue:

☞ **Click** Continue

In most cases you will now see a message asking you if you really want to uninstall this program:

In this case you do not want to uninstall the program:

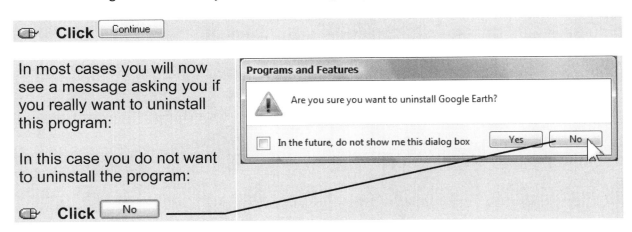

☞ **Click** No

If you cannot find the program you want to remove, and if the program does not have its own uninstall program, then it is possible that this program is a *Windows Vista* feature. You may be able to find the program in the *Turn Windows features on or off* window:

☞ **Click**
Turn Windows features on or off

Your screen goes dark and you will need to give permission to continue:

Click [Continue]

Now you will see a list containing the various *Windows* features.

Look up the program you want to remove, for example a game:

Click ⊞ next to [Games]

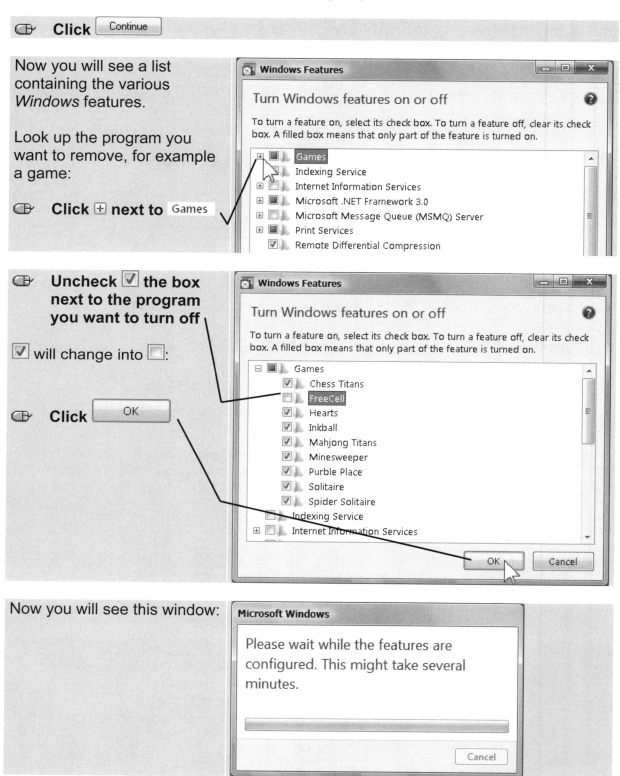

Uncheck ☑ the box next to the program you want to turn off

☑ will change into ☐:

Click [OK]

Now you will see this window:

Microsoft Windows

Please wait while the features are configured. This might take several minutes.

[Cancel]

After that, you will return to the *Control Panel*:

Because you have not uninstalled a program, but have merely turned off a *Windows* feature, you will not see any changes in this window.

☞ **Close the window** ✐¹

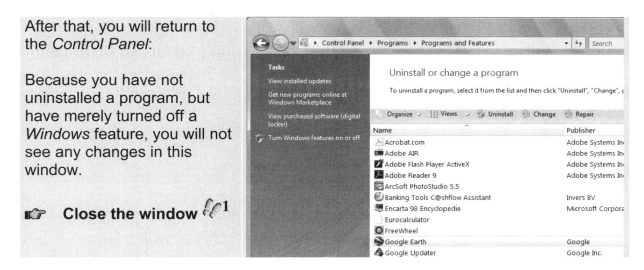

Turning on *Windows* features works the same way. All you need to do is check the box and it will change from ☐ into ☑.

If you cannot find the program you want to remove in the *Control Panel* list, or in the *Windows* features list, then the program is probably not a *Windows* program. In this case you need to remove the program folder manually.

⇨ **Please note:**

A program may be an auxiliary program, used for supporting another program. If you uninstall such a program, the main program will no longer function properly. So pay close attention when removing programs, especially if you are unfamiliar with the program.

🖰 **Click**

🖰 **Click** Computer

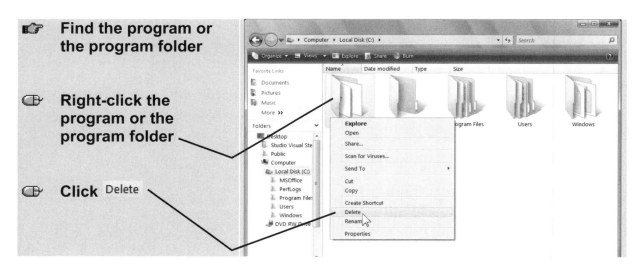

☞ **Find the program or the program folder**

☞ **Right-click the program or the program folder**

☞ **Click** Delete

⇨ **Please note:**

If you delete a folder, all of its contents will be deleted as well. Always check the contents of a folder, before deleting it.

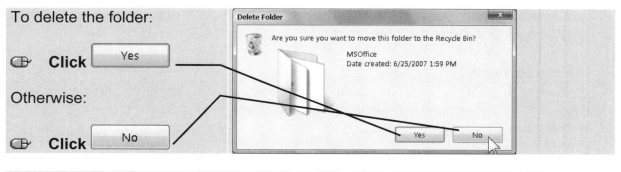

To delete the folder:

☞ **Click** Yes

Otherwise:

☞ **Click** No

☞ **Close the window** 1

⇨ **Please note:**

If you have deleted a program folder (without uninstalling the program first), then all shortcuts and program changes will remain stored in the *Windows* registry. With a special program, such as *Cleansweep* or *CClean* you can clean up the registry and remove all references to deleted programs.

💡 **Tip**

If a program is damaged, it may not be possible to uninstall this program in the usual way. The uninstall procedure will be interrupted and some of the files and shortcuts will remain stored on the hard disk. In this case, first try to install the program again. If this works, you can usually uninstall the program afterwards, without any difficulty.

3.5 Background Information

Dictionary

Disk cleaner	Special program that deletes partially removed programs and unused programs from your hard disk. For example, *Cleansweep* and *CClean* are cleanup programs.
Program	A set of instructions that a computer uses to perform a specific task, such as word processing, accounting, or data management. Also called an application.
Program compatibility	*Program Compatibility* is a *Windows* mode, used to run programs that were written for earlier editions of *Windows*. Most programs that are written for *Windows XP* will also run in *Windows Vista*, but older programs may run partially or not run at all. If an older program does not run properly, you can open the *Program Compatibility Wizard* to simulate earlier versions of *Windows*.
Uninstall program	Program that removes another program from the computer.
Windows features	Programs that are a standard, integral part of *Windows Vista* and that can be turned on or off by the user.
Wizard	Program that helps the user perform complicated tasks, such as installing or uninstalling a program.

Source: Windows Help and Support

Which older programs should not be uninstalled?
Many programs that were written for earlier editions of *Windows* will run in *Windows Vista* without any problem. The *Program Compatibility Wizard* will help you solve any minor problems.
However, the underlying software of the *Windows Vista* operating system is very different from earlier editions of *Windows*. That is why it is best to refrain from installing programs that use a variety of internal *Windows* functions and procedures. For example, the following programs:

- antivirus programs;
- antispyware programs;
- disk utility programs, such as programs that help you with partitioning your hard disk;
- programs that speed up your computer or hard disk;
- backup programs;
- various driver programs (drivers).

For these tasks you should only use programs that were specifically written for *Windows Vista*, unless the documentation for an older program expressly states that the program is suitable for *Windows Vista*.

Installing programs to another location
Usually the installation procedure lets you choose the disk and the folder to which the program will be installed. Only when you do not have enough space on the default disk drive, is it better to choose another location. Occasionally a program will not run properly if it is installed to another location, and automatic updating may also pose a problem.

Keep in mind that even if you install a program to another disk, the program will often store certain files to your default disk.

After installing a program, you should never move the program files to another location. If you do this, the program may not run properly anymore and most likely you will need to reinstall the program once again.

Compatibility settings

The *Program Compatibility Wizard* lets you select a number of different settings:

Setting	Description
Compatibility mode	The program will run with the settings of an earlier edition of *Windows*. Try this setting if you are sure that the program was written for (or performed well with) an older version of *Windows*.
256 colors	A limited number of colors will be used in the program. Various older programs use fewer colors.
640 x 480 screen resolution	The program will run in a smaller window. Try this setting if the graphics on your screen are deformed or incorrect.
Disable visual themes	The themes will be disabled for this program. Try this option if you are experiencing problems with menus or buttons on the title bar of the program.
Disable desktop composition	Windows transparency and other advanced display options will be disabled. Select this setting if you experience problems with the display while running a program.
Disable display scaling on high DPI settings	The automatic scaling of the screen while using large letters will be disabled. Try this setting if the large letters cause problems with the program display.
Administrator privileges	The program will be executed with administrator privileges, as if the user were an administrator. Certain programs will only run correctly if they are run with administrator privileges. This setting is only available if you are logged on as an administrator.
View settings for all users	Here you can select the settings that are valid for all users on your computer.

Source: Windows Help and Support

3.6 Tips

 Tip

After installing a program, check for updates
Many programs you purchase on CD or DVD will already have been updated by the time you buy the program. Most programs provide free updates for registered users. For example, the program *Google Earth*:

⊂⊳ **Click** Help

⊂⊳ **Click**
Check for Updates Online

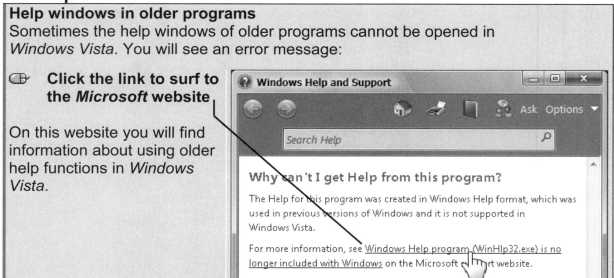

 Tip

Help windows in older programs
Sometimes the help windows of older programs cannot be opened in *Windows Vista*. You will see an error message:

⊂⊳ **Click the link to surf to the *Microsoft* website**

On this website you will find information about using older help functions in *Windows Vista*.

4. Hardware Troubleshooting

Even though modern computers are more reliable than ever before, you may still experience a problem now and then. This could happen with a device that is connected to the computer (the peripherals) or with one of the built-in components (the hardware). For example, you may run into a technical problem such as a missing driver. Each type of hardware has its own specific set of drivers. Since hardware is made by different manufacturers, even computers of the same type will not always have the same features. And a Canon deskjet printer for example will work a little differently than a Hewlett Packard deskjet printer.

Troubleshooting means analyzing the problem first, and then following the necessary steps that will lead to a solution. In this process, your own experience is crucial. This chapter will show you a number of steps you can take to solve common hardware issues and driver problems. You will also learn about additional programs that can help you find a solution.

In this chapter you will learn how to:

- solve problems with new equipment;
- solve problems with older equipment;
- solve frequently occurring hardware problems;
- use the device manager;
- download new driver programs;
- check the computer's memory;
- solve printer problems;
- solve audio problems.

 Please note:

A number of problems are circumvented by downloading the most recent drivers and *Windows Vista* updates. Always make sure you install the latest *Windows Vista* updates to your computer, and if you experience device problems, always check if there are new drivers available.

Please note:

The procedures described in this chapter require administrator privileges and you will need the administrator password. If you are logged on as a standard user, you will be able to read about certain procedures, but not execute them.

4.1 General Hardware Problems

Before undertaking dramatic action in the case of a hardware problem, take a look at the following items. Often you will be able to solve the problem by following a few simple steps. For example, many people tend to forget to search the manufacturers' website first. The product's creators will naturally have the most expertise available. They often provide recent information and support for common occurring problems.

Sometimes a problem cannot be solved. A computer is a complicated device which uses different parts made by different manufacturers. In spite of the standards the manufacturers have agreed to, it may happen that two components or devices really cannot work together well. Both devices are installed correctly and comply with all the technical specifications, but they simply cannot work together. Always try to make a deal with your supplier about returning a new device in case it does not work with your computer.

Also, pay attention to the minimal requirements. Keep in mind that these minimal requirements only apply to the specific *Windows Vista* edition when the computer is not executing any other tasks at that moment and is not running other programs. If you want your computer to work properly, it should exceed the requirements and often have more capacity than is specified. As for the specified free disk space, you need to remember that part of the disk needs to be available for various temporary files.

 Please note:

In this paragraph you will read about some general problems and solutions. Depending on the type of device and the type of connection, you may need to follow different steps. Always carefully follow the instructions given by the manufacturer.

Installing new hardware
A lot of problems can be prevented by correctly installing the hardware. Follow these general instructions:

- Compare the (minimal) requirements of your computer for hardware and software. A device that will work with *Windows Vista* will not always work with *Windows XP,* and vice versa. How much disk space do you need, how much RAM memory is required, how fast should the processor be, etcetera.
- Always read the installation instructions provided by the manufacturer first, even when you have installed similar devices before. Sometimes the order of the actions has changed, due to previous issues being addressed.

- Continue reading on the next page -

If you must install software that your hardware requires, always execute a 'clean' installation. Close other programs and reboot the computer after the installation has finished. It may even be necessary to temporarily shut down your antivirus program and firewall. In that case, also disconnect your Internet connection, so your computer will not contract viruses while installing the program.

After installation, the device does not function properly
You have installed the device and the software according to the instructions, but still the device does not function properly. You can try the following things:

- Check if the device is switched on and if it is properly connected.
- Reboot your computer and switch the device off and on again.
- In the installation instructions or in the manual the manufacturer often lists frequently occurring problems. Check the manual for your problem.
- Visit the manufacturers' website and try to find the solution to your problem. Check the FAQs (Frequently Asked Questions).
- Search for new driver software and install the new drivers (for installing new drivers see also *paragraph 4.3 Device Management*).
- Search the Internet for a solution with the help of a search engine, such as *Google*. Use keywords such as the make or type of your device, and a short description of the problem. You may find various websites with solutions.
- Uninstall the device's software and then re-install. Reboot your computer before installing the device for a second time.
- Phone or send an e-mail to the manufacturer's helpdesk.

Problems with other devices after installing a new device
The new device works fine, but now other devices do not function properly anymore. Follow these steps:

- In *Windows Device Manager* (see *paragraph 4.3 Device Management*), temporarily disable the new device and check if the problem still occurs.
- If the new device is of the same type as an older device, for example, a mouse, then you can sometimes use only one of these devices at a time. You can check this by following the previous step.
- Uninstall the software of the device that did function properly and re-install the software again. First reboot the computer, before installing the device for the second time.
  Please note: only uninstall the device's software if you still have the installation CD or DVD and all other necessary information for installing the device.
- If the problem persists even after uninstalling, use *System Restore* to return the system and settings to an earlier point in time, before you started installing the new device.

- Continue reading on the next page -

- Visit the manufacturer's websites of both conflicting devices and look for a solution. For example in the FAQs (Frequently Asked Questions).
- Search for new drivers and install these (see also *paragraph 4.3 Device Management*).
- Search the Internet for a solution with the help of a search engine, such as *Google*. Use keywords such as the make or type of your device, and a short description of the problem. You may find various websites with solutions.
- Phone or send an e-mail to the manufacturer's helpdesk.

Problems with a device that previously functioned normally
A device has always worked fine, but suddenly it does not function anymore. It is important to determine if anything has changed:

- Turn off the device, check the connections and turn the device on again.
- Does the device have a self test or reset feature? Try this feature.
- Use the System Health Report (see *paragraph 2.7 System Health Report*). The information in this report is not always important or understandable, but it is worth a try to check this report. If necessary, you can send this report to the manufacturer's helpdesk by e-mail.
- Does the problem occur only after you have used your computer for a while? The device may be overheating. Built-in devices such as disks and cards are known to have problems with overheating.
- What has changed recently? Have you connected a new device, have you installed a new operating system, a *Vista* update or an antivirus program?
- Perhaps the problems are caused by a *Windows* update. See if you can find a new version of the driver software (see *paragraph 4.3 Device Management*) that is compatible with the new situation. If necessary, you can use *System Restore* to return the system to an earlier point in time.
- An update to an antivirus program or a firewall can also be the cause of the problem. Disconnect the Internet connection and temporarily disable these programs, and see if the problem persists. Do not forget to restart these programs before connecting to the Internet again or retrieving your e-mail.
- Uninstall the device's software, then re-install the software and the device. First reboot your computer before installing the device for the second time.
- Visit the manufacturer's website and look for a solution. For example in the FAQs (Frequently Asked Questions) section.
- Search the Internet for a solution with the help of a search engine, such as *Google*. Use keywords such as the make or type of your device, and a short description of the problem. You may find various websites with solutions.
- Phone or send an e-mail to the manufacturer's helpdesk.

In the next section you can read more about solving hardware problems. First you will learn how to solve frequently occurring problems. Then you will learn how to use various programs that can help you find a solution.

Tip

Solving problems with Windows Help and Support

In *Windows Help and Support* you will find the solution to a variety of common problems. This is how you look up these problems:

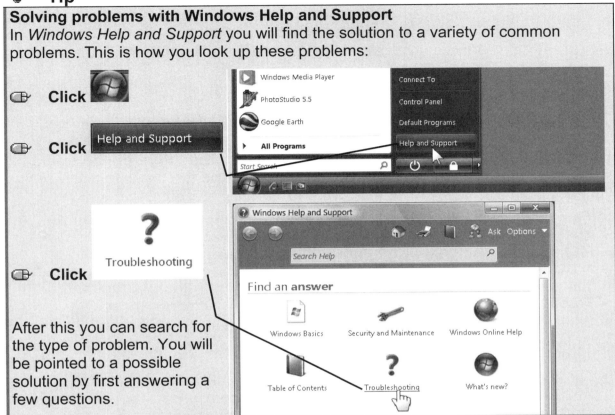

Click

Click **Help and Support**

Click **Troubleshooting**

After this you can search for the type of problem. You will be pointed to a possible solution by first answering a few questions.

 Tip

Microsoft help on the Internet

On the website http://support.microsoft.com you can select your operating system and find solutions for frequently occurring problems with *Windows Vista*, or with hardware and software.

☞ **Open *Internet Explorer*** 🦶19

☞ **Go to http://support. microsoft.com** 🦶22

Click **Windows Vista**

4.2 Frequently Occurring Hardware Problems

In this section you will learn how to solve various problems you may be experiencing with the most important components of your computer, and with some of the devices connected to it.

> **Problem: the computer keeps shutting down, or reboots spontaneously.**

If a computer shuts down occasionally, or reboots all by itself, there can be several reasons. First of all, this is a good time to stress how important it is to routinely save your documents as you work so as to avoid losing important data. Well-known causes for this problem are:

- The computer is not plugged in properly: check to make sure all plugs are properly connected.
- A virus causes the computer to reboot continuously: use your antivirus program to scan the complete hard disk.
- Problems with the RAM memory: see *paragraph 4.4 Memory Checks*.
- Part of the motherboard is faulty, or one of the components of your computer has a bad connection to the motherboard. Repairs (if possible) will have to be made by your supplier.
- The computer overheats. Does the computer only shut down after you have used it for a while? See if you can hear the fan that is built-in at the back of the machine. The fan could be clogged by dust, which causes it to malfunction. Check your computer's manual to see if it is possible to clean the fan. Often you can do this from the outside, with a vacuum cleaner.
- Irregular power supply. Although a computer is usually equipped to handle power surges, if the fluctuations are too large, the computer may shut down and start up again all by itself. Try to find out if the problem occurs whenever you (or your neighbor) have switched on other heavy duty electrical equipment. If necessary, buy a *UPS* (*Uninterruptible Power Supply*).

HELP! What is a UPS?

A UPS (Uninterruptible Power Supply) is a device which connects a computer to a power supply and which makes sure that the power supply will not be interrupted. A UPS or emergency power supply contains a battery which lets you use the computer for some while after the electricity has been cut off.
UPS devices usually also offer protection against short-lived power surges and short interruptions of the power supply, or against lightning strikes in the electricity grid.

Problem: sometimes the hard disk cannot be found.

Your hard disk may contain a tremendous amount of data, so if the disk seems to become unreliable you should take precautions. Here are some of the reasons why the hard disk may not be detected:

- Your hard disk's connector is loose. If you have an external hard disk, you will be able to check this quite easily. Checking an internal hard disk is trickier. It is probably better to leave this to your computer supplier.
- A conflict has arisen between the hard disk and another device or driver. In *paragraph 4.3 Device Management* you will read how to check for this.

If you have experienced problems with your hard disk, you need to back up this disk right away. If the hard disk cannot be found at all and this problem persists, there usually is a problem with the *Windows Vista* device management.

Problem: reading/writing to or from the hard disk takes too long, or the computer reports read/write errors.

If the computer is taking a longer and longer time to read or save data, the cause could be:

- A hard disk that is full. Clean up all unused files, let *Windows Vista* clean up your hard disk (see *paragraph 2.5 Cleaning Up the Hard Disk*) and defragment the disk (*paragraph 2.6 Disk Defragmentation*). To free up more space on your hard disk you could also transfer files to another disk.
- The surface of the hard disk is damaged. Check the hard disk with the *Disk Error Check Tool* (*paragraph 2.8 Checking Your Disk*).
- The hard disk's connector is loose. If you have an external hard disk, you will be able to check this quite easily. Checking an internal hard disk is trickier. It is probably better to leave this to your computer supplier.

If you experienced this kind of problem, make sure you regularly back up important data and use the save command more frequently as you work.

Problem: burning data to CD or DVD.

CDs and DVDs can cause problems while burning data. Here are some things to consider:

- There are many different kinds and qualities of CDs and DVDs. You could try using a different brand or type.
- A CD or DVD of the RW type (read/write) will cause more problems than a simple R type (recordable) CD or DVD.
- Try using a lower burning speed.
- Antivirus programs and screensavers may disrupt the burning process. If necessary, temporarily disable these programs.

- Some programs will finalize a disk after burning, which means that you cannot add data to the disk anymore.
- The CD or DVD writer may be dirty. In a computer store you can buy special cleaning sets.

 Please note:

If the speed of your CD or DVD player is too high for the disk you use, the disk may even explode inside the player. When using an older disk be sure to check its maximum burning speed. You can find this information on the disk packaging.

 Tip

The CD or DVD player will not open
There may be a time when it is not possible to open the CD/DVD drive using the eject button (for example, when the computer is shut down). Carefully insert a stiff wire such as a straightened paper clip into the manual eject hole until you feel resistance. Gently press harder until the drive tray opens slightly and then slide the tray out.

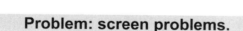 **Problem: screen problems.**

There are two kinds of screen problems:
1. Problems with the *Windows Vista* settings: you can read about these problems in *paragraph 5.6 Problems with Screen Settings*.
2. Hardware problems: these are the most frequently occurring hardware problems:
- The screen stays dark: check all the connections, jacks and plugs, and the power switch.
- Does the computer emit several short bleeps while starting up? The graphics card may be malfunctioning, or may not be properly connected to the computer. The connection problem may be caused by a loose monitor cable, or the monitor cable is plugged into the wrong jack.
- The screen image has moved, or is too large or too small: check the monitor's manual and find out how to move, enlarge or reduce the image.

- The colors are not right (1): check your monitor's manual and find out how to adjust the color settings, or how to calibrate the colors. Calibrating means testing and adjusting the settings according to the manufacturers color specifications.
- The colors are not right (2): are the screen settings correct? Check if the graphics card is connected properly (check the monitor and the card). If it is a separate card, also check the connection. Move the cable and see if this makes a difference.

Problem: mouse and keyboard.

If your mouse and keyboard are not functioning properly, you can barely operate your computer. If the keyboard does not work, check the following:
- First check the cables and connectors.
- If the keyboard or mouse is a wireless device, then check the batteries.
- Some keyboards have a key with which you can disable the keyboard, a so-called Lock key. If the Lock key is activated, you will not be able to use the keyboard. De-activate this key.
- Check if the NumLock and CapsLock indicators on the keyboard light up when pressed. If they do not, the keyboard is probably not connected properly.
- There may be a conflict with another device, or with a built-in mouse (in a notebook). Check the device manager (see *paragraph 4.3 Device Management*).

 Tip

Operating Windows without a mouse
If the mouse does not work anymore, you can still perform many common tasks by using the keyboard. You will find a list of keyboard shortcuts for operating *Windows* in the *Tips* section at the end of this chapter

Problem: no sound.

If you cannot hear sounds, then check the following:
- Check if the speakers are switched on and if the volume control is in the right position.
- Check if the speakers are connected to the proper outlet in the computer. Pay attention to the color coding (pink, green and/or blue).
- Find out the exact situation in which you cannot hear sounds: does it occur only when using certain programs or when starting up or shutting down *Windows Vista*? In the first case, you need to check the manual or help tools for the program first. Are you still not hearing any sounds when starting up and shutting down *Windows*? Then read *paragraph 4.3 Device Management* and *paragraph 4.6 Sound Problems*.

Problem: printer problem.

With a printer you can encounter many different kinds of problems. Problems concerning printers are treated separately, in *paragraph 4.5 Printer Problems*.

4.3 Device Management

If a device does not perform correctly when working with *Windows Vista*, you can temporarily disable the device in the *Device Manager* window, or search for new drivers. An old, out-of-date driver is often the cause of the problem.

⇨ **Please note:**
If you want to load new drivers, you will need to connect to the Internet.

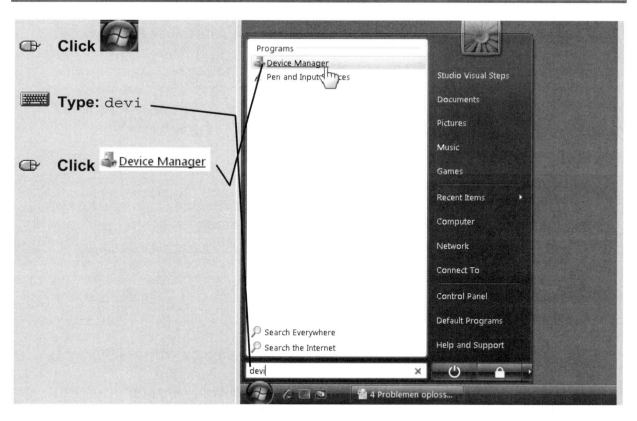

Your screen goes dark and you will need to give permission to continue:

Now you will see extensive information about the components that are installed on your computer:

☞ **Click ⊞ next to** ▉ **Display adapters**

Now you will see the make and type of your display adapter:

☞ **Click your display adapter**

☞ **Click** ▤

Here you will see that, according to *Windows Vista*, the device is working properly: ———

☞ **Click the** Driver **tab**

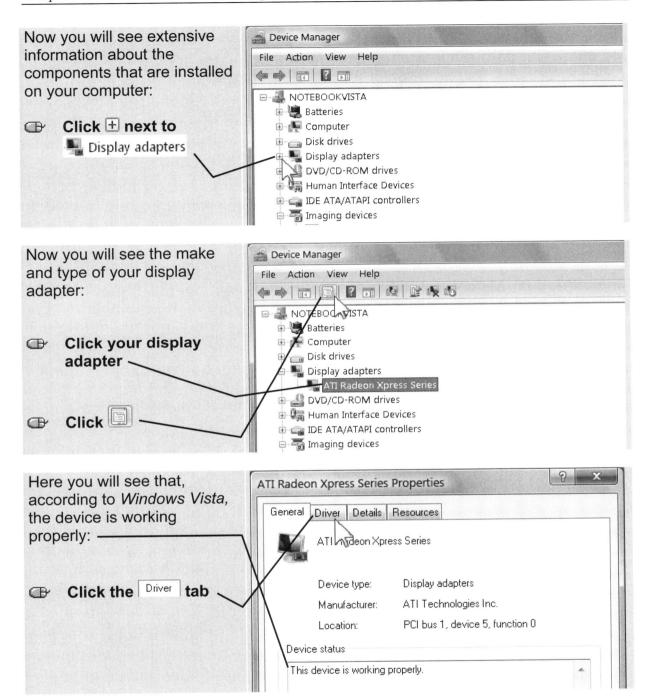

➡ **Please note:**

If you want to update the driver software you will need to be connected to the Internet.

⇨ **Please note:**

If a device or component is working properly, you do not need to search for driver updates. New updates regularly cause problems on older computer equipment. If everything is working correctly, it is better to keep the old driver, unless you have information that the new driver has extra, interesting features.

You can do this step and click the button ⬚ Cancel ⬚ in the next window.

Here you will see the driver details:

If you do not wish to update the driver:

☞ **Click** ⬚ Cancel ⬚ **and continue on page 138**

If the component is not working properly, or if you want to update the driver:

☞ **Click** ⬚ Update Driver... ⬚

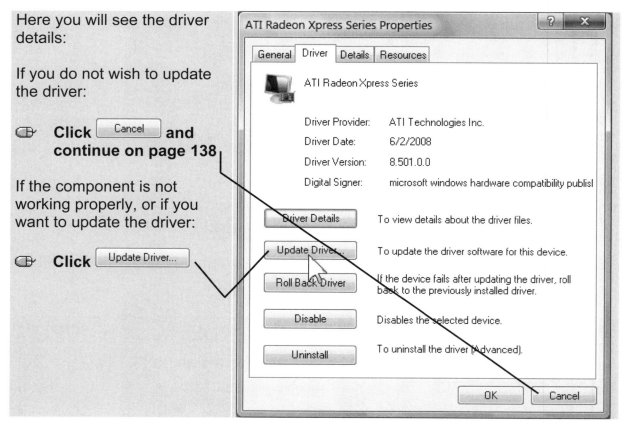

If you want to check for new drivers:

☞ **Click**

➜ Search automatically for updat
Windows will search your computer and t
software for your device.

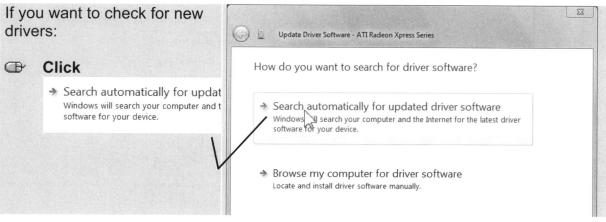

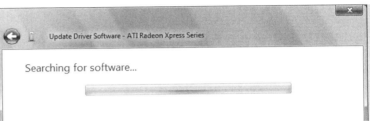

→ Browse my computer for driver software
Locate and install driver software manually.

If you choose   , *Windows* will search
for the driver software on your hard disk, or on another disk drive. Usually the driver
on your hard disk will be the driver that is currently in use. If you have downloaded a
more recent driver from the manufacturer's website, you can search for it now. If
your driver software is stored on a CD, you can use the CD to re-install the driver.
You may need the driver for a new installation of the operating system to your
computer.

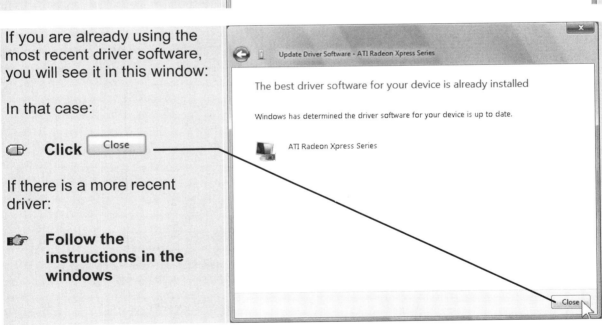

Windows will now connect to the *Microsoft* website, to check if there are more recent drivers available.

If you are already using the most recent driver software, you will see it in this window:

In that case:

☞ **Click** Close

If there is a more recent driver:

☞ **Follow the instructions in the windows**

⇨ **Please note:**

In this case you have only looked for new driver software on the *Microsoft* website. The manufacturer of your hardware may be able to provide a newer driver program. If the problem persists, check the manufacturer's website.

If your computer does not work properly and you suspect that this is caused by one of the components, you can temporarily disable a component by clicking Disable .

Please note:

If you disable important components in the computer, such as your monitor, keyboard, or mouse, you will not be able to operate the computer very well. Use this option only to disable extra components, such as network adapters or DVD drives. If you are using a second monitor or mouse, for example, you can try to disable these as well.

If the problem has been solved by disabling a device or component, you need to uninstall that device by clicking Uninstall . If necessary, you can install the device again later, and see if the problem occurs again.

HELP! I am experiencing problems with the new driver.

If you experience problems after having installed a new driver, return to a previous version by clicking the button Roll Back Driver .

After the new driver has been installed, you will see the details in this window:

 Click Close

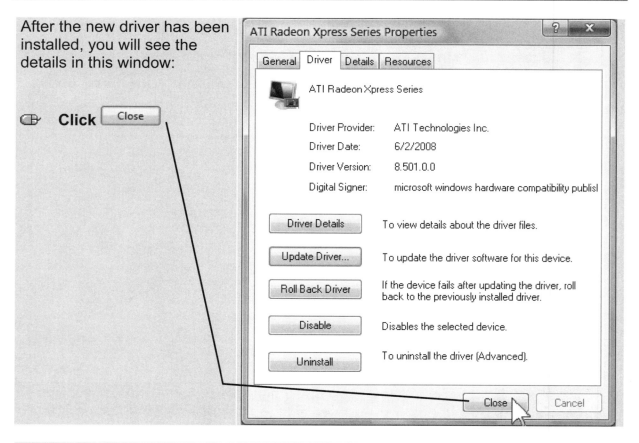

☞ **Close the *Device Manager* window** 1

4.4 Memory Checks

A lot of unexpected hardware errors occur due to insufficient or malfunctioning memory. Most often this is the case with RAM memory and cache memory. With the *Memory Diagnostics Tool*, *Windows Vista* can check these types of memory and provide an error report if something is wrong. If you get a *Windows Vista* message about a memory problem, you should always check the memory. You can also use the tool to perform checks yourself:

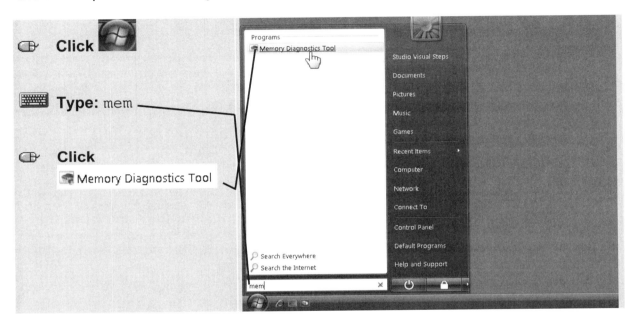

Your screen goes dark and you will need to give permission to continue:

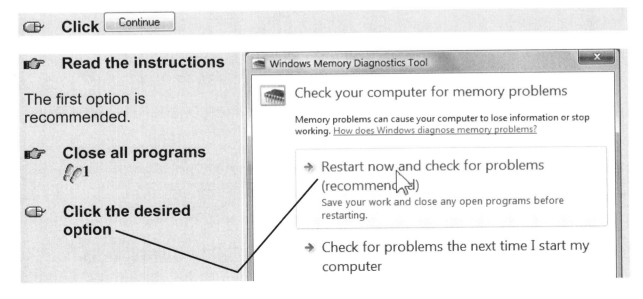

The computer will reboot and you will see a blue screen. The memory check will start. The test will take anywhere's from a few minutes to half an hour. Do not touch your computer until *Windows Vista* starts up by itself again. Afterwards you will see your desktop:

In the right bottom corner of your desktop you will see a message concerning the results of the memory check:

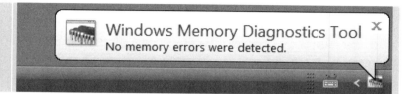

 HELP! There is a memory problem.

If a memory problem has been found, it will depend on the type of memory whether or not you can solve the problem yourself.

In most computers you can easily replace the RAM memory, but be sure to replace it with the right type of memory, because different types of RAM memory within the same computer can cause problems. Also check first if the memory cards are well connected, before replacing any cards. Beware of static electricity. If you prefer not to do these things yourself, then your supplier will be able to do this for you.

Is the cache memory faulty? Replacing this will be more difficult. Depending on the type of cache memory, it is possible that the chip or device will need to be replaced. It is best to let your supplier do this.

Start the *Memory Diagnostics Tool* for a second time to see if all problems are really solved.

All the electronics in your computer are very sensitive to static electricity. We all are charged with static electricity. This static electricity can originate from the friction between your shoes and the rug, for example, or from your clothes. In dry weather you may notice the static electricity when you touch a metal object. When you touch the car or the door handle, you will see a small spark and feel a light shock. As a result of that shock you will get rid of your static charge.
That same spark is strong enough to damage or destroy computer chips. Always make sure to get rid of your static charge, before opening up your computer. You can do this by touching a metal object first, or you can use an anti-static wristband that is connected to a metal object.
The strongest discharge of static electricity is caused by lightning. Sometimes a computer can even be damaged when lightning has struck somewhere in the neighborhood.

4.5 Printer Problems

Unlike a computer, a printer is a device that has more moving mechanical parts rather than electronic. This is why printer problems occur more often than computer hardware problems. In this section you will learn how to recognize and solve some common problems.

Problem: the printer does not work.

If a printer does not work properly, check the following:
- Are the cables connected correctly? Turn off the printer and turn it back on again.
- Are the LED lights burning? If not, the printer may be disconnected in some way.
- Do you see any warning lights indicating that the ink, toner or paper has run out? Replace the ink or toner cartridge, or add paper.
- Check if the printer's self test feature is working properly.
- Check if the right printer has been selected.

Does it seem like everything works fine, but you still cannot print a document? Then check the *Control Panel* for error messages:

☞ **Open the *Control Panel*** 14

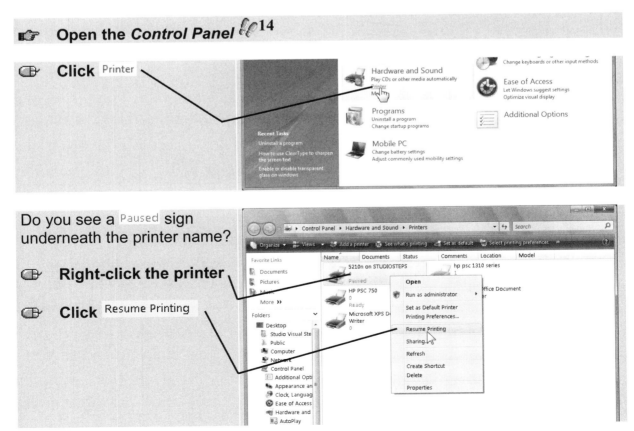

Click Printer

Do you see a Paused sign underneath the printer name?

Right-click the printer

Click Resume Printing

HELP! I am getting an error message.

If you are not logged on as an administrator, you will see the following message:

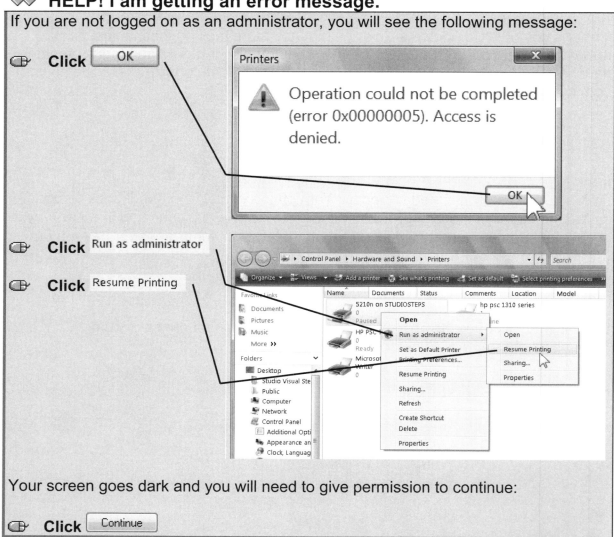

☞ **Click** OK

☞ **Click** Run as administrator

☞ **Click** Resume Printing

Your screen goes dark and you will need to give permission to continue:

☞ **Click** Continue

 Tip

Note the default printer

You will recognize the default printer by the ✔ symbol. This printer will always be the one used by the system, unless you select another printer (in the case that you have a second printer).

Does it say Offline underneath the printer name?

☞ **Right-click the printer**

☞ **Click** Use Printer Online

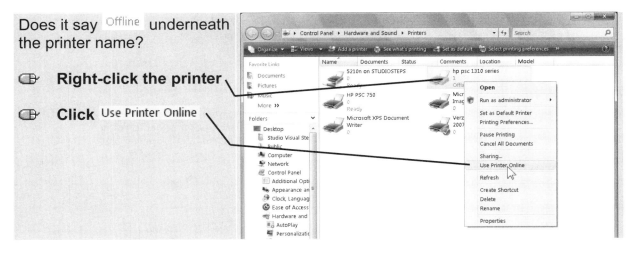

☞ **Right-click the printer**

☞ **Click** Properties

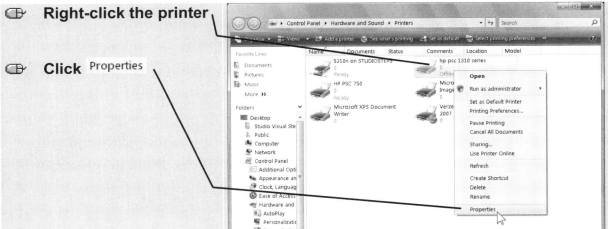

If these two settings are correct, you can print a test page:

At the bottom of the window:

☞ **Click** Print Test Page

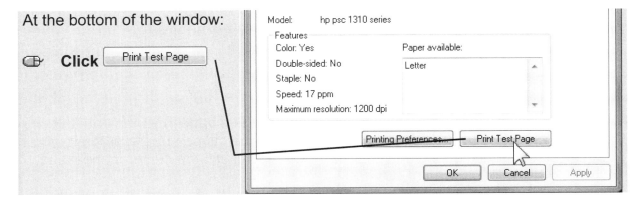

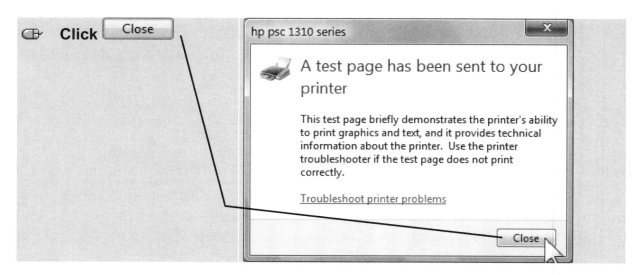

☞ **Close all windows** $\ell\ell^1$

If the test page has been printed, you will know that the printer is properly connected and the settings are correct.

If the test page has not been printed, there might be a problem with the connection, or with the printer itself. Have you already checked the connection? Then try to use the printer with another computer. If the printer still does not work, it is probably due to some technical error.

Problem: the printed page has smudges or stripes on it.

Look up how to clean the ink cartridges in your printer manual. Most inkjet printers have a built-in function that cleans the ink cartridges. You can operate this function from the *Control Panel*, or from a separate printer software program.

Problem: the colors are wrong.

Clean the ink cartridges. Look up how to print a color test page in your manual. If the colors on the test page are correct, the problem may be caused by the program you are using. If the colors on the test page are incorrect, check the printer manual and find out how to adjust the color settings.
If you have an inkjet printer which uses separate cartridges for each color, check every color. Usually you will see a warning message, if one of the color cartridges has run out, or does not function correctly.

Problem: the black color is not really black.

If the printer uses color cartridges as well as a black cartridge, then black should be really black. If that is not the case, then the black color will be made with the color cartridges. Check if the black cartridge is installed correctly, and is not empty. Check the manual and see if you can find a setting you can use to indicate that black colors should be printed by using the black cartridge.

Problem: the print contains strange symbols.

First compare the paper print with the print preview option in your program.

⇨ Please note:

While printing, check if the printer name in the window is the correct name of the printer you use. If you are not sure, re-install the printer.

☞ Open the print preview

Do you see strange symbols here as well? If so, try other programs and see if they also show these strange symbols. If not, then there might be a problem with the communication between your printer and the program you use. Check the program manufacturer's website, you might find more information there.

Tip

Use Paint and WordPad to test the printer
It is best to use simple *Microsoft* programs to test your printer. This way you will probably experience the fewest problems. Use *WordPad* to test printing texts and *Paint* to test printing images.

You could also open the *Device Manager* (see *paragraph 4.3 Device Management*) to look for a new driver for your printer. If there are no new drivers available, check the manufacturer's website for new driver software.

Problem: I want to cancel the print job.

If you have already sent the document to the printer, but want to cancel the print job, follow these steps:

On the taskbar:

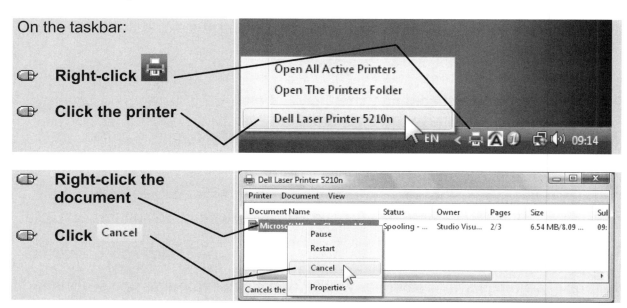

Right-click

Click the printer

Open All Active Printers

Open The Printers Folder

Dell Laser Printer 5210n

Right-click the document

Click Cancel

Dell Laser Printer 5210n

Printer Document View

Document Name	Status	Owner	Pages	Size	Sul
Microsoft W...	Spooling - ...	Studio Visu...	2/3	6.54 MB/8.09 ...	09:

Pause
Restart
Cancel
Properties

Cancels the

Give permission to cancel the print job

⇨ Please note:

It may take some time before the printer stops printing, because part of the document has already been sent to the printer.

4.6 Sound Problems

If your speakers do not produce any sound, and you have already checked the speaker cables and plugs, you can check the following:

⇨ **Please note:**

The windows you will see here, are default *Windows Vista* windows. Some sound cards may show different windows.

☞ **Click** [Windows logo]

☞ **Click** Control Panel

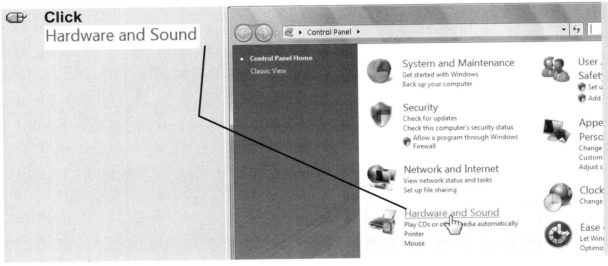

☞ **Click**
Hardware and Sound

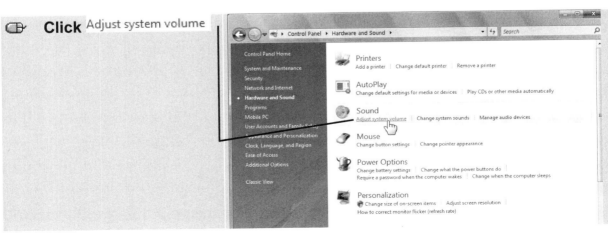

☞ **Click** Adjust system volume

Do you see the 🔇 symbol under `Device` or `Applications`? This indicates that the speakers are switched off.

In your window you might see various slide controls under `Applications`.

👉 **Click** 🔇

🔇 will change into 🔊:

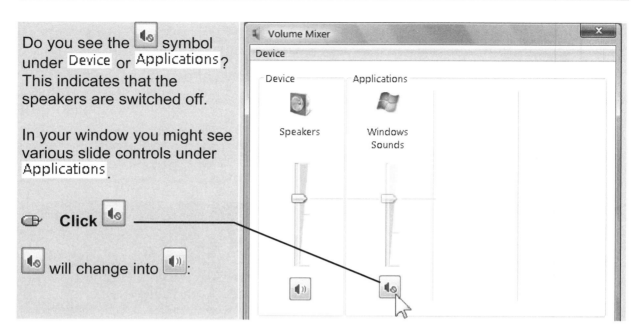

❋ HELP! All the settings are changing at once.

If you move the slide control under `Device`, this setting will also apply to *Windows* and all the programs you are using. If you change a setting under `Applications`, then the setting will apply to the program you have chosen, and to *Windows*, but not to other programs, for example playing an audio CD. If you want to change the sound settings for individual programs, you need to use `Applications`. If you want to change the settings for all applications, you need to use `Device`.

The speakers are switched on and are used by *Windows Media Player*.

The *Windows Sounds* are disabled:

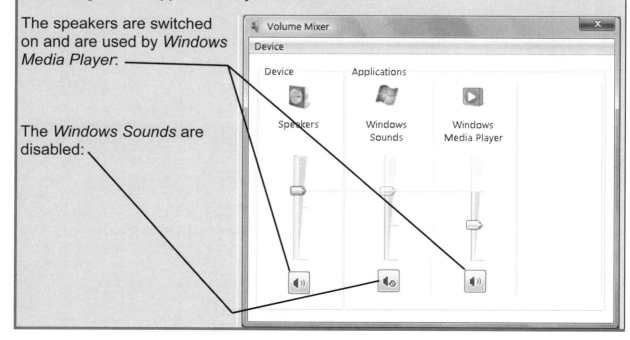

Is one of the slide controls pushed down? This indicates the sound is enabled, but you may not be able to hear it.

 Drag the slide control upracewards

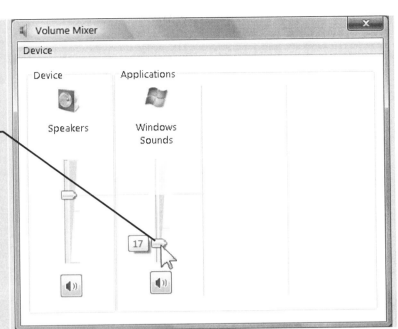

If you move the slide control under `Device`, all other sliders will move along with it. If you move a slide control under `Applications`, then this setting will only apply to that specific program.

 Close the window $\ell\ell^1$

❌ HELP! The slide control under `Device` is moving as well.

The `Applications` slide control cannot be set higher than the volume of the `Device` slide control. If you move the `Applications` slide control higher than the `Device` slide control, that slider will automatically move up with it. This only applies when you move the slide control up.

When you move the `Device` slide control down the sliders of all applications will move along with it, if they were set higher than the `Device` slide control.

💡 Tip

First test the Windows Sounds
If you do not hear any sounds while using a program, this may be caused by the settings in this window, or by the program itself. This is why you need to try and solve the problem for the *Windows Sounds* first. If you can hear those sounds but cannot hear the program sounds, you need to look for the sound settings in that program.

In some cases a particular program may not be able to work with your sound card. Check the manufacturer's website for a solution, or contact their helpdesk.

💡 Tip

Quick launch of the Volume Mixer

On the right side of the taskbar you see an 🔊 icon. You can use this icon to check or change your sound settings.

☞ **Point the mouse arrow at** 🔊

Now you will see information about your speakers and sound card:

☞ **Click** 🔊

Now you see the current setting for the Device. You can adjust the volume here, too.

If you want to see the other volume settings:

☞ **Click** Mixer

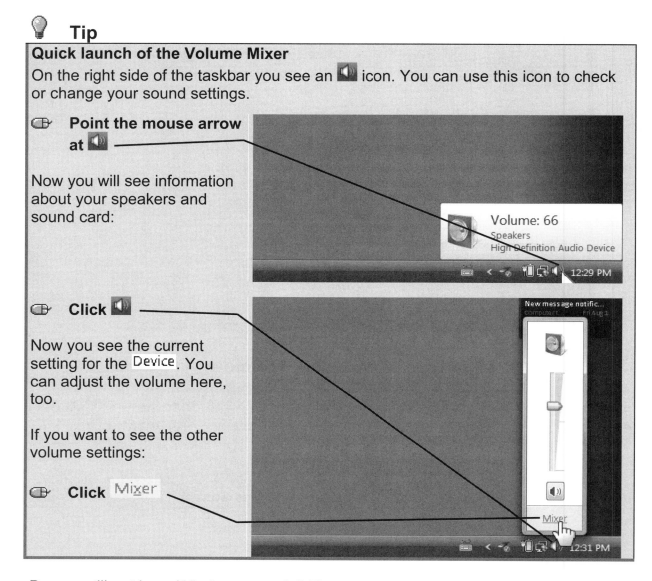

Do you still not hear *Windows* sounds? Then you can do the following:

☞ **Click** Change system sounds

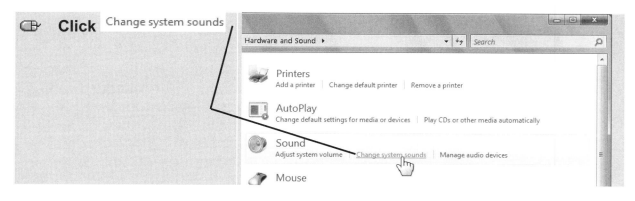

Look and see if a sound scheme is set. If you see No Sounds:

☞ **Click** No Sounds

☞ **Preferably, click** Windows Default

☞ **If necessary, check the box ☑ next to** Play Windows Startup sound

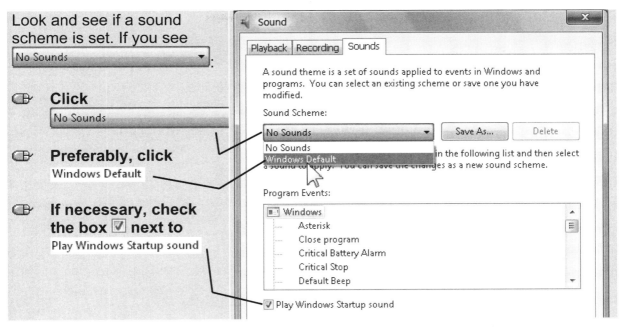

You will be able to test your sound right away:

☞ **Click a task with a 🔊 symbol**

☞ **Click ▶ Test**

If the speakers are enabled, you will hear a sound.

☞ **Click OK**

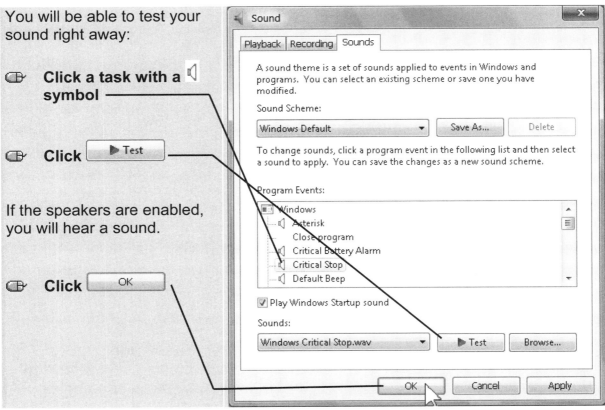

Tip

Changing the sounds
Do you want to hear a different sound for a certain task? Then click the button with the name of the sound, in this example it is called `Windows Hardware Fail.wav ▼`. You will be able to choose a different *Windows Sound*. If you want to insert your own sounds, you can search for sound files by using the `Browse...` option.

Does the problem still persist? Then check the following:

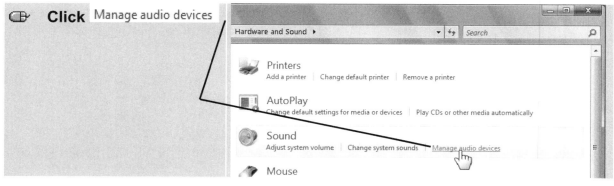

Click Manage audio devices

Now you will see the audio equipment inside your computer:

Click a device

Click `Properties`

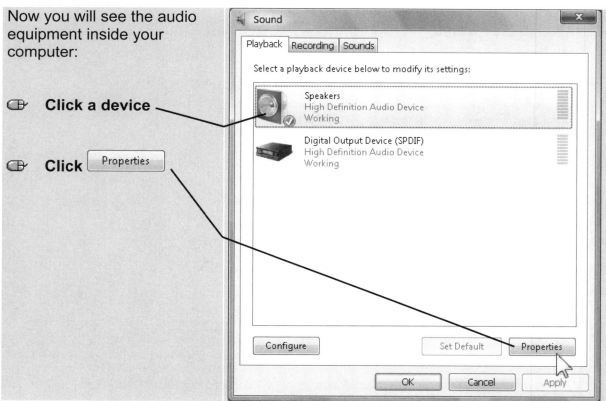

The window that you see now will depend on the make and type of the audio device. Take a look at this window and see if you can find settings that can help you solve your problem.

Here you will see your speakers' properties:

Is the device enabled? If not:

☞ **Click**

Don't use this device (disable)

☞ **Click**

Use this device (enable)

When the device is enabled:

☞ **Click the** Levels **tab**

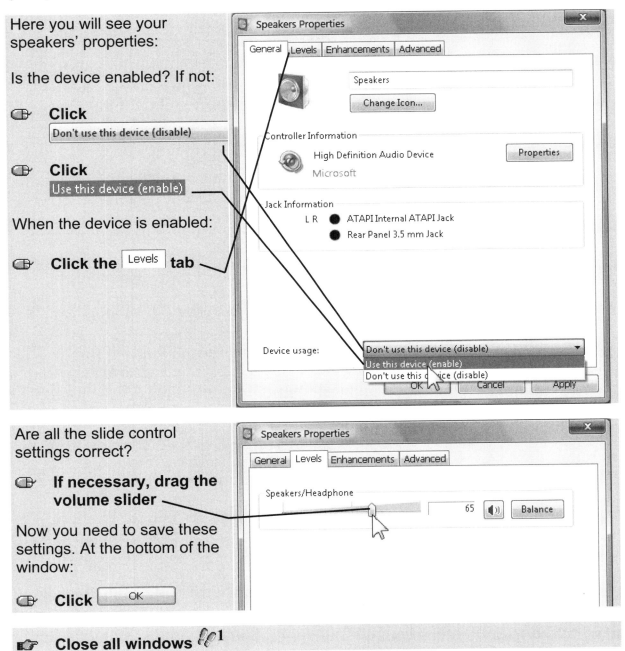

Are all the slide control settings correct?

☞ **If necessary, drag the volume slider**

Now you need to save these settings. At the bottom of the window:

☞ **Click** OK

☞ **Close all windows** ℓℓ1

If you still do not hear sounds, the problem could be caused by the sound card. Check if there are new drivers available for the sound card (see *paragraph 4.3 Device Management*), also look up the manufacturer's website, or let your supplier check your computer.

4.7 Background Information

Dictionary	
Device Manager	Using *Device Manager*, you can determine which devices are installed on your computer, update driver software for your devices, check to see if hardware is working properly, and modify hardware settings.
Driver	Software that enables hardware or devices (such as a printer, mouse, or keyboard) to work with your computer. Every device needs a driver in order for it to work.
Main volume	The volume setting for the speakers.
Print queue	The list of documents that are waiting to be printed.
Sound scheme	You can have your computer play a sound when certain events happen, such as when you log on or when you receive a new e-mail. *Windows* comes with several sound schemes that play for common program events. Additionally, some desktop themes have their own sound schemes.
Test page	You can print a test page to check if a printer is printing graphics and text correctly. A test page also displays information, such as the printer name, model, and driver software version that can help you troubleshoot printer problems.
Update	Updates are additions to software that can prevent or fix problems, enhance the security of the computer, or improve the computer's performance.
Upgrade	An upgrade is a transition to a new, enhanced edition of a software program.
Source: Windows Help and Support	

Video and sound cards

Every computer contains a video and a sound card. These cards send signals to your screen and to your speakers. Sometimes these are separate cards, but they may also be integrated into the motherboard (*onboard*).

These cards are very important in determining your computer's performance when creating and playing sound and video files. Even if you have a very fast computer, a slow video card can cause delays while processing images and sounds. You also may experience that sound and vision are not synchronized.

Do you like working with video images? Then you should choose a computer with a separate video card. Such a card will not be integrated into the motherboard. Separate cards usually contain more and faster memory. Moreover, the drivers of these cards are easier to upgrade, which may be necessary when you are going to use new software. Mobile computers (laptops and notebooks) nearly always have cards that are integrated into the motherboard. This is because of the restricted space inside.

 Tip

Connecting speakers

To connect speakers and microphones three jacks are used that are differentiated by color. These jacks are:

- Pink: microphone jack

- Blue: device line-in jack

- Green: speaker line-out jack

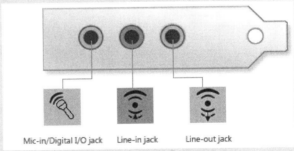

Picture: Windows Help and Support

Most sound cards have at least one line-out connection to connect to speakers, and one line-in connection to connect to a microphone. If you pay good attention to the colors of the jacks, connecting speakers and microphones is very simple.

4.8 Tips

 Tip

A device does not work after a Windows Vista update has been installed
If a device does not function properly after having updated *Windows Vista,* and if there are no new drivers available, you can try the following:

☞ **Open the *Device Manager* window** 7

☞ **Find the device**

☜ **Click** Uninstall

Afterwards, reboot the computer. *Windows Vista* will detect a new device and will again try to install this device.
Please note: during this procedure you may need to use the installation CD that came with the device.

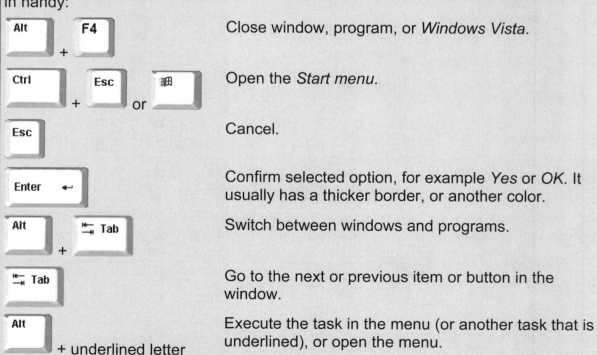 **Tip**

The mouse does not work anymore
Almost all of the actions you perform with the mouse can also be done using the keyboard. If you cannot use your mouse, the following key combinations may come in handy:

Alt + **F4**	Close window, program, or *Windows Vista.*
Ctrl + **Esc** or ⊞	Open the *Start menu.*
Esc	Cancel.
Enter ←	Confirm selected option, for example *Yes* or *OK.* It usually has a thicker border, or another color.
Alt + **Tab**	Switch between windows and programs.
Tab	Go to the next or previous item or button in the window.
Alt + underlined letter	Execute the task in the menu (or another task that is underlined), or open the menu.

5. Solving Software Problems and Windows Vista Problems

Many problems you experience while using your computer are caused by software. Software is still mostly human-made, as opposed to hardware, which is mostly machine-made. A software program consists of millions of instructions. Despite best efforts, some errors are inevitable. This goes for *Windows Vista* as well. Whether or not you run into an error depends on the kinds of things you are trying to do with the program and what type of computer you have. Even though most of these errors will be minor in nature, they can still be very annoying. If you stay calm and try to discover what is actually happening, the solution is usually easy to find.

In this chapter you will learn about common software problems and some of the common complaints regarding *Windows Vista*. Even though each problem is different, you will learn how to detect an error and where to search for a possible solution. You will also learn how to resolve some of the problems that may occur with a folder window or the display screen.

In this chapter you will learn:

- general tips for solving software problems;
- what to do when a program is not responding anymore;
- creating problem reports for software;
- how to search the *Microsoft* website for solutions to software problems;
- how to set up automatically generated problem reports;
- about the system registry;
- how to back up the system registry;
- how to solve problems with file, folder and screen settings;
- what to do when *Windows Vista* does not work properly.

➡ **Please note:**

Many problems will be solved by updating *Windows Vista*. Always make sure that you have installed the most recent *Windows Vista* updates on your computer.

➡ **Please note:**

To be able to execute the tasks in this chapter, you need to be logged on as an administrator and therefore know the administrator password. If you are logged on as a standard user because you do not know the administrator password, you can just read through this chapter.

5.1 Common Software Problems

When a program fails to install correctly, or refuses to open, there may be several causes. Perhaps the program starts up all right, but then suddenly stops responding after a while. This can be very annoying when you are in the middle of something and you lose all your work.
In most cases a program that has always worked correctly, will go on working as it should. If a problem does arise, it could be caused by changes in the system, such as a *Windows Vista* update or an update of the program itself, or even from new hardware.

In this section you will read about possible solutions for common software problems. As with hardware problems, it is possible to distinguish between different situations:

Installing new software
It is very important that a program is correctly installed. Here are some guidelines:

- Compare the suggested (minimum) system requirements for hardware and software to that of your own computer. A program that is written for *Windows Vista* will not always work with *Windows XP*, or vice versa. Note how much disk space and RAM memory is required, how fast the processor needs to be, etcetera.
- Always read the installation manual, even if you have installed a similar program before. Very often a wizard will guide you through the installation process.
- It is preferable to install a program using standard drive settings. Most often this is the C drive.
  Please note: if you install a program on a drive other than the standard drive where the operating system (*Windows Vista*) is installed, some data will be stored on the standard drive as well. This means you need to be able to access the standard drive.
- Make sure you are logged on as a user with administrator privileges. A standard user is not always allowed to make changes to the system files needed while installing software.
- Make sure you perform a 'clean' installation: before installing a program, first close all other programs and reboot the computer. It may even be necessary to temporarily shut down your antivirus program and firewall. In that case, you should also disable the Internet connection, to prevent viruses from infecting your computer.

In *Chapter 3 Installing and Removing Programs* you can read more about installing programs.

The program does not work properly after it has been installed

If the program does not work correctly after installation, you can follow these steps:

- Reboot your computer and see if the program then works properly.
- In the manufacturers' installation manual, the most frequently occurring problems are often listed. Check the manual for a description of your problem.
- Visit the manufacturers' website and look for clues to finding a solution. For example, in the FAQs (Frequently Asked Questions) section. Also check to see if any updates or new software editions are available and install them.
- Does the problem report contain information about this program, and have you already sent this report to *Microsoft*? (see *paragraph 5.3 Software Problem Reports*).
- Try to find the solution on the Internet. Type the name of the program, which version it is plus a short description of the problem as a keyword phrase in a search engine such as *Google*. You may find a number of different websites offering a solution to your problem.
- Uninstall the program, and re-install it again. Make sure to reboot your computer before installing the program a second time.
- Contact the manufacturers' helpdesk by e-mail or telephone.

Problems with other programs, after having installed a program

Most of the time, your other programs should not be affected when you install a new program. But if you do run into problems, you can try the following things:

- Certain types of programs such as firewalls, antivirus programs, burning software and communication programs will not work properly if other programs of the same kind are running simultaneously. If you have installed more than one program of the same kind, try removing one.
- Uninstall the program that is causing the problem, and re-install it. Make sure to reboot your computer before installing the program for a second time. **Please note:** make sure you still have the original installation CD, and the proper registration codes, before uninstalling the program.
- If the problem persists after having re-installed the program, then uninstall and re-install the new program. You may be able to find the cause of the problem by checking the installation options. It's possible that existing file extensions will be automatically associated with the new program.
- Visit several other websites and look for clues to the solution. For example, in the FAQs (Frequently Asked Questions) section. Also check to see if any updates or new software editions are available and install them.
- Try to find the solution on the Internet. Type the name of the program, which version it is plus a short description of the problem as a keyword phrase in a search engine such as *Google*. You may find a number of different websites offering a solution to your problem.
- Contact the manufacturers' helpdesk by e-mail or telephone.

Problems with a program that has always functioned properly
If a program suddenly stops working properly, your computer system may have changed in some way:

- What has changed? Have you connected a new device? Have you installed a *Vista* update, a *Service Pack* or an antivirus program?
- A *Windows Vista* update may cause problems. You could try to solve the problem by installing an update to your program as well. Check if you can find a more recent edition of your program or an update.
- An update of an antivirus program or firewall can also cause trouble. Disable your Internet connection and temporarily disable the antivirus program and firewall while using the program. Do not forget to enable these programs again before you connect to the Internet or retrieve your e-mail.
- Uninstall the program that is causing the problem, and re-install it. Make sure to reboot your computer before installing the program for a second time.
- Visit the manufacturers' website and look for clues to finding a solution. For example, in the FAQs (Frequently Asked Questions) section. Also check to see if any updates or new software editions are available and install them.
- Try to find the solution on the Internet. Type the name of the program, which version it is plus a short description of the problem as a keyword phrase in a search engine such as *Google*. You may find a number of different websites offering a solution to your problem.
- Contact the manufacturers' helpdesk by e-mail or telephone.

There can be many different reasons why a program stops working. The steps we have described will help you check for the most common causes. This still leaves a number of special situations that may cause problems, such as program errors or conflicts with *Windows Vista*. These problems cannot be solved easily. In most cases you will need to wait for an update of the program that causes the problem.

 HELP! Update or upgrade?

Many programs offer regular updates, and occasionally an upgrade. An update is an extension or enhancement for a certain edition of a program. An upgrade is a transition to a new edition which may contain a number of new features. An update is usually free of charge, but you may have to pay for an upgrade. Licensed or registered users will often get a discount when buying upgrades.

5.2 A Program Is Not Responding

Sometimes, when you are in the middle of working, a program suddenly freezes. It doesn't react anymore to your keyboard or mouse clicks. If the program still does not react after you've waited a while, you can try to close the program or programs.

⇨ **Please note:**

Sometimes *Windows Vista* is performing tasks in the background, such as saving files. This is why you should always wait a little before attempting the following steps. Shutting down programs or shutting down *Windows Vista* too quickly might result in loss of data.

This will probably not work, but you can always try to close the program in the usual way:

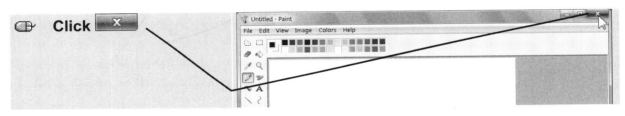

⊕ **Click** [X]

💡 **Tip**

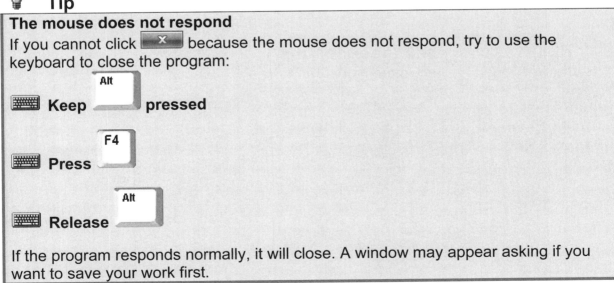

The mouse does not respond

If you cannot click [X] because the mouse does not respond, try to use the keyboard to close the program:

⌨ **Keep** [Alt] **pressed**

⌨ **Press** [F4]

⌨ **Release** [Alt]

If the program responds normally, it will close. A window may appear asking if you want to save your work first.

If the program cannot be closed, or clicking [X] does not work, you can close the program by using the *Windows Task Manager*.

⌨ **Simultaneously press** [Ctrl] , [Alt] **and** [Delete]

Your screen will turn blue:

☞ **Click *Start Task Manager***

The *Windows Task Manager* window appears. The left side shows the programs that are running. Their status is indicated on the right. One of the programs shows the status Not Responding :

☞ **Click the program that causes the error message** ———

☞ **Click** End Task ——

The other programs will continue to work normally.

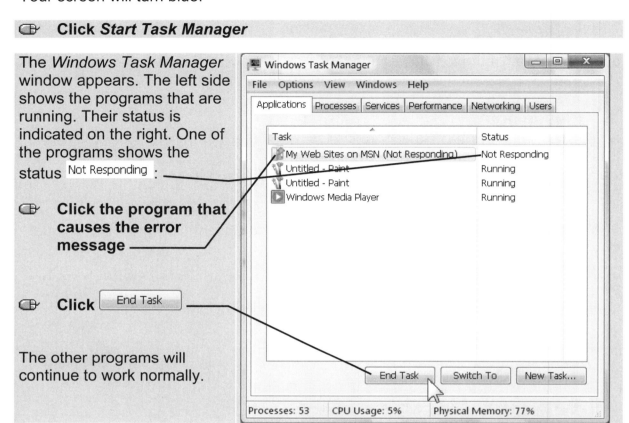

HELP! I cannot see the programs.

If you have opened a different tab in the *Windows Task Manager*:

☞ **Click the** Applications **tab**

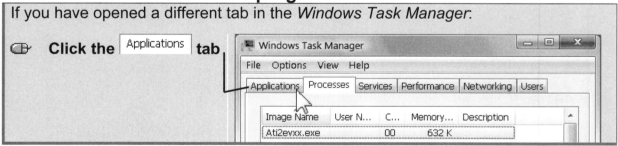

You may be asked if you want to save the file:

If you want to save the file:

☞ **Click** Save ——

Otherwise:

☞ **Click** Don't Save ——

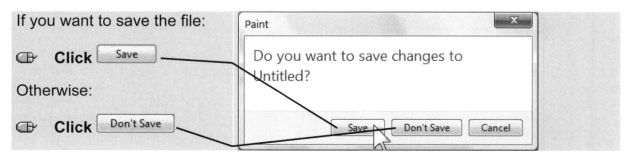

☞ **If necessary, choose a location and file type**

Here you see the *Windows Task Manager* window. The task that has been closed is no longer listed:

☞ **Click** [X]

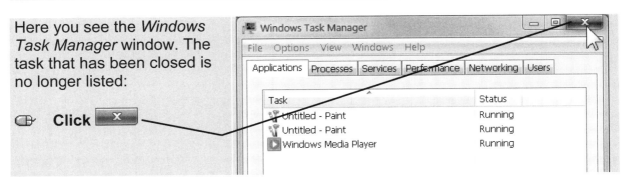

5.3 Software Problem Reports

There are different kinds of software problems. If a problem occurs between *Windows Vista* and another program, *Microsoft* can sometimes provide the solution.

Each time your computer experiences problems with software, such as when a program doesn't start up or when it doesn't respond anymore, a problem report is generated. If you send this report to *Microsoft* via the Internet, they might be able to find a solution for you.
The problem report also tells you which programs have caused problems before, and which possible solution was offered:

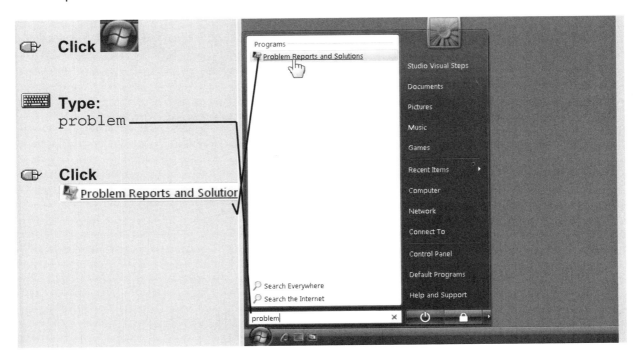

☞ **Click**

⌨ **Type:**
problem

☞ **Click**
🔧 Problem Reports and Solution

Now you will see a list of problems:

Most likely the problems in your window will be different than the ones shown here.

☞ **Click a problem**

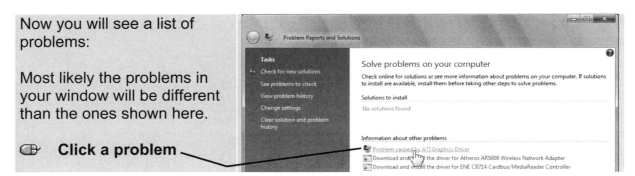

Here you will see the solution that *Microsoft* has provided:

☞ **Click** OK

You can print this information by clicking 🖶 Print this solution.

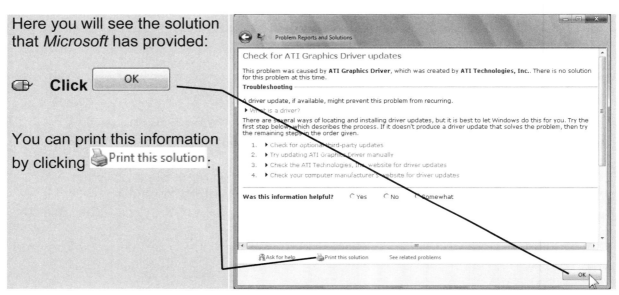

You can send the reports to *Microsoft* via the Internet to check if any solutions have been found:

☞ **Click** Check for new solutions

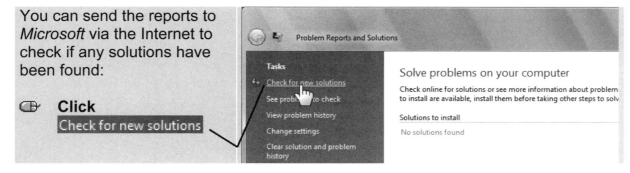

Windows is looking for a solution:

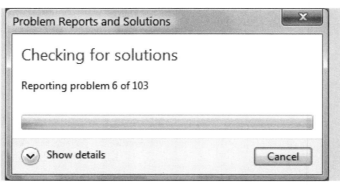

In this example, a solution has not yet been found:

☞ **Click** `Close`

Here you will see the date the last report was sent:

If you want to view older problems, you will need to check the problem history.

☞ **Click** `View problem history`

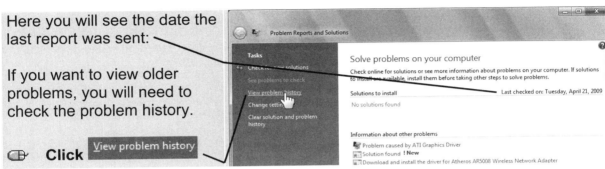

Here you see the problems that have occurred earlier:

The problems that appear in your window may be different than the ones shown here.

☞ **Double-click a problem**

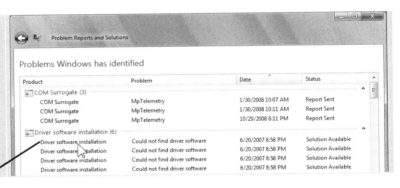

Now you will see the technical details of the problem:

Use `Copy to clipboard` to paste the report into an e-mail message. This way you can send it to the helpdesk of the program manufacturer, for example:

☞ **Click** `OK`

In the next window:

⬚ **Click** `    OK    `

It is possible that the problems you see are not caused by the program, nor by *Windows Vista*, but by something else, such as shutting down the program in an irregular way, for example. In that case *Microsoft* cannot provide the answer.

If a problem occurs, a report is sent to *Microsoft* automatically. As soon as the problem has occurred, *Microsoft* will receive this report and, if possible, the solution will be sent to you. If you do not want to use this service, or change the settings for other users, you will need to do the following:

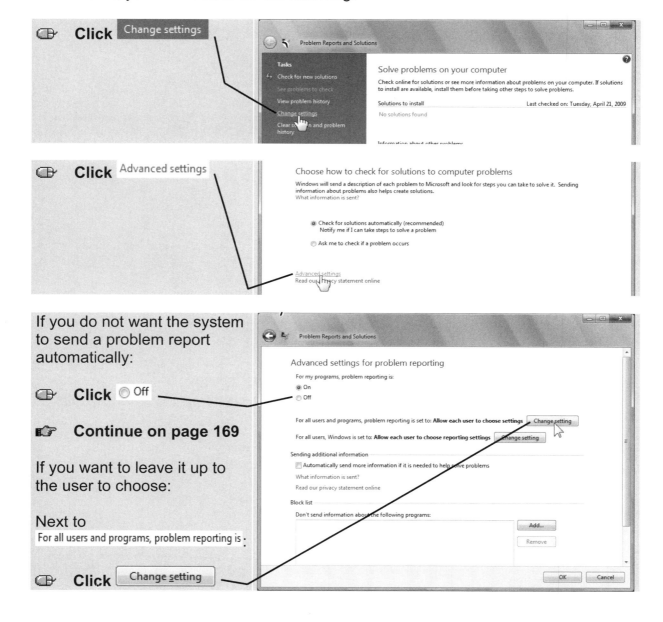

⬚ **Click** `Change settings`

⬚ **Click** `Advanced settings`

If you do not want the system to send a problem report automatically:

⬚ **Click** ○ Off

☞ **Continue on page 169**

If you want to leave it up to the user to choose:

Next to
`For all users and programs, problem reporting is` ·

⬚ **Click** `Change setting`

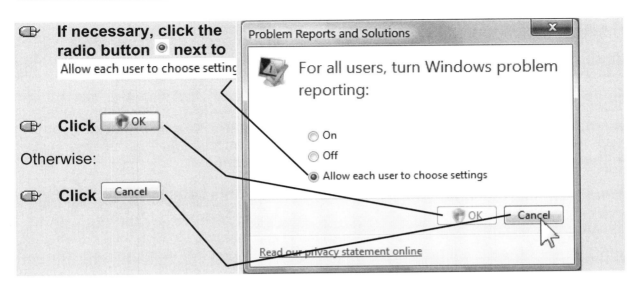

If necessary, click the radio button ◉ **next to** Allow each user to choose setting

Click OK

Otherwise:

Click Cancel

Your screen goes dark and you will need to give permission to continue:

Click Continue

You can also determine whether reports and other information may be sent for other users:

Next to For all users, Windows is set to: :

Click Change setting

Make your choice

Click OK

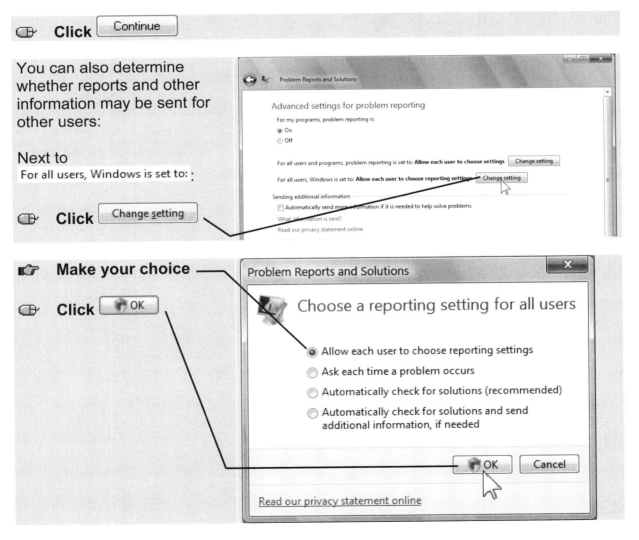

Your screen goes dark and you will need to give permission to continue:

Click [Continue]

If *Microsoft* needs additional information regarding the problem, for example about other programs you were using at the time, this information can be retrieved if you give your permission. Usually you will need to give permission every time data will be retrieved, but you can also let the system send this information automatically:

If you allow *Microsoft* to retrieve the information automatically:

Check the box ☑ next to
Automatically send more informatic

Click [OK]

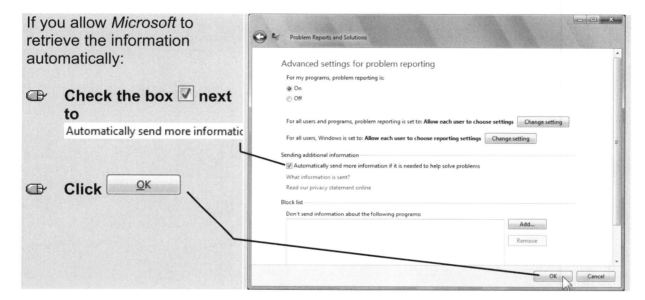

In the next window:

Click [OK]

 Tip

Excluding programs from the problem report
Use the [Add...] button to add programs you want to exclude from the report. For example, if you already know you have older programs that generate error messages while you are using them.

The problem history will always be saved. This means that older problems, and problems that you have already solved, will be sent to *Microsoft* over and over again. If you want to delete the problem history, this is how to do it:

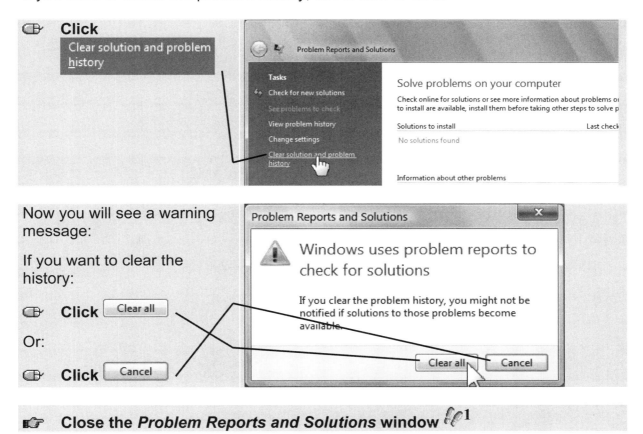

☞ **Close the *Problem Reports and Solutions* window** 📖¹

5.4 The System Registry

The system registry consists of a number of files in which *Windows Vista* stores specific data about the hardware, programs and users of the system. When you open a program, *Windows Vista* checks the registry to see which specific settings apply to this program, how it should be started, etcetera. The registry is updated every time new hardware is installed, or when a program is installed or removed. Sometimes the registry will not be updated correctly. This may be because of a computer failure, because you have closed a program in the wrong way, or because of unknown causes. If this happens you can update the registry yourself, but only if you know where the error is located and how to correct it.

Instructions for changing the registry often can be found on the website of antivirus program manufacturers. A virus often changes the registry, and you need to undo such a change yourself. In the following section you will learn how to open and back up the registry.

Please note:

The system registry is a highly complicated file. Changing the registry may lead to hardware malfunctioning, software problems or even *Windows Vista* failures. In this section you will only take a look at the registry and not make any changes.

 Tip

Create a restore point
To be on the safe side, you should create a restore point before continuing with this section *ℓℓ*[13].

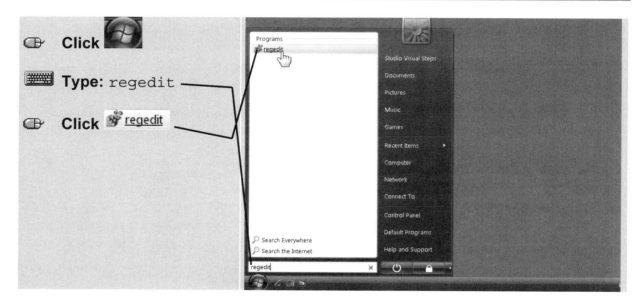

Click

Type: regedit

Click regedit

Your screen goes dark and you will need to give permission to continue:

Click [Continue]

Here you will see the *keys* in the registry:

The items displayed in your window may look different than what is shown here. There may also be items showing in the right pane.

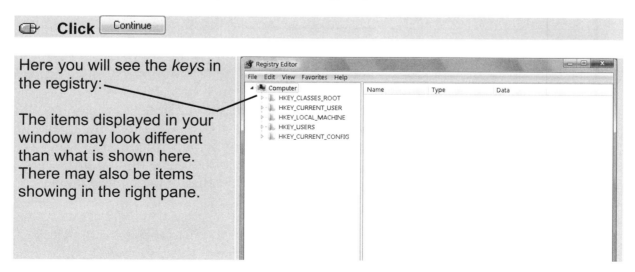

First you need to back up the registry:

☞ **Click** File

☞ **Click** Export...

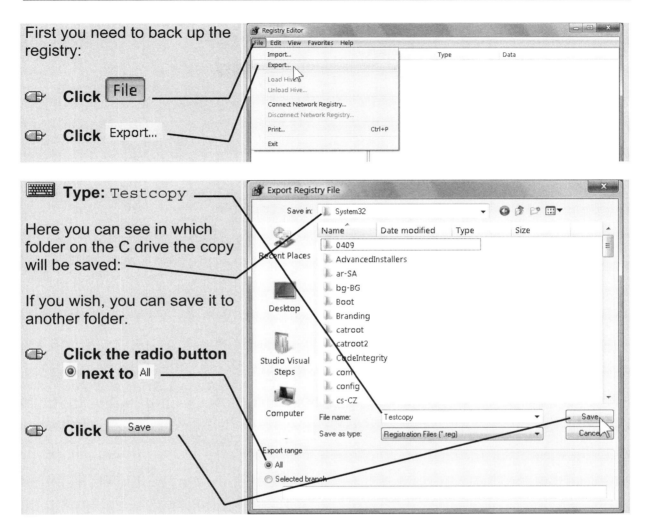

🖮 **Type:** Testcopy

Here you can see in which folder on the C drive the copy will be saved:

If you wish, you can save it to another folder.

☞ **Click the radio button** ◉ **next to** All

☞ **Click** Save

Now the backup will be made and when it has finished you will see the registry again. The registry consists of a number of keys which are comparable to folders. These keys contain the settings for all programs and devices in *Windows Vista*.

☞ **Click** ▷ **next to** HKEY_CURRENT_USER

The folder will open:

☞ **Click** Console

Now you will see the *subkeys Windows Vista* is using:

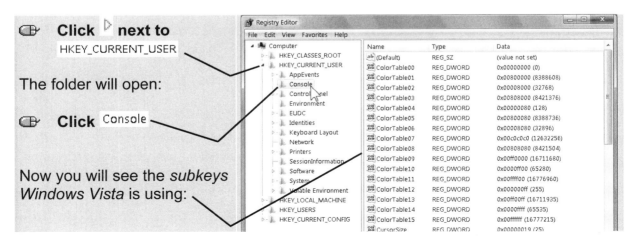

To change the value of a subkey:

  Double-click a subkey

In this case you are not going to change anything:

  Click [Cancel]

In general, it is best not to change anything in this window.

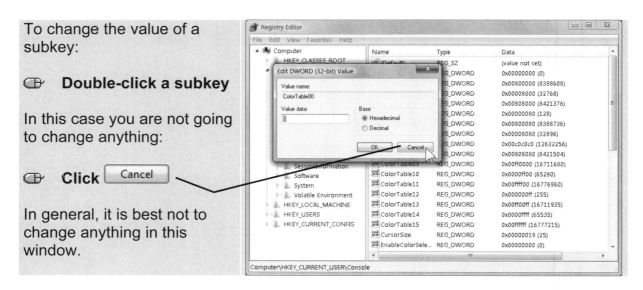

☞ **Close the *Registry Editor* window** 📖¹
   If you are asked if you want to save the changes, do not do so.

You should only change registry settings if you really know what you are doing, or if you have been given specific written instructions. If the instructions are on screen, it is a good idea to print them first. Otherwise there is a chance that you will not be able to read the instructions while working in the registry. Always back up your registry settings first. If you are not sure that you have changed the registry correctly, close the window without saving the changes.

💡 **Tip**

Manually deleting viruses from the registry
Viruses are known to change registry settings, in order to bypass security settings. If you have found a virus on your computer, check the antivirus program manufacturers' website for information on how to change the registry:

Here you see part of a website instruction page for the anitivirus program *Symantec*:

Note the warning:

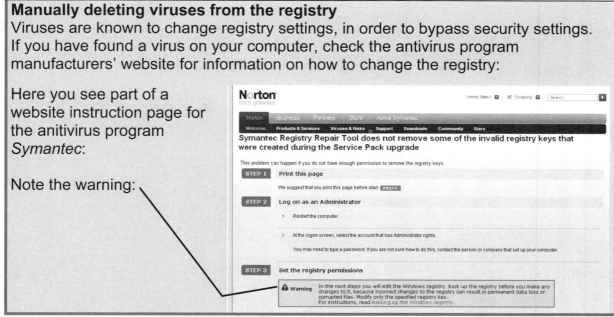

HELP! I have accidentally changed something in the registry.

If you have saved a registry change by accident, you can import the old registry from the backup you have made:

☞ **Close all programs**

☞ **Open the *Registry Editor* window**

☞ **Click** `File`

☞ **Click** `Import...`

☞ **If necessary, drag the scroll bar down**

☞ **Click the registry file you want to import**

☞ **Click** `Open`

If there are any other programs open, you may see a warning message:

☞ **Click** `OK`

☞ **Close the *Registry Editor* window**

In some cases you may need to reboot your computer.

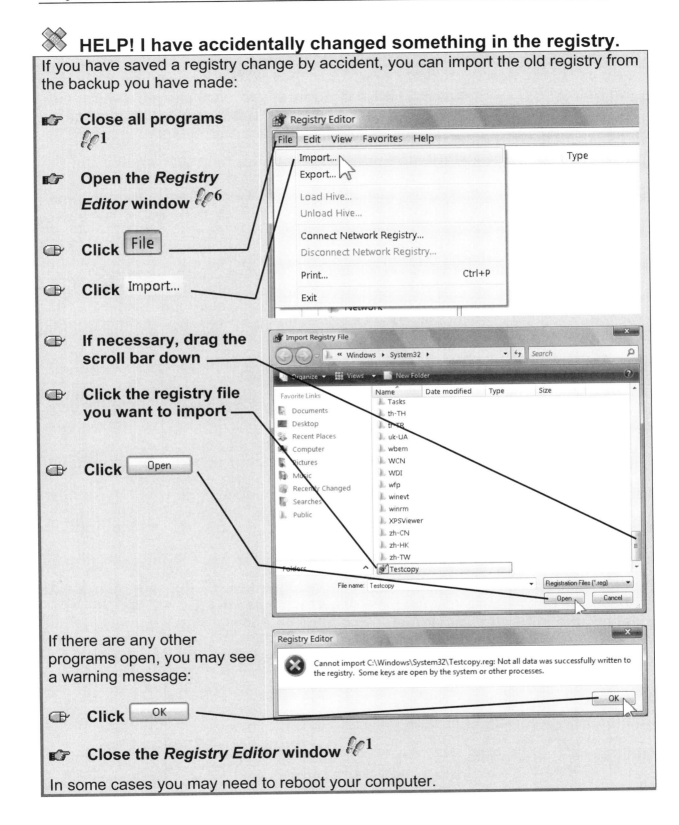

5.5 Problems with Files and Folders

When you open *Windows Explorer,* or use the *Open* or *Save* file options to open and save files, you will see the drives, files and folders of your computer. As a user, you can change the settings with which to view these files and folders. In this section you will learn how to solve some common problems with files and folders.

 Tip

The exercises in this section are presented in such a way that you can do them one after the other, in order to learn how to solve the problems that are discussed here.

Problem: the file names do not show the file types (extensions).

The file type, also called the extension, indicates what kind of file it is. By default, *Windows Vista* does not show file extensions. If you do want to show them, this is how to do it:

☞ **Open a folder or disk station** 🖐10

In this example you see an open folder with several program files.
The file names do not show the known file extensions:

 Tip

Recognizing the file type by its icon
Even if you do not see the file extension, you can often recognize the file type by its symbol. The icon often symbolizes the file type or the program that is used to open this type of file.

🖯 **Click** ⬛ Organize ▾

🖯 **Click**
Folder and Search Options

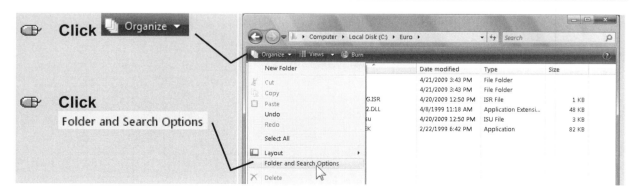

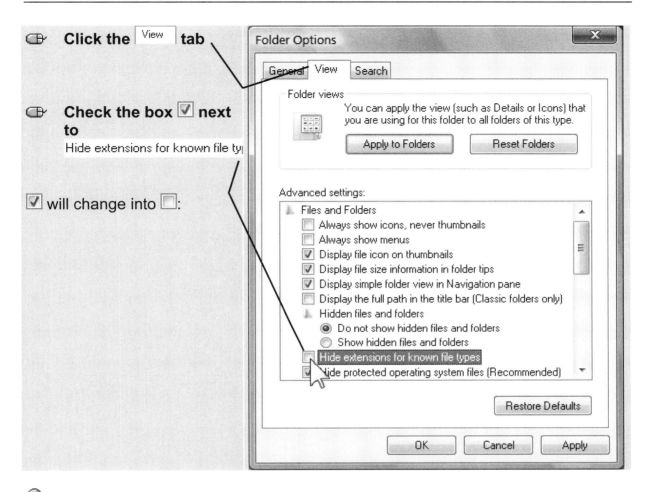

Click the `View` **tab**

Check the box ☑ **next to**

Hide extensions for known file ty|

☑ **will change into** ☐:

Folder Options

General View Search

Folder views

You can apply the view (such as Details or Icons) that you are using for this folder to all folders of this type.

[Apply to Folders]   [Reset Folders]

Advanced settings:

Files and Folders
☐ Always show icons, never thumbnails
☐ Always show menus
☑ Display file icon on thumbnails
☑ Display file size information in folder tips
☑ Display simple folder view in Navigation pane
☐ Display the full path in the title bar (Classic folders only)
Hidden files and folders
◉ Do not show hidden files and folders
○ Show hidden files and folders
☐ Hide extensions for known file types
☑ Hide protected operating system files (Recommended)

[Restore Defaults]

[OK]   [Cancel]   [Apply]

💡 Tip

Apply to all folders
To apply the new folder settings to all folders:

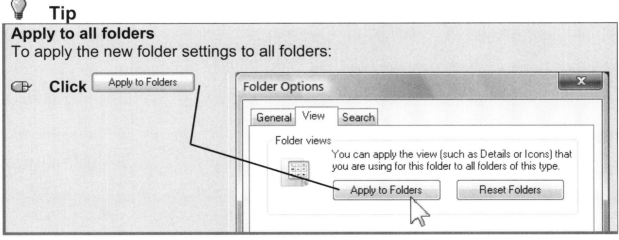

Click [Apply to Folders]

Folder Options

General View Search

Folder views

You can apply the view (such as Details or Icons) that you are using for this folder to all folders of this type.

[Apply to Folders]   [Reset Folders]

At the bottom of the window:

☞ **Click** [OK]

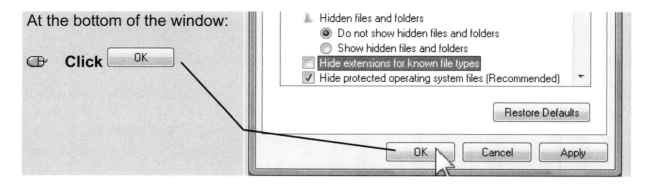

🩹 HELP! The new settings are wrong.

If you do not like the settings, you can return to the default settings:

To apply the default settings
to all folders:

☞ **Click** [Reset Folders]

To apply the default settings
to the active folder only:

☞ **Click** [Restore Defaults]

☞ **Click** [OK]

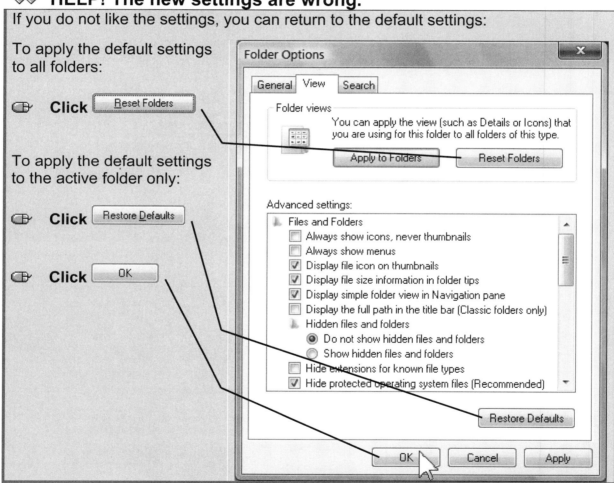

Now you will see the known file extensions listed next to the file name:

Problem: when I change the file type, I get a warning message.

Many file types are associated with the program you use to open a file. If you change the file type, the file will not be opened with that specific program anymore and you may therefore not be able to use the file any longer.

⇨ Please note:

You will only see this warning message when you have chosen to show known file types. If you have not chosen this setting, you will be able to change the file name without changing the file type.
In order to perform the next exercise you need to disable the option
Hide extensions for known file types .

Open a folder or disk drive ✍10

You should see the file extensions next to the file names:

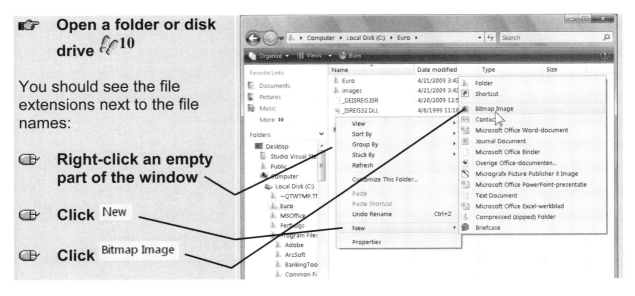

☞ **Right-click an empty part of the window**

☞ **Click** New

☞ **Click** Bitmap Image

HELP! I cannot create a bitmap image.

If you cannot create a bitmap image in the folder you are currently using, then choose another folder, for example the *Documents* folder.

Type: Image

Press Enter ⏎

Now you will see a new file of the type .BMP:

The file type is Bitmap Image :

Right-click 🖼 Image.bmp

Click Rename

Click next to 'bmp'

Press ← Backspace **three times**

Type: xyz

Press Enter ⏎

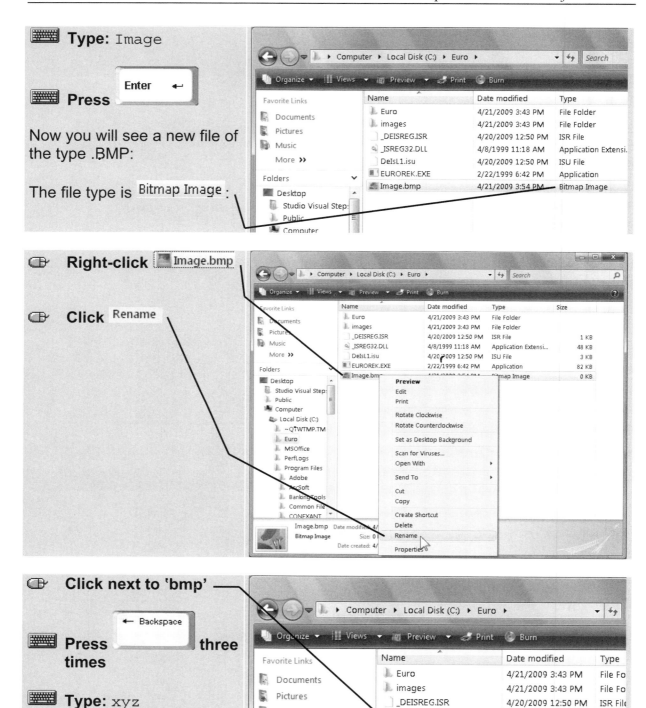

You will see this warning:

☞ **Click** [Yes]

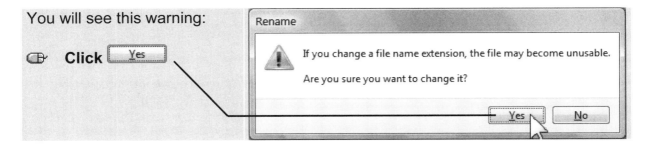

➡ **Please note:**

Never change the file types of *Windows* features, programs or system files.
Changing them may result in program failures or problems with *Windows Vista*.

The file extension has
changed, and therefore also
the file type:

⊙ **Problem: the file cannot be opened.**

If a file has an unknown file type, *Windows Vista* will not know how to open this file.
You need to choose a program with which you can open this file:

☞ **Double-click**
  Image.xyz

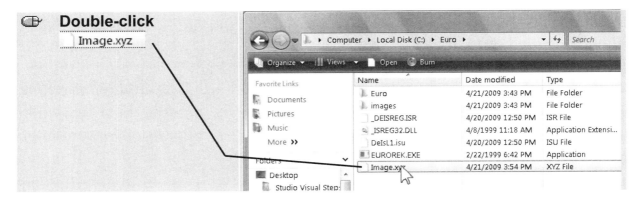

You will see that the file cannot be opened automatically:

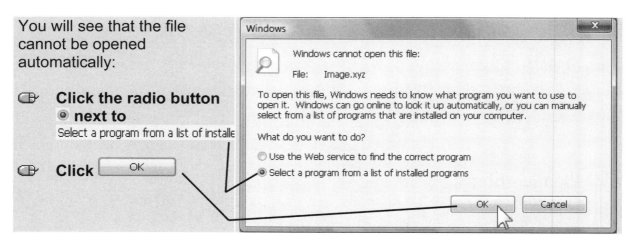

☞ **Click the radio button ⊙ next to**
Select a program from a list of installe

☞ **Click** [OK]

Because you know this is a picture, you want to open the file in *Paint*:

☞ **Click** Paint

☞ **Check the box ☑ next to**
Always use the selected program to op

☐ will change into ☑:

☞ **Click** [OK]

 Tip

Using a default program for a specific file type
If you always want to open files of a specific file type with a specific program, you need to check the box ☑ next to Always use the selected program to open this kind of file .

HELP! The program I need is not listed.

Not all programs will appear in this window. Sometimes you will only see the programs you have used last. If you want to open the file with a program that is not listed, then follow these steps:

If your program is not in this list:

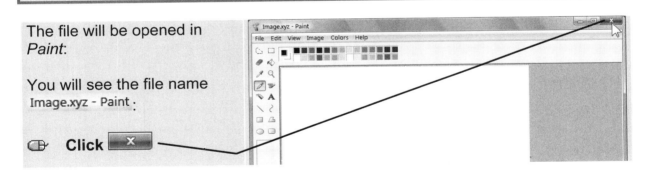

Click   Browse...

Now you can search the computer for the program yourself.

The file will be opened in *Paint*:

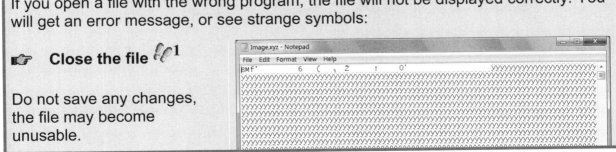

You will see the file name Image.xyz - Paint :

Click   X

HELP! I only see strange symbols.

If you open a file with the wrong program, the file will not be displayed correctly. You will get an error message, or see strange symbols:

Close the file &1

Do not save any changes, the file may become unusable.

Problem: the file cannot be found by clicking the shortcut.

A shortcut can be used to open a program or a file on your computer, in a network, or on the Internet. If you double-click a shortcut to a file that does not exist anymore, you will get an error message. We will demonstrate this here:

Right-click Image.xyz

Click Send To

Click
Desktop (create shortcut)

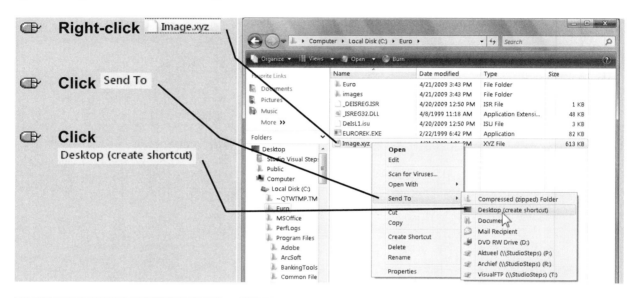

Right-click Image.xyz

Click Delete

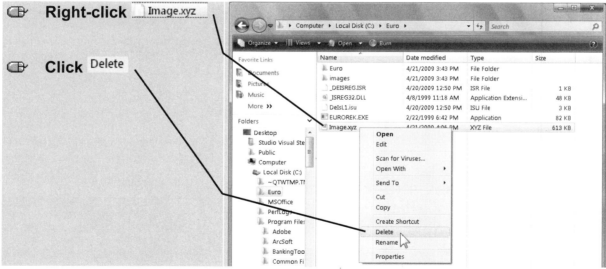

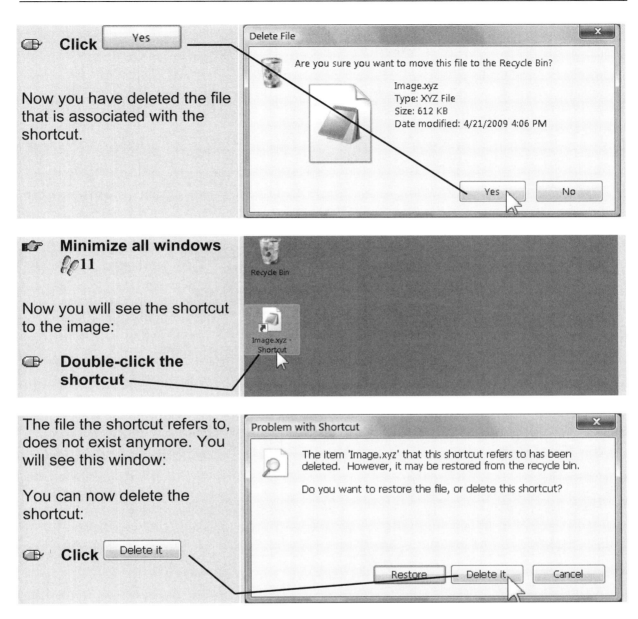

☞ **Click** Yes

Now you have deleted the file that is associated with the shortcut.

Delete File

Are you sure you want to move this file to the Recycle Bin?

Image.xyz
Type: XYZ File
Size: 612 KB
Date modified: 4/21/2009 4:06 PM

Yes   No

☞ **Minimize all windows** 𝄃𝄃11

Now you will see the shortcut to the image:

☞ **Double-click the shortcut**

Recycle Bin

Image.xyz - Shortcut

The file the shortcut refers to, does not exist anymore. You will see this window:

You can now delete the shortcut:

☞ **Click** Delete it

Problem with Shortcut

The item 'Image.xyz' that this shortcut refers to has been deleted. However, it may be restored from the recycle bin.

Do you want to restore the file, or delete this shortcut?

Restore   Delete it   Cancel

It is best to delete shortcuts that refer to files that do not exist anymore. This will prevent you from getting error messages. *Windows Vista* also becomes sluggish on start up if you have a lot of invalid shortcuts.

If there is no connection to the Internet, or if the shortcut refers to a webpage that can no longer be found, you will see this message in *Internet Explorer*:

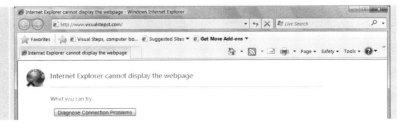

⚙ **Problem: deleting a file is not possible, because the file is in use.**

You can only delete a file which is not in use. It also depends on the type of file and on the program, whether or not you are allowed to delete the file. If the file is opened, you will see the *File In Use* window:

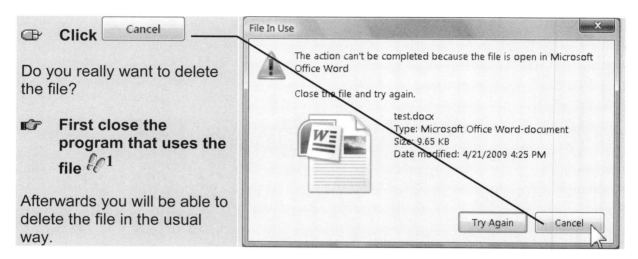

🖱 **Click** Cancel

Do you really want to delete the file?

☞ **First close the program that uses the file** ℓℓ¹

Afterwards you will be able to delete the file in the usual way.

⇨ **Please note:**

It is possible that files are being used by a program, or by *Windows Vista,* that you yourself haven't opened, for example, system specific files. You should never delete these types of files.

⇨ **Please note:**

Sometimes a file stays in use for a short while, even after closing the program that used it. You will still be getting the error message when you try to delete it. You can try to delete the file later.

⚙ **Problem: I cannot see all of the files.**

Besides the visible files, some folders also contain hidden files. Usually, these files are hidden because they are system critical files and therefore should not be tampered with. This is how you can view these files:

🖱 **Click the minimized folder on the taskbar**

Or:

☞ **Open another folder** ℓℓ10

Right-click an empty part of the window

Click New

Click Text Document

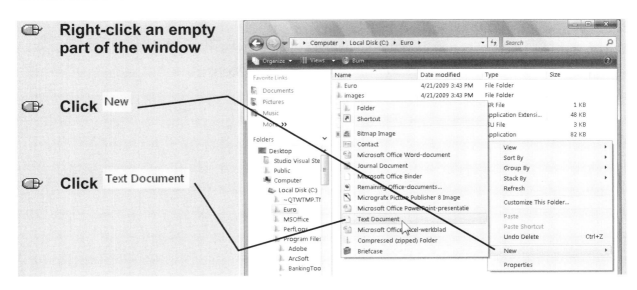

HELP! I cannot create a text document.

If you are not able to create a text document in the folder you are currently using, then choose a different folder, such as the *Documents* folder.

Type: Secret

Press Enter ←

Now you will see a new file with the file type .TXT:

This file is a Text Document .

Right-click Secret.txt

Click Properties

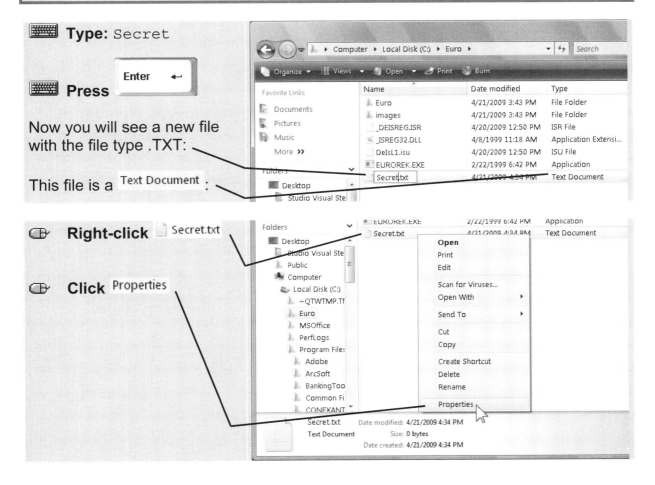

Here you will see the properties of 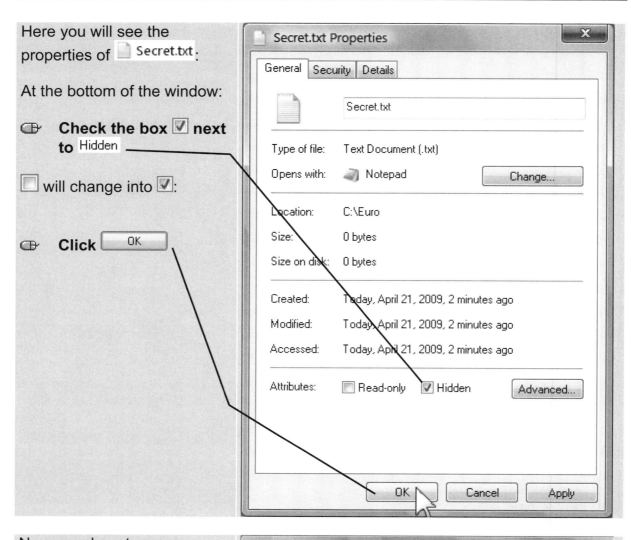 Secret.txt:

At the bottom of the window:

☞ **Check the box ☑ next to** Hidden

☐ will change into ☑:

☞ **Click** OK

Now you do not see Secret.txt in the folder window anymore:

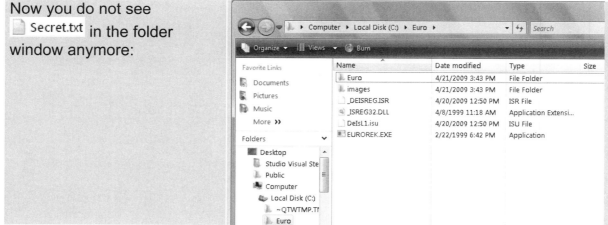

This is how you can display the hidden files:

☞ **Open the *Folder Options* window** 🐾¹²

🖱 **Click the** `View` **tab**

🖱 **Drag the scroll bar down**

🖱 **Click the radio button** ◉ **next to** `Show hidden files and folders`

○ **will change into** ◉:

🖱 **Click** `OK`

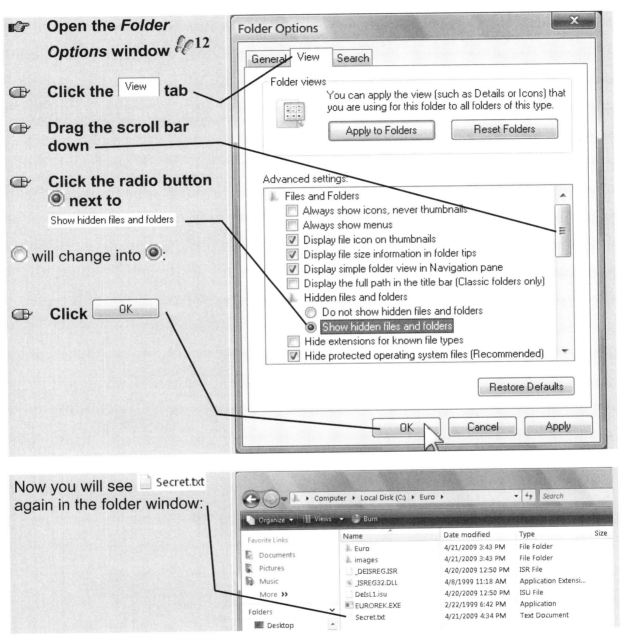

Now you will see 🔲 Secret.txt again in the folder window:

💡 **Tip**

Recognizing hidden files

You can also recognize hidden files by their slightly different appearance in the icon that is associated with them. The icon next to the file name has a lighter hue:

🖼 Hidden.bmp
🖼 Visible.bmp

Problem: when I select a file, I do not see any file information.

When you select a file, you will see a default pop-up window which contains information about the file. This is how you enable or disable these pop-up windows:

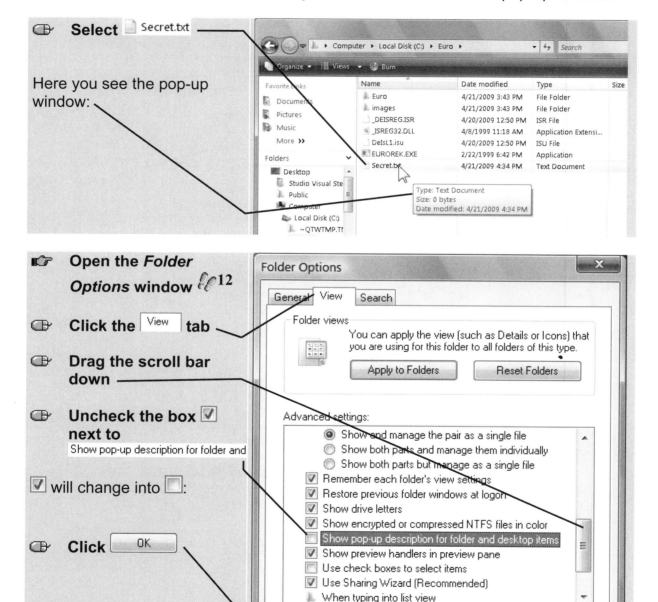

Select ▢ Secret.txt

Here you see the pop-up window:

☞ Open the *Folder Options* window ℰℓ12

⊕ Click the ▢ View ▢ tab

⊕ Drag the scroll bar down

⊕ Uncheck the box ☑ next to
Show pop-up description for folder and

☑ will change into ▢:

⊕ Click ▢ OK ▢

☞ **Select** ⬜ Secret.txt

Now you no longer see a pop-up window when you select ⬜ Secret.txt :

To display the pop-up window again, follow the same steps as above.

⬤ **Problem: I do not see the check boxes to select the files and folders.**

In *Windows* you can select multiple files or folders at once by pressing ⬚ Ctrl and ⬚ ⇧ Shift . To do this, you press one of these keys while selecting the files. It may be a little easier for you to do this if you use check boxes. First you need to enable these check boxes:

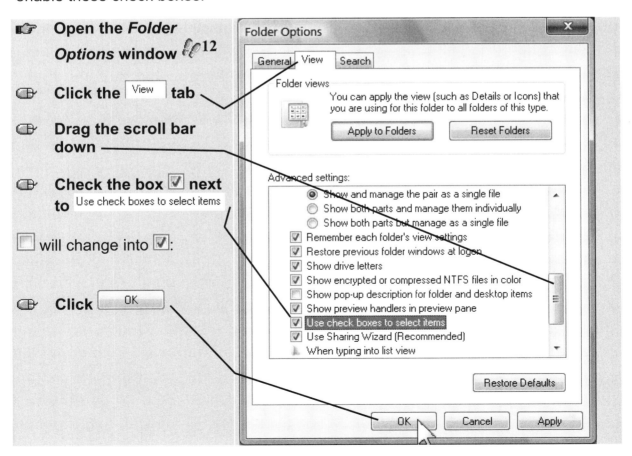

☞ **Open the *Folder Options* window** ✍12

☞ **Click the** ⬚ View **tab**

☞ **Drag the scroll bar down**

☞ **Check the box** ☑ **next to** Use check boxes to select items

⬜ will change into ☑ :

☞ **Click** ⬚ OK

☞ **Point to** Secret.txt

Now you will see a check box:

☞ **Check the box ☑ next to** Secret.txt

Now the file is selected.

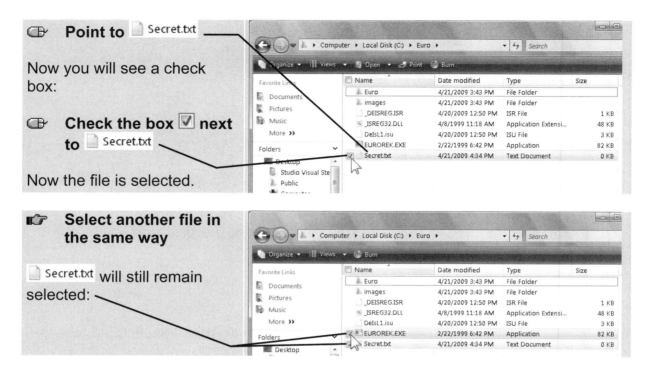

☞ **Select another file in the same way**

Secret.txt will still remain selected:

This is the way to select multiple files if you want to move, copy or delete them. If you do not check the box but click the file name instead, or another part of the window, the selection will be undone:

☞ **Click somewhere under the file list**

The checkmarks will disappear:

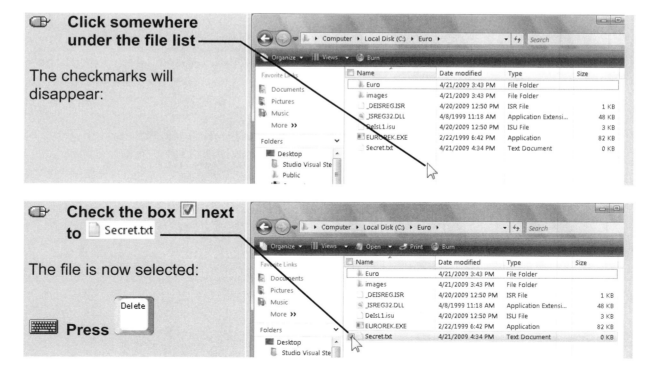

☞ **Check the box ☑ next to** Secret.txt

The file is now selected:

⌨ **Press** Delete

Now you will see a window and you will be asked if you really want to delete this file:

☞ **Click** [Yes]

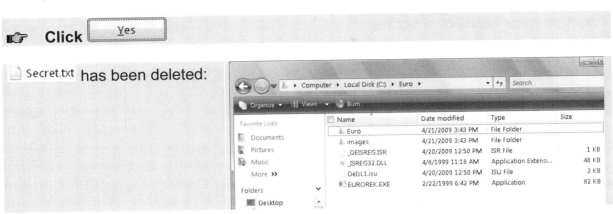

📄 Secret.txt has been deleted:

💡 **Tip**

Opening folders with a single click
You can also open folders with a single click instead of double-clicking them:

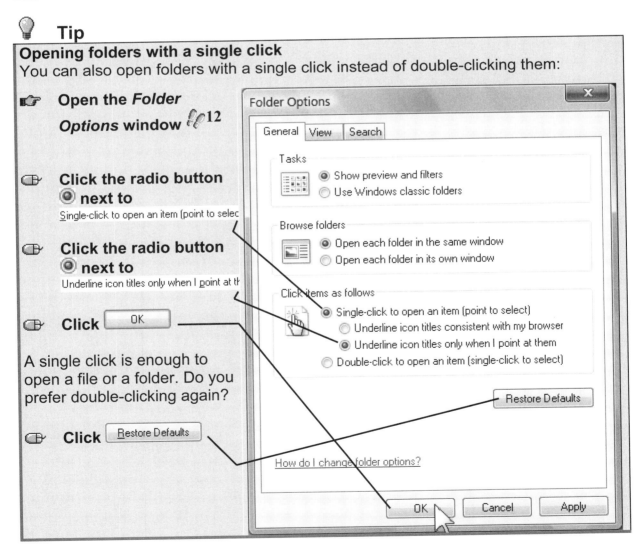

☞ **Open the *Folder Options* window** 👣12

☞ **Click the radio button ⦿ next to**
Single-click to open an item (point to selec

☞ **Click the radio button ⦿ next to**
Underline icon titles only when I point at th

☞ **Click** [OK]

A single click is enough to open a file or a folder. Do you prefer double-clicking again?

☞ **Click** [Restore Defaults]

Problem: I would like to restore the default settings.

After you have changed several settings, you can always revert back to the default settings if you wish:

☞ **Open the *Folder Options* window** *𝓵𝓵*12

☞ **Click the** View **tab**

☞ **Click** Restore Defaults

Have you changed the settings in several different folders?

☞ **Click** Reset Folders

☞ **Click** OK

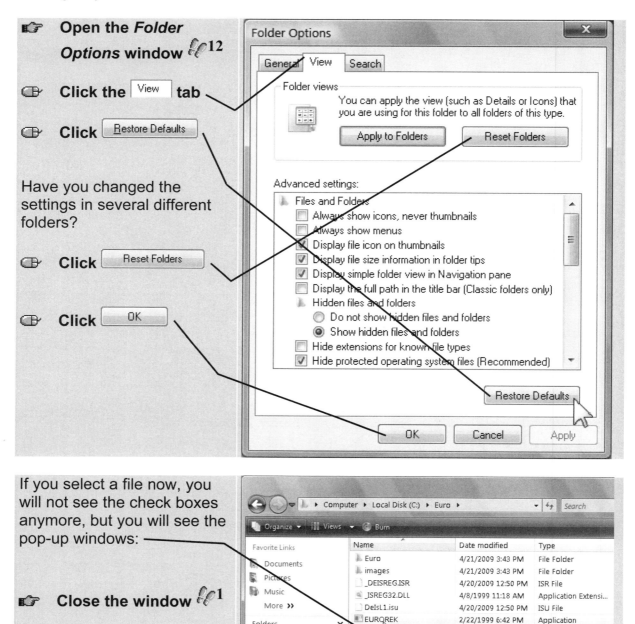

If you select a file now, you will not see the check boxes anymore, but you will see the pop-up windows:

☞ **Close the window** *𝓵𝓵*1

5.6 Problems with Screen Settings

The desktop in *Windows Vista* is the main screen (or space) that you see after you turn on your computer. It serves as a surface for your work. Many problems are caused by incorrect desktop/screen settings. In this section you will read about common problems and their solutions.

⚙ Problem: the desktop is bigger than the screen.

When the desktop is larger than the screen, certain parts of the screen may be off screen, such as the taskbar. First check to see if you have accidentally enlarged or moved the display with the buttons on the monitor. Try to use these buttons first to restore the display. If necessary, check the monitor's manual.

If this does not work, the screen resolution settings may be incorrect. Your graphics card may be set to a resolution that is not suitable for your monitor. For example, a resolution intended for widescreens when you don't have a widescreen monitor.

☞ **Right-click an empty spot on the desktop**

Please note: be careful not to click an icon or the taskbar.

☞ **Click** Personalize

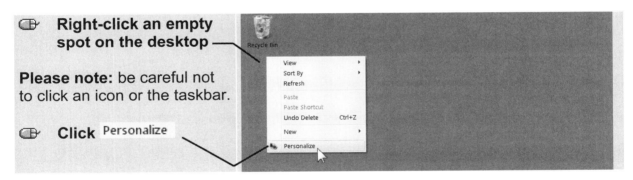

Now you will see the *Personalization* window:

☞ **Click** Display Settings

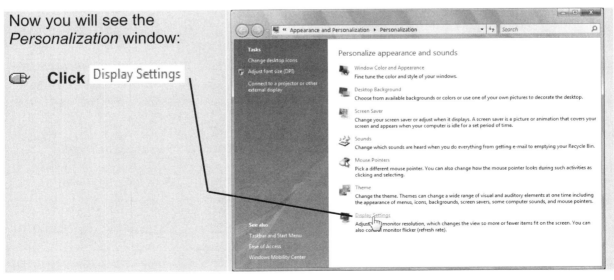

Under Resolution::

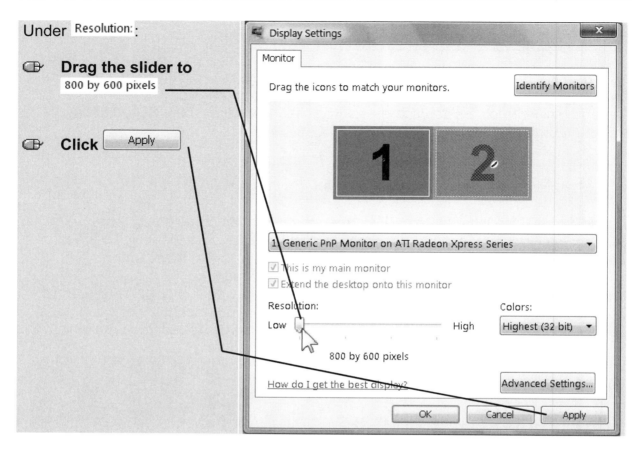

🖱 **Drag the slider to** 800 by 600 pixels

🖱 **Click** Apply

Now you can see what the desktop will look like if you choose this resolution.

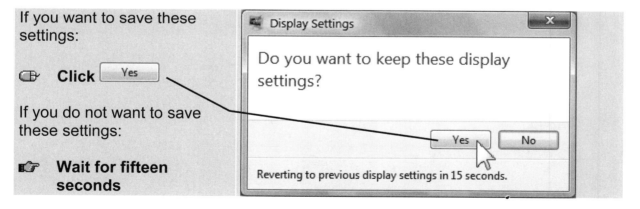

If you want to save these settings:

🖱 **Click** Yes

If you do not want to save these settings:

☞ **Wait for fifteen seconds**

If the desktop is fully visible again, you can try other resolutions in the same way. Experiment a little until you are satisfied with the results.

☞ **Close all windows** 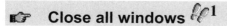 [1]

Problem: the desktop is smaller than the screen.

Usually you will see dark borders next to, above or below the display. You will be able to solve this in the same way as the previous problem. First try to use the buttons on your monitor again to correct the display, otherwise choose a different screen resolution.

Problem: no icons.

Although you can set your desktop to hide all icons, icons can be very useful to open the programs you frequently use. If you cannot see any icons at all, including the *Recycle Bin*, first check if the icons are enabled:

- **Right-click the desktop**

- **Click** View

If the box next to Show Desktop Icons is not

checked ✓ :

- **Check the box** ✓ **next to** Show Desktop Icons

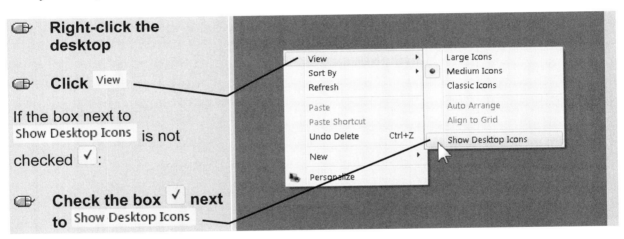

Problem: I do not see the default icons.

Usually your desktop will contain some default icons, such as the *Recycle Bin*. If you cannot see these icons, this is how to make them appear:

- **Right-click the desktop**

- **Click** Personalize

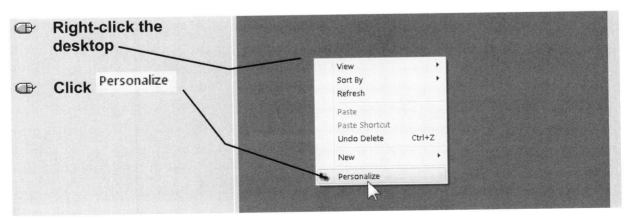

Click Change desktop icons

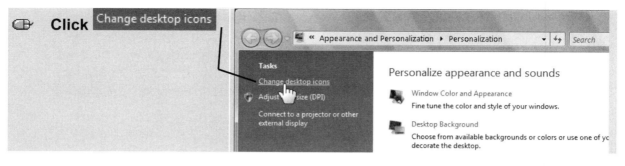

Check the box(es) ☑️
next to the icon(s) you
want to show

Click OK

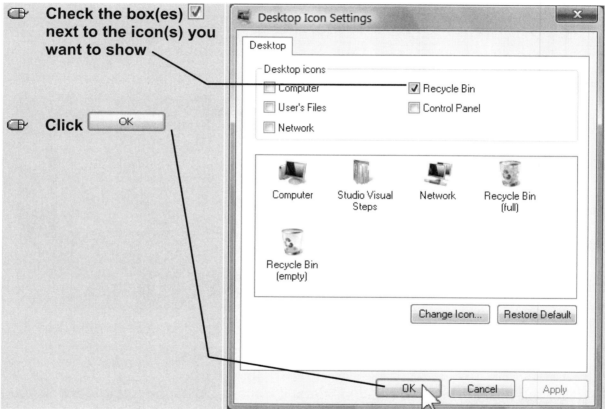

☞ **Close the next window** 🖐️1

Now you will see the selected
icons appear on your
desktop:

⊙ Problem: the icons are too large or too small.

If you do see the icons, but they are the wrong size, you can change them as follows:

☞ **Right-click an empty spot on the desktop**

Please note: be careful not to click an icon or the taskbar.

☞ **Click** View

☞ **Click the desired size**

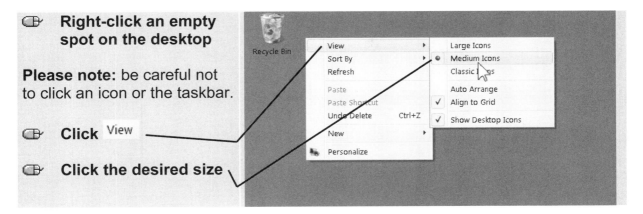

⊙ Problem: the letters on the desktop are too large or too small.

A high resolution causes everything on your desktop to be reduced in size, including all of the text. The text may therefore become harder to read. This is how you can change the size of the text:

☞ **Open the *Personalization* window** $\ell\ell^8$

☞ **Click** Adjust font size (DPI)

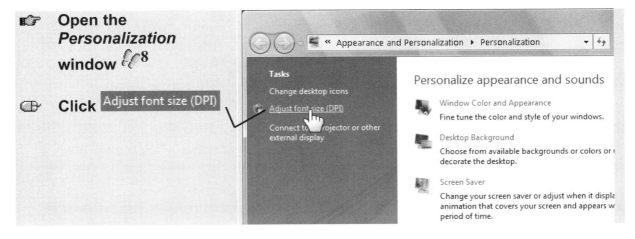

Your screen goes dark and you will need to give permission to continue:

☞ **Click** Continue

Click the radio button next to
Larger scale (120 DPI)

Or click Custom DPI... at the bottom of the window, if you want to choose the size yourself:

Click OK

If you want to save these settings, you will need to reboot your computer.

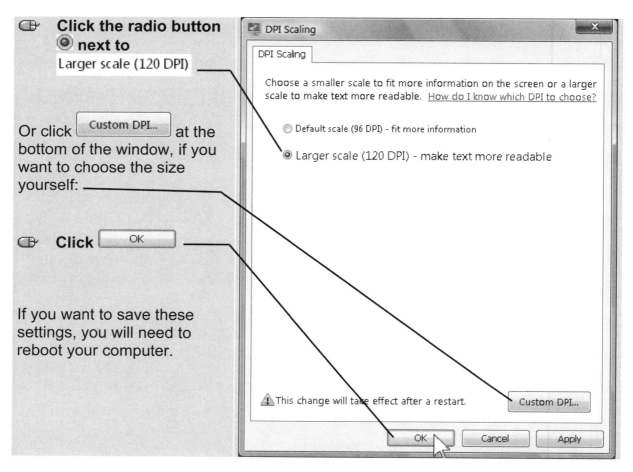

☞ **Close the windows** ℓℓ¹

⇨ **Please note:**

If you choose letters that are too big, you may not be able to see the full text in a given window. Also the text next to a button may only be partially visible. This could become a hindrance as you work.

Adjustments made to the DPI setting will only change the letter size for the desktop and for the standard *Windows Vista* windows. The size of the letters in the programs you use will not change. Some programs allow you to change the letter size in the program itself.

⚪ Problem: the letters are not clear.

Windows Vista uses *ClearType* to improve the smoothness of text. If the letters on your screen are fuzzy or frayed (this is often the case with LCD screens), then check to make sure ClearType is enabled:

⇨ **Please note:**

ClearType will slow down your screen a little.

⇨ **Please note:**

In the *Windows Vista Home Basic* edition, ClearType is not available.

⇨ **Please note:**

In *Internet Explorer* you need to use separate settings to enable ClearType. The *Tip* at the end of this chapter will tell you how to do this.

👉 **Open the Personalization window** 👣 8

🖱 **Click**
Window Color and Appearance

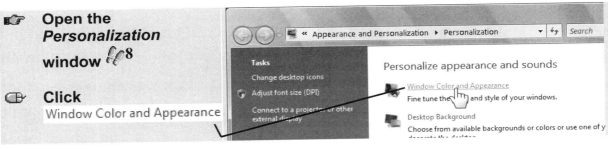

🖱 **Click**
Open classic appearance properties

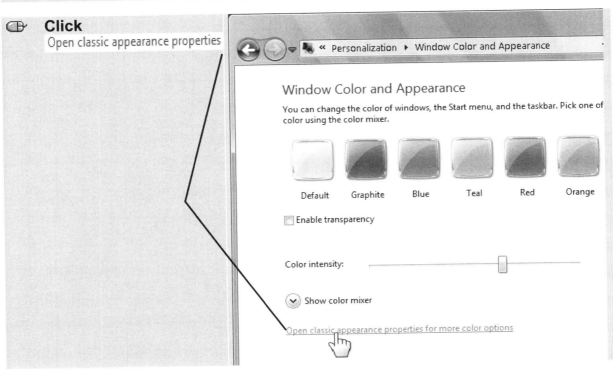

Click Effects...

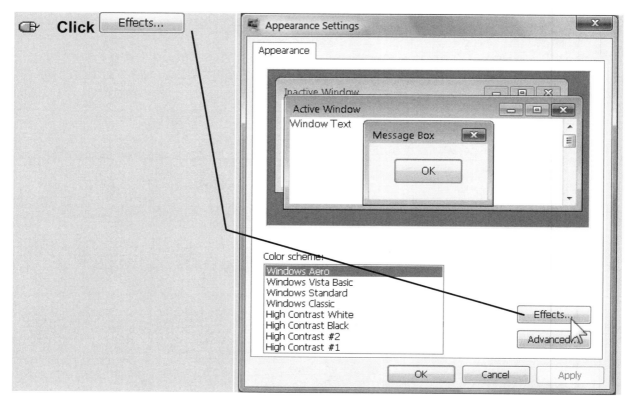

Check the box ☑ next to
Use the following method to sm

Click OK

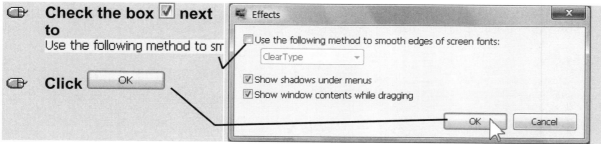

✂ HELP! I do not see the ClearType option.

If you see Standard instead of ClearType :

Click Standard ▼

Click ClearType

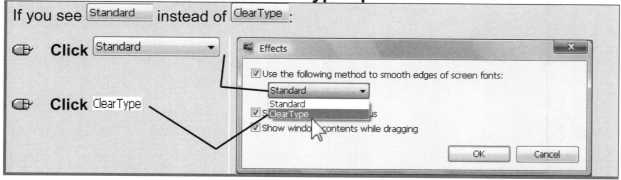

☞ **Close all windows** ✍¹

Problem: I cannot see the *Desktop* icon on the *Quick Launch* toolbar.

By default the *Desktop* icon ■ can be found on the *Quick Launch* toolbar next to the *Start* button. You can use this icon to quickly minimize all active program windows. If you do not see this icon on your toolbar, you can make it appear by doing the following:

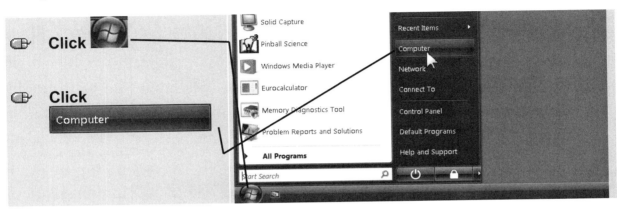

Click 🖱️

Click 🖱️
Computer

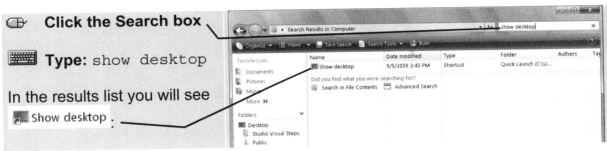

Click the Search box 🖱️

Type: show desktop ⌨️

In the results list you will see
🖳 Show desktop .

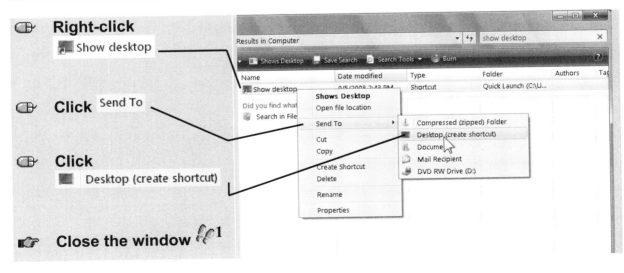

Right-click 🖱️
🖳 Show desktop

Click Send To 🖱️

Click 🖱️
■ Desktop (create shortcut)

Close the window 👣1

The shortcut will be placed on the desktop:

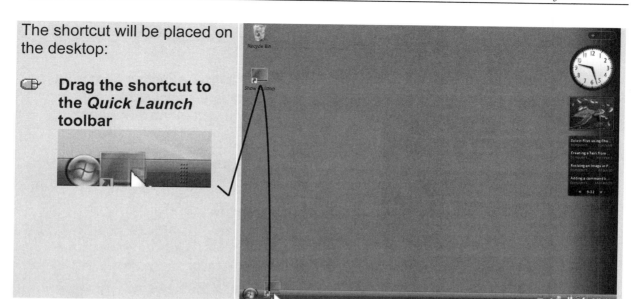

☞ **Drag the shortcut to the *Quick Launch* toolbar**

Now the icon is back again:

The location of the icon on the toolbar depends on the place where you let go of the mouse button. On your screen this might be a different location.

☞ **Delete the shortcut on your desktop** 🐾⁹

✖ HELP! I cannot see the icon.

If you have already placed several icons on the *Quick Launch* toolbar, you may not be able to see some of the icons. To the right of the toolbar you will see :

☞ **Click**

Now you will see the other icons:

You can drag the icon to a different place on the toolbar where it will always be visible.

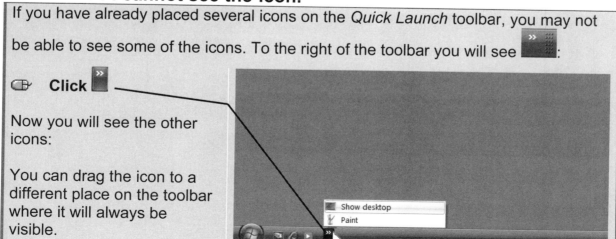

HELP! I do not see the Quick Launch toolbar.

If the *Quick Launch* toolbar is not visible on the taskbar, you can make it appear by doing the following:

☞ **Right-click the taskbar**

☞ **Click** Toolbars

☞ **Click** Quick Launch

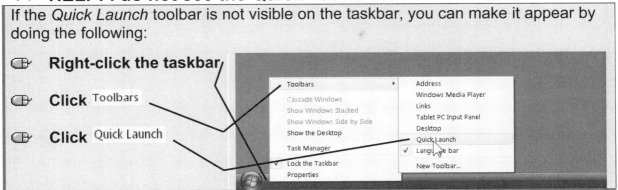

5.7 Windows Vista Does Not Work Properly Anymore

If *Windows Vista* does not function properly anymore, the best thing to do is to reboot the computer. If the keyboard and the mouse are not responding either, you can use the reset button, or just turn the computer off and on again. When you have turned off the computer, wait a moment before turning it back on.

Start *Windows Vista* again and check if everything is back to normal and that you have not lost any data. If there really is a problem with *Windows Vista*, you need to find the cause of the problem. The *Windows* diagnostics can help you do this:

☞ **Click**

⌨ **Type:** msconfig

☞ **Click** msconfig

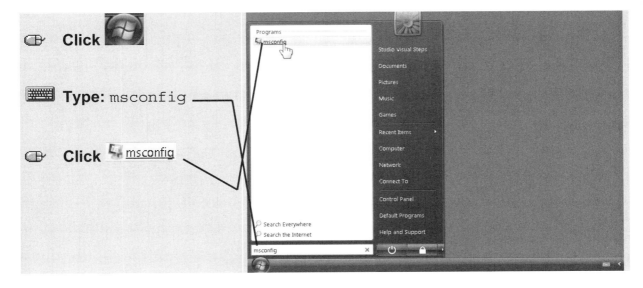

Your screen goes dark and you will need to give permission to continue:

☞ **Click** Continue

Now you will see the startup options:

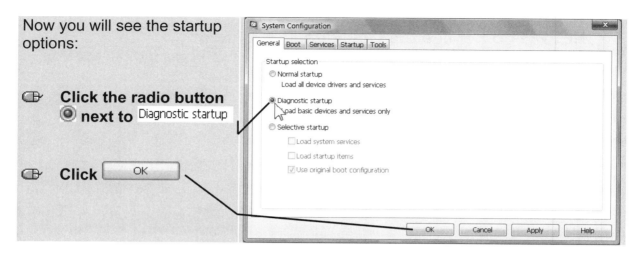

☞ **Click the radio button** next to Diagnostic startup

☞ **Click** OK

After this you will be asked to reboot the computer. *Windows Vista* will now start up in a simpler environment called *Safe Mode*, and only the necessary components will be loaded. Now you can see if *Windows Vista* works properly in this mode. If *Windows Vista* is working as it should, the problem is caused by one of the programs that is loaded when you start up *Windows Vista* in the normal manner.

⇨ **Please note:**

In this mode the security settings will be disabled. So do not connect to the Internet.

After having rebooted you will see a simple screen:

All special features are disabled 🛢️📵🔇 10:13 AM.

☞ **Click** 🪟 Start

⌨️ **Type:** msconfig

☞ **Click** 📄 msconfig

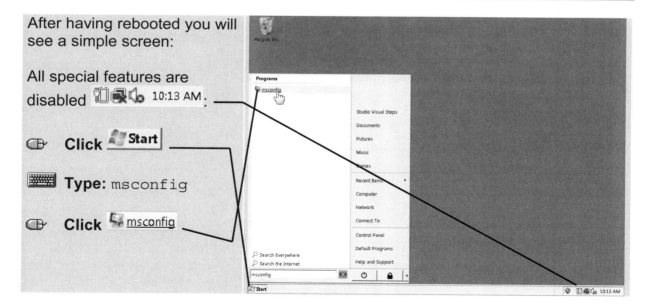

Your screen goes dark and you will need to give permission to continue:

Now you need to revert to the normal startup mode for *Windows Vista,* but you can choose an option that will show you all the boot information during the *Windows Vista* startup:

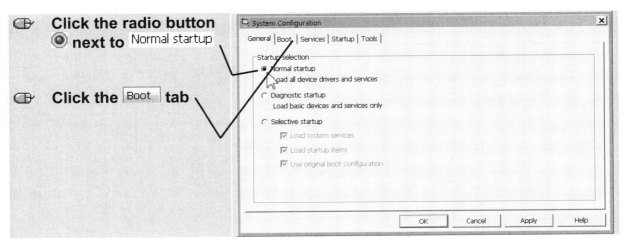

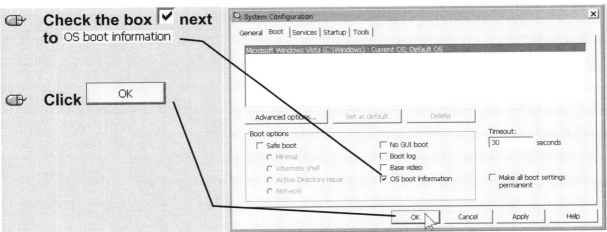

Afterwards you need to reboot the computer. Now you will see what happens when *Windows Vista* starts up and loads the startup programs. If you see an error message, make sure to remember it.

🩹 HELP! I am getting an error message about a certain program.

If the error messages are about programs that start up along with *Windows Vista*, you can temporarily disable these programs:

👉   **Start *MSConfig*** ✍20

👉   **Click the** Startup **tab**

👉   **Check the box ☑ next to the program you want to disable**

👉   **Click** OK

👉   **Reboot the computer**

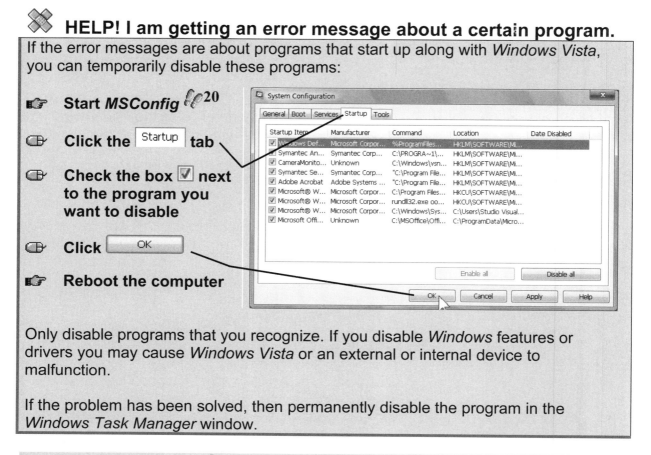

Only disable programs that you recognize. If you disable *Windows* features or drivers you may cause *Windows Vista* or an external or internal device to malfunction.

If the problem has been solved, then permanently disable the program in the *Windows Task Manager* window.

👉   **Close all windows** ✍1

Advanced startup options

In the previous situation it was still possible to (partially) startup *Windows Vista*. If this is not possible anymore, then reboot your computer and press [F8] a few times, before *Windows Vista* starts loading. After pressing [F8] a few times a black screen appears with a boot menu and *Advanced Startup Options*.

Some of these options, like the *Safe Mode,* will let *Windows Vista* start up with only the bare minimum of necessary components. If a problem does not recur after you have rebooted the computer in *Safe Mode*, you can be sure that the operating system is not the cause of the problem. The other options will let *Windows Vista* start up with advanced features that are meant to be used by system administrators and IT professionals.

Restoring the computer

If you choose this option, you will see a list with auxiliary programs (tools) that will help you repair the system by solving startup problems, running diagnostic tests or restoring the system. This option will only be available if these tools were installed on your hard disk. If you have a *Windows* install disk, you will be able to find the *System Repair Programs* on this disk. Insert the disk into the disk drive and wait until you see the main menu.

Safe mode

If you choose this option, *Windows Vista* will be started with a minimum set of drivers and services. The graphical user interface will be restricted, as well as certain desktop features.

Safe mode with networking

If you choose this option, *Windows Vista* will be started in *Safe Mode*, but the drivers and services you need for networking or using the Internet will be started as well.

Safe mode with alternate shell

This option will start up *Windows Vista* in *Safe Mode*, but you will see the black *Windows Command Prompt* window instead of the usual *Windows* user interface. This option is used most often by IT professionals and system administrators.

- Continue reading on the next page -

Enable boot logging

This option will store all information from the boot process in the *ntbtlog.txt* file. This file will list all the drivers that are installed during the startup process. You will be able to use this file to solve any startup problems.

Enable low resolution video (640 x 480 resolution)

If you choose this option, *Windows Vista* will start up the current video driver program in minimal VGA mode. This mode uses a low screen resolution and refresh rate. You need to use this mode if you want to change the screen settings.

Last known good configuration (advanced)

This startup option uses the most recent system settings that worked properly. These settings include the registry settings and all the drivers to be loaded.

Directory services restore mode

This option will start up the *Windows Vista* domain controller running *Active Directory*, which makes it possible to repair the directory service. This option is meant for IT professionals and system administrators and only applies to servers.

Debugging mode

This mode will start up *Windows Vista* in an advanced troubleshooting mode, which will enable IT professionals and system administrators to solve system problems.

Disable automatic restart on system failure

This option prevents *Windows* from automatically restarting if an error causes *Windows Vista* to fail. Choose this option only if *Windows* is stuck in a loop where *Windows* fails, attempts to restart, and fails again repeatedly.

Disable driver signature enforcement

This option allows drivers containing improper signatures to be installed.

Start Windows normally

This option starts *Windows Vista* in its normal mode.

Source: Windows Help and Support

5.8 Background Information

Dictionary	
ClearType	A technology for displaying fonts so that they appear clear and smooth on LCD monitors.
File type	The format of a file, commonly indicated by its file name extension. The file type indicates what program the file is associated with.
Frequently Asked Questions (FAQ)	These are questions frequently asked by users, for example about the way a program works, or about solving a problem. Most manufacturers' websites contain pages with answers to these questions and possible solutions.
Notifications	Notifications are small pop-up windows that are displayed in the notification area of the taskbar. They provide information about a variety of things, including status, progress, and the detection of new devices.
Problem report	Problem reports contain information such as the name of a program that does not function correctly, the date and time when the problem occurred and the version of a program. The problem report helps to establish the kind of problem it is. It contains information about the problem and may even provide a possible solution.
Registry key	A stored information set within the *Windows* registry. The information contained within the key controls shows how specific parts of *Windows* look and function.
Subkey	An element of the registry that contains entries or other subkeys. A tier of the registry that is immediately below a key or a subtree (if the subtree has no keys).
System registry	A database in *Windows* which contains important information about the system configuration.

Source: Windows Help and Support

Re-installing Windows Vista
If *Windows Vista* continues to cause problems, or will not start up at all, your last hope is to install *Windows Vista* once more.
It is always best to try to repair *Windows Vista* first (see *paragraph 5.7 Windows Vista Does Not Work Properly Anymore*).

Warning
It is always a good idea to backup your files before running a new installation of *Windows Vista*. When you execute a clean installation, the current edition of *Windows* will be replaced, as well as all personal files.

This is how to run a complete new installation of *Windows Vista*, which will restore all default settings.
1. Turn your computer on and insert the *Windows Vista* DVD into the drive.
2. Follow the instructions on the *Install Windows* window and click *Install now*.
3. It is recommended to download the latest updates, by using the option on the *Get important updates for installation* window. This will help to ensure a successful installation and help to protect your computer against security threats. You will need an Internet connection to get installation updates.
4. On the *Type your product key for activation* window, we strongly recommend that you type your 25-character product key to help avoid problems during activation.
5. On the *Please read the license terms* window, if you accept the license terms, click *I accept the license terms*.
6. Follow the instructions on each window. On the *Which type of installation do you want?* window, click *Custom*.
7. On the *Where do you want to install Windows?* window, click *Drive Options (advanced)* and select the partition (normally C) where you want to install *Windows*.
8. Click *Next* to begin the installation. You might see a compatibility report.
9. Follow the instructions.

Please note: Be sure to install antivirus software after the installation is complete.

Source: Windows Help and Support

5.9 Tips

  Tip

Work faster without using icons and preview panes
If you disable the icons view in the folder windows, image files will be displayed much faster. Then you will see a standard icon with the file name and type, instead of a miniature image of the file.

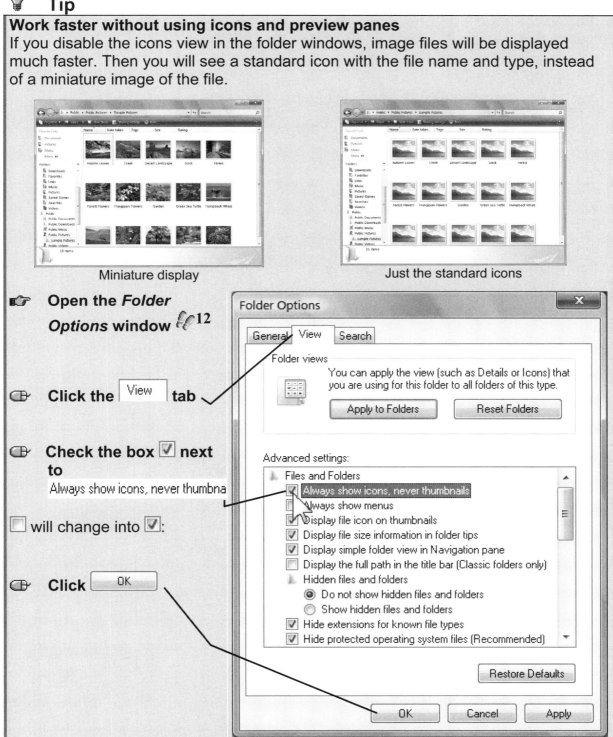

Miniature display   Just the standard icons

☞ **Open the *Folder Options* window** 👣**12**

🖱 **Click the** View **tab**

🖱 **Check the box ☑ next to**
Always show icons, never thumbna

☐ **will change into ☑:**

🖱 **Click** OK

Folder Options

General | **View** | Search

Folder views
You can apply the view (such as Details or Icons) that you are using for this folder to all folders of this type.

[Apply to Folders]   [Reset Folders]

Advanced settings:

- Files and Folders
  - ☑ Always show icons, never thumbnails
  - ☐ Always show menus
  - ☑ Display file icon on thumbnails
  - ☑ Display file size information in folder tips
  - ☑ Display simple folder view in Navigation pane
  - ☐ Display the full path in the title bar (Classic folders only)
  - Hidden files and folders
    - ⦿ Do not show hidden files and folders
    - ○ Show hidden files and folders
  - ☑ Hide extensions for known file types
  - ☑ Hide protected operating system files (Recommended)

[Restore Defaults]

[OK]   [Cancel]   [Apply]

Tip

For administrators only
If you see the *Windows* symbol next to a task or a button, such as this example
[🛡 OK], you will need to be logged on as an administrator and know the
administrator password, in order to be able to execute the task.

 Tip

Disable ClearType in Internet Explorer
This is how you disable ClearType in *Internet Explorer*:

☞ **Open *Internet Explorer* ✆¹⁹**

☞ **Click** 🔧 Tools ▼ , Internet Options

☞ **Click the** [Advanced] **tab**

☞ **Uncheck the box** ☑
next to
[Always use ClearType for HTML]

☑ will change into ☐:

☞ **Click** [OK]

ClearType will now be
disabled in *Internet Explorer*.

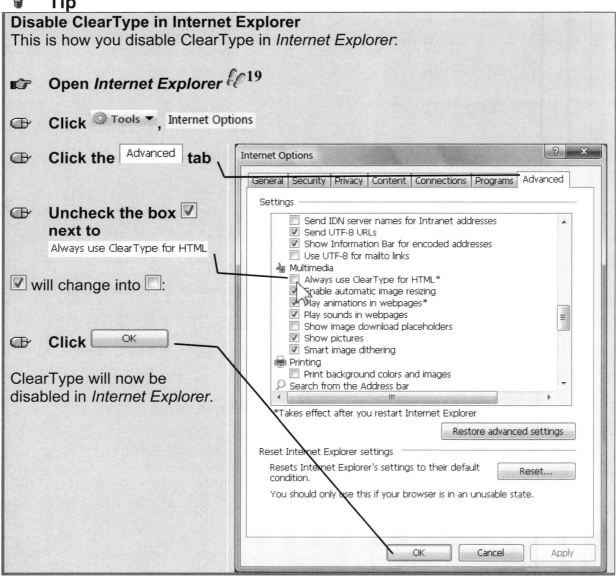

6. Cleaning Up Windows Mail and Internet Explorer

A common problem with e-mail programs such as *Windows Mail* is that it gradually takes longer to process the commands. This is often caused by the large amount of accumulated messages in the received and sent folders. Cleaning up and organizing your e-mails once in a while will usually speed things up again so you can read your messages more quickly and easily. *Windows Mail* itself does not have a built in feature to do this. In this chapter you will learn how to export old messages to other folders. In this way you will reduce the number of old messages to be loaded each time you start your e-mail program while at the same time providing you with a backup copy.

You will also learn different ways of blocking unwanted e-mail messages. Unfortunately, you will discover that none of these methods will block each and every unwanted message. Furthermore, setting security levels too strict can be a problem, because that will sometimes also block the messages you do want to receive.

The Internet browser *Internet Explorer* deserves some attention as well, because undesirable software can reach your computer via the Internet connection. This too can result in your computer processes slowing down, and create all sorts of problems with various other software programs, or with *Windows Vista* itself.

In this chapter you will learn how to:

- delete messages;
- create folders in mail boxes;
- define rules for your messages;
- export messages to an archive;
- import messages;
- block unwanted e-mail messages;
- define safe senders;
- block certain domains;
- delete *Internet Explorer*'s history;
- manage add-ons;
- remove spyware with *Windows Defender*.

6.1 Organizing and Cleaning Up Your E-mail Messages

Keeping your e-mail messages in order will mean you need to organize and clean up these messages from time to time. If you do not do this, you will notice that after a while it will take *Windows Mail* longer to perform its tasks.

☞ **Open *Windows Mail* ℓℓ¹⁸**

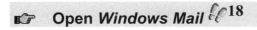 **Delete messages.**

You can delete unimportant messages.

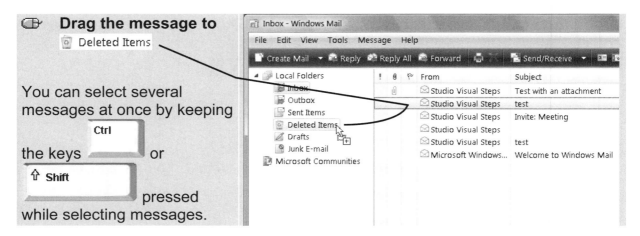

Do not forget to empty the *Deleted Items* folder from time to time:

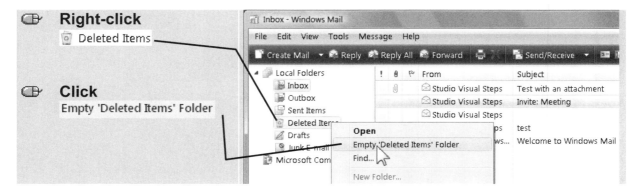

Now you will be asked if you really want to delete these messages:

Organizing messages in folders.

You can create different folders for the messages you want to save.
For example folders for a specific subject or a specific sender:

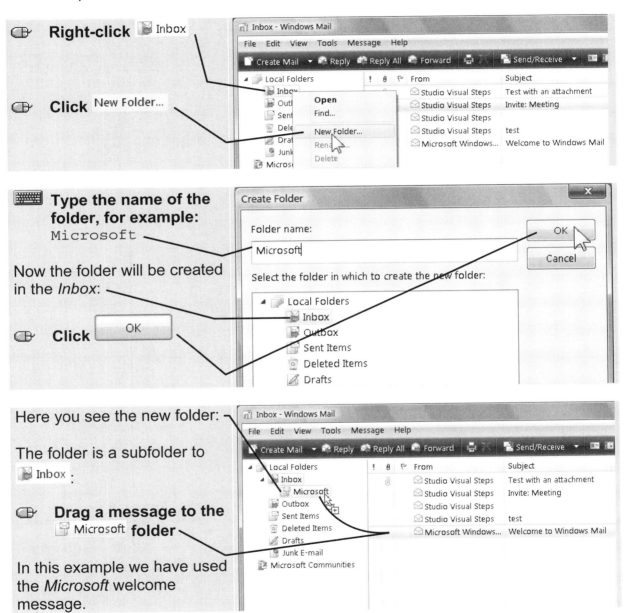

Right-click Inbox

Click New Folder...

Type the name of the folder, for example: `Microsoft`

Now the folder will be created in the *Inbox*:

Click OK

Here you see the new folder:

The folder is a subfolder to Inbox.

Drag a message to the Microsoft **folder**

In this example we have used the *Microsoft* welcome message.

In the new subfolder you can create subfolders again. You can do this in the same way as shown above.

 Please note:

If you delete a subfolder, all the messages in this subfolder will be deleted as well.

 Tip

Collect messages from all folders
If you want to organize your messages in a structured way, it is best to remove messages from both the *Sent Items* folder and the *Inbox* folder. This way, you can save those messages separately and you can have complete collections on a specific subject or sender.

6.2 Message Rules

You can define several rules for your messages, for example if you want to save specific messages in a specific folder automatically. You can define such folder rules based on the sender, the subject or the content of a message. This will help to keep your e-mails organized much better. The easiest way to define a message rule is by selecting a message first:

☞ **Click the** Microsoft
    folder

Now you will see the
message:

☞ **Click the message**

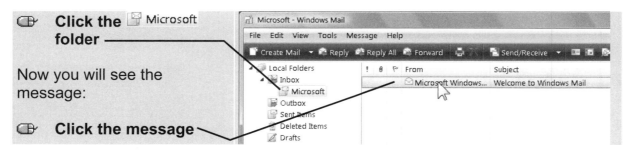

You want to save all
messages from this sender in
this folder:

☞ **Click** Message

☞ **Click**
    Create Rule From Message...

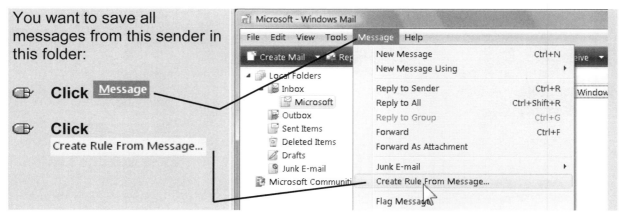

A rule will be defined for all messages from this sender:

You can also define different conditions for the other messages. Click one of the other conditions:

Here you will see that the sender's e-mail address is automatically filled in:

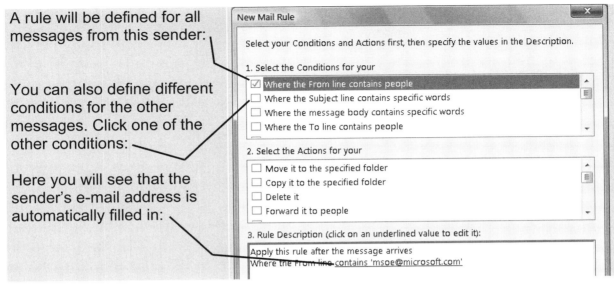

Now you need to select the actions for this rule:

- ☞ **Check the box ☑ next to** Move it to the specified folder

Next, you will need to specify to which folder you want to move the messages:

- ☞ **Click** specified

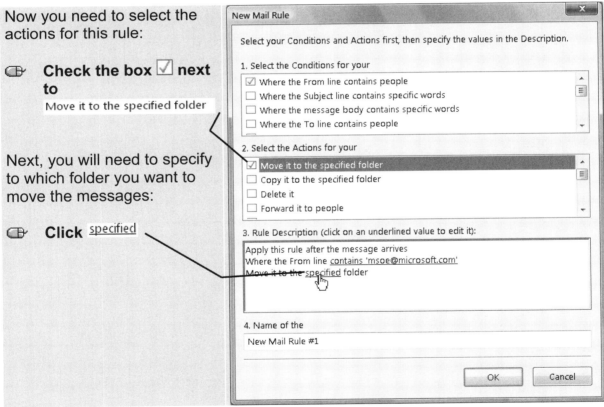

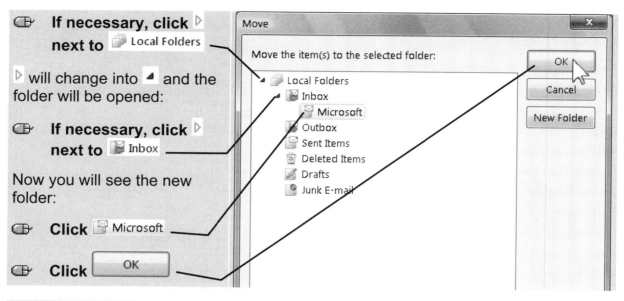

If necessary, click ▷ next to 📄 Local Folders

▷ will change into ◢ and the folder will be opened:

If necessary, click ▷ next to 📧 Inbox

Now you will see the new folder:

Click 📧 Microsoft

Click [OK]

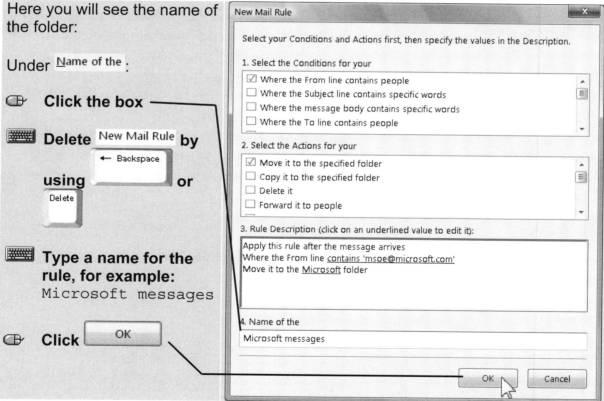

Here you will see the name of the folder:

Under Name of the .

Click the box

Delete New Mail Rule **by**

using [← Backspace] **or**

[Delete]

Type a name for the rule, for example: Microsoft messages

Click [OK]

In the next window:

Click [OK]

All new messages from this sender will be moved to the folder you have defined.

⇨ **Please note:**

Because of this rule you will find new messages in different folders. Watch all your mailboxes carefully. If you have new messages, the folder name will be displayed in **bold** letters and you will see the number of new messages, like this: 📧 **Microsoft** (1) .

💡 **Tip**

Changing message rules

If you want to change a rule, or add a new rule without an existing message, you need to:

👆 **Click** Tools

👆 **Click** Message Rules

👆 **Click** Mail...

To change a rule:

👆 **Click the rule**

👆 **Click** Modify...

To add a new rule:

👆 **Click** New...

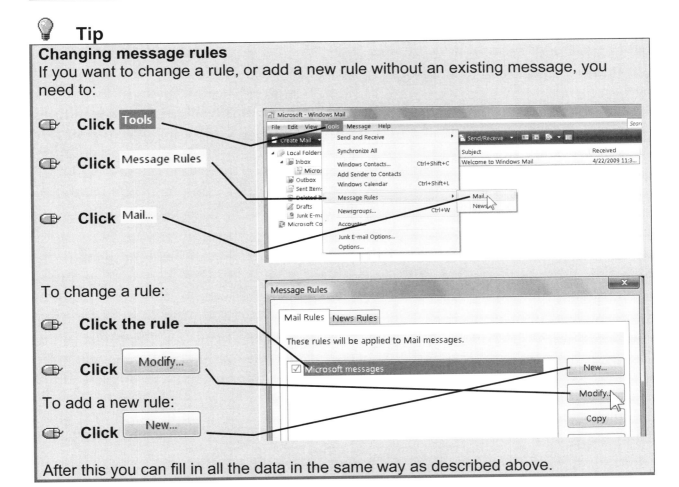

After this you can fill in all the data in the same way as described above.

6.3 Exporting and Importing Messages

Even if you are very organized and regularly clean up your mailbox, the number of messages may increase rapidly over time. Most likely you want to save some of these messages, but a lot of them you will probably never need again. By exporting old messages to backup folders you will then be able to delete them from the regular mailboxes and so speed up the program again.

This is how you export messages:

 Create a new folder in
📧 Inbox **and call it** *Old*
messages 2009 🖐[15]

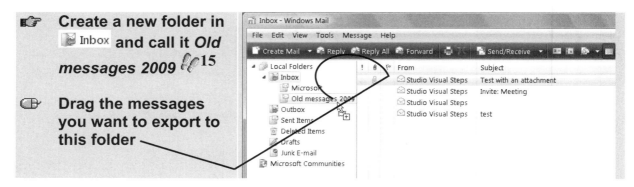

📥 **Drag the messages**
you want to export to
this folder ⟵

💡 **Tip**

Organizing old messages
It is a good idea to create subfolders in the folder you created with specific names for different kinds of messages. If you need to find these messages later on, you will know in which subfolder to look. In the subfolders you will be able to search by date and subject of the messages.

If you still need a message, you can leave it where it is. Only export messages you do not need anymore, but still want to save in a backup folder.
When you have collected all your old messages in the folder, you can export the folder:

📥 **Click** File

📥 **Click** Export

📥 **Click** Messages...

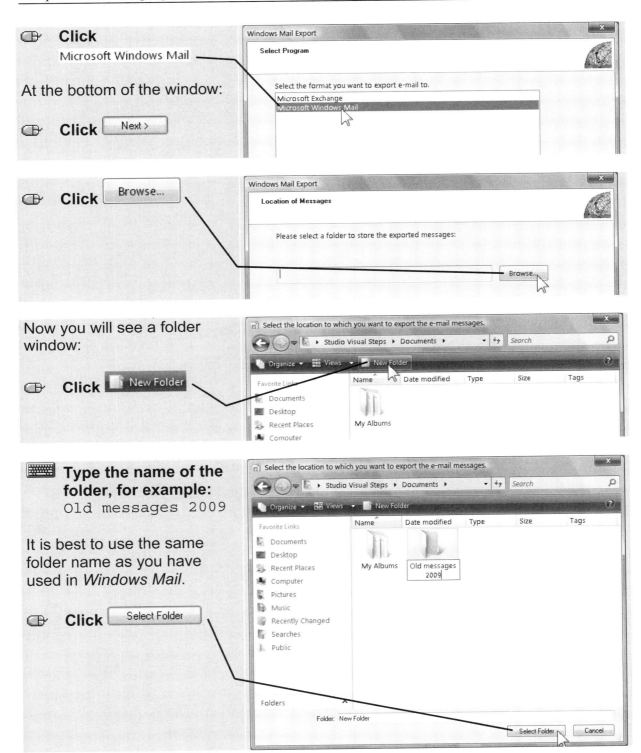

Click Microsoft Windows Mail

At the bottom of the window:

Click Next >

Click Browse...

Now you will see a folder window:

Click New Folder

Type the name of the folder, for example:
Old messages 2009

It is best to use the same folder name as you have used in *Windows Mail*.

Click Select Folder

In the next window:

☞ **Click** [Next >]

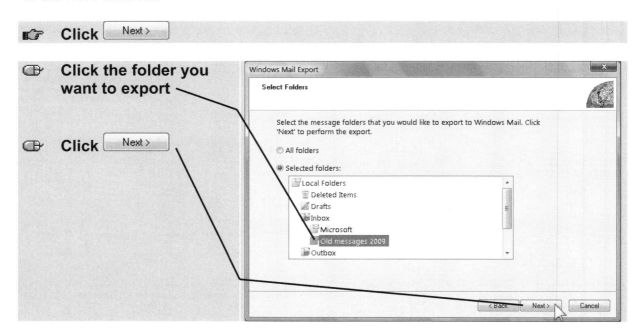

☞ **Click the folder you want to export**

 Click [Next >]

💡 **Tip**

Exporting all messages
With the option ⦿ All folders you will be able to export all of the folders and this way you will get a backup of all your messages.

Now the messages will be exported:

Afterwards you will see this:

At the bottom of the window:

☞ **Click** [Finish]

☞ **Delete the folder with the exported messages** ℓℓ**17**

Now *Windows Mail* will work faster and your mailboxes will be better organized.

If you want to find an older message later on, you will not be able to find this message in your regular mailboxes, or by searching *Windows Mail*. You will need to import the exported folder first:

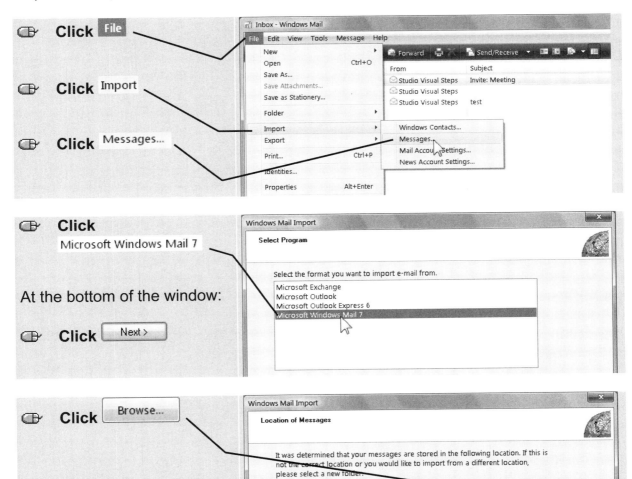

Click the folder you want to import, for example

Old messages 2009

Click Select Folder

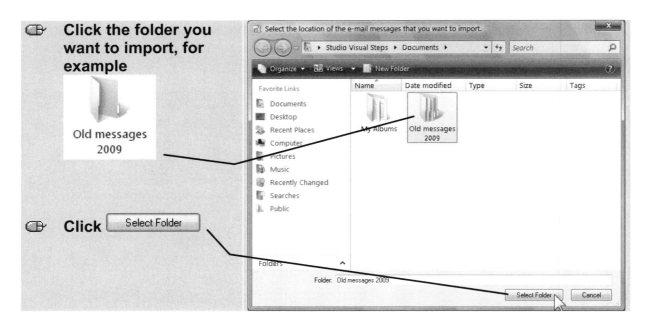

In the next window:

Click Next >

Click the folder you want to import, in this case Old messages 2009

If you have created subfolders, you will not need to import all subfolders separately.

Click Next >

Now the messages will be imported. Afterwards you will see this:

At the bottom of the window:

Click Finish

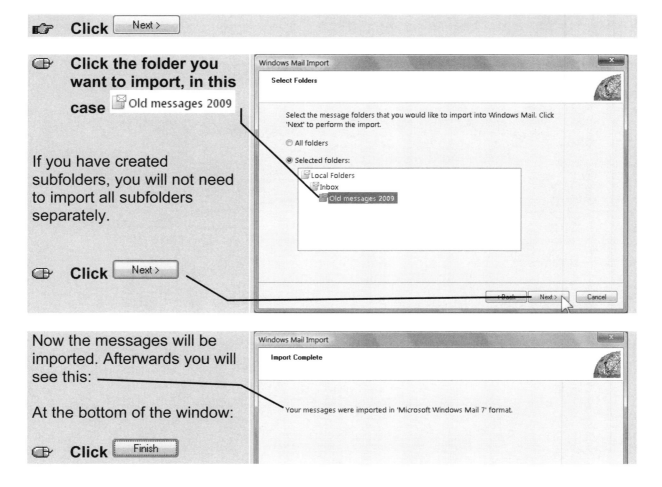

The imported folder will not be placed in the *Inbox*, but in the *Imported Folder* box:

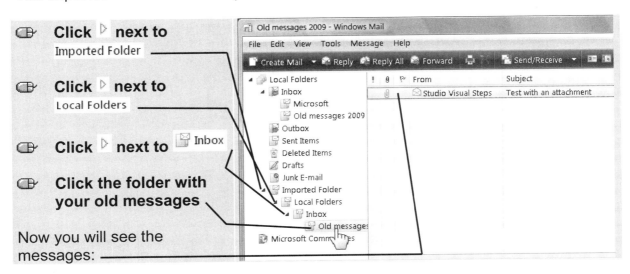

 Click ▷ **next to**
Imported Folder

 Click ▷ **next to**
Local Folders

 Click ▷ **next to** 🗐 Inbox

 **Click the folder with
your old messages**

Now you will see the
messages:

After you have imported the folder with old messages, the original exported folder will still remain stored on your hard disk. This means you can delete the imported folder from *Windows Mail* when you do not need it anymore.

💡 **Tip**

Backup your messages
When you export your messages, you have automatically created a backup copy of your messages on your hard disk. However, if your computer crashes, you will have lost this backup. But if you save your copy of the messages folder in the *Documents* folder, this folder will be automatically included in the regular backup procedure of your computer. It is best to store these computer backups on an external disk. That way, you will always have a copy of your e-mail messages, even if you cannot use your computer anymore.

6.4 Unsolicited E-mail Messages

The spam filter of your Internet service provider will block the bulk of these unwanted messages. But it is impossible to block every message. So you might still find some unwanted messages in your mailboxes. You could define a message rule to move these messages to the *Junk E-mail* folder, but you can also block the sender. This is how you do it:

⇨ **Please note:**

Blocking a message will not stop the message coming in, but will move it to the
 folder.

Click an unwanted message

Click **Message**

Click **Junk E-mail**

Click
Add Sender to Blocked Senders List

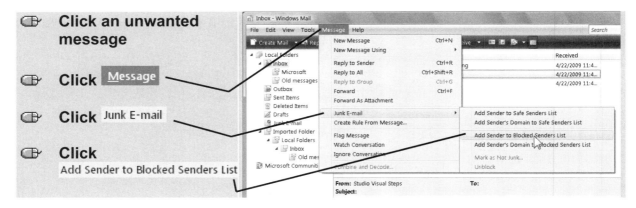

You will see a confirmation window:

Click **OK**

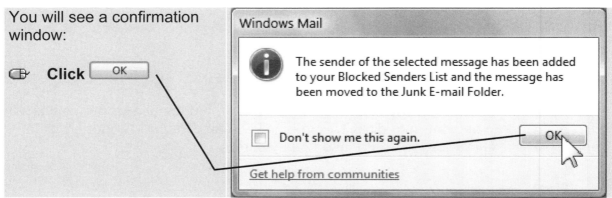

➡ **Please note:**

All messages from this sender will be moved to the 🔲 Junk E-mail folder, including previous messages from this sender.

➡ **Please note:**

In the same way you will be able to block domain names. This means you can block the country name or the Internet address of a sender, such as .com of .uk. Keep in mind that blocking a domain name will block all other messages you receive from this domain. For example, if you block .uk, all your e-mail messages from England will be marked as junk e-mail.

In the *Tools* menu you will find the settings for unwanted e-mail messages, in the *Junk E-mail* options:

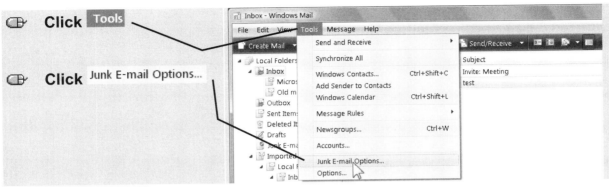

Click Tools

Click Junk E-mail Options...

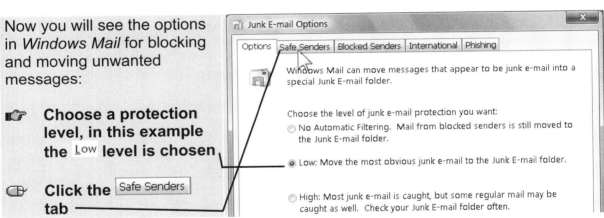

Now you will see the options in *Windows Mail* for blocking and moving unwanted messages:

☞ **Choose a protection level, in this example the** Low **level is chosen**

Click the Safe Senders **tab**

⇨ **Please note:**

If you choose ☐ Permanently delete suspected junk e-mail instead of moving it to the Junk E-mail folder , you risk losing e-mail messages that you might have wanted to see.
This may happen when normal e-mail messages are mistaken for spam. If you choose to delete suspected e-mail messages immediately without checking, you might also delete some bona fide messages. If you move suspected messages to the Junk E-mail folder, you will always be able to check them first.

Messages from these senders will always be accepted:

Of course you want to receive messages from your own contacts. That is why you should enable the Also trust e-mail from my Windows Cont. option:

Now you will add new, safe addresses:

☞ **Click** Add...

Leave the option Automatically add people I e-mail to disabled. When you sent a message to an address that you do not want to receive any messages from, this option would mark the sender as a safe sender.

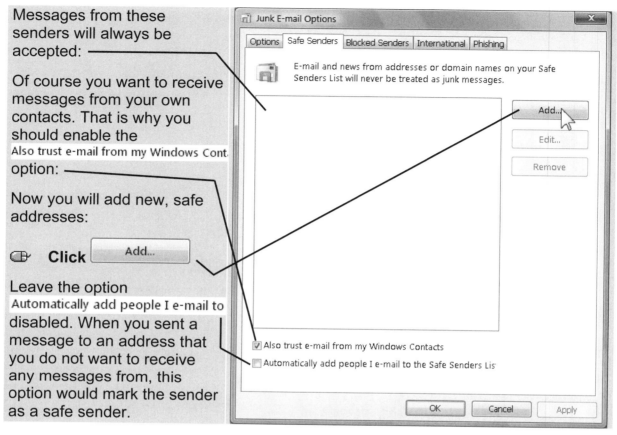

⌨ **Type the address of the safe sender, for example:** info@visualsteps .com

☞ **Click** OK

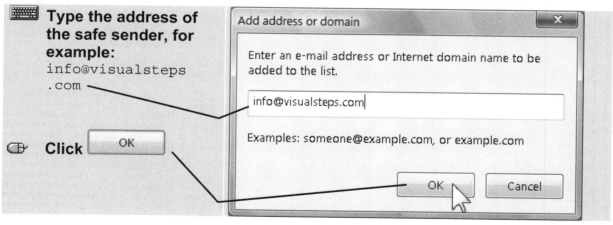

Now the address has been added to the list.

To remove an address:

 Click the address

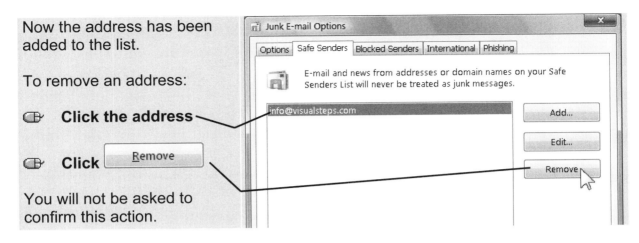

 Click Remove

You will not be asked to confirm this action.

Tip

Add safe senders to the Inbox
You can also add safe senders to the *Inbox*, by selecting the senders from the messages you have received:

 Right-click the message

 Click Junk E-mail

 Click Add Sender to Safe Senders List

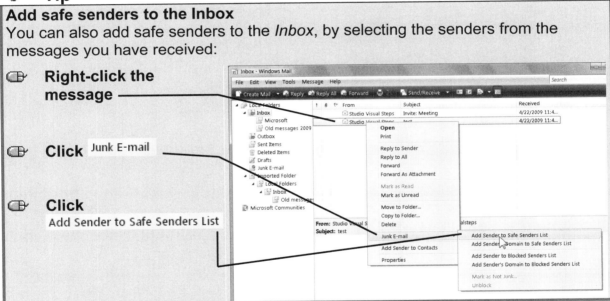

 Click the Blocked Senders **tab**

Now you will see the list with blocked senders.

To unblock the sender:

 Click the address

 Click Remove

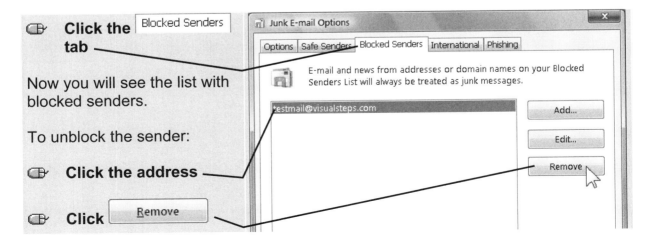

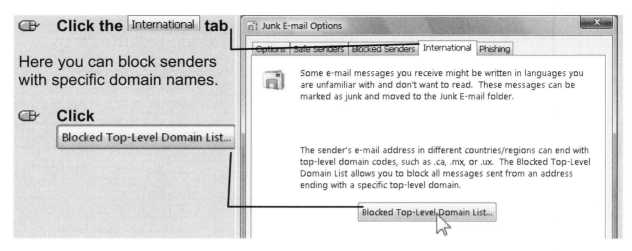

Click the | International | tab

Here you can block senders with specific domain names.

Click

Blocked Top-Level Domain List...

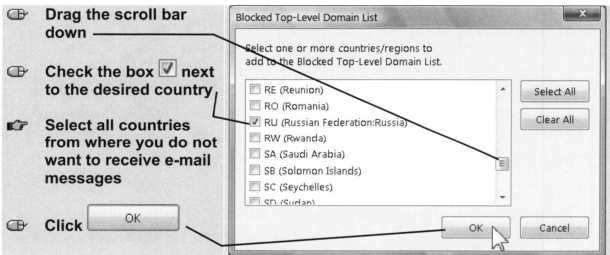

Drag the scroll bar down

Check the box ☑ next to the desired country

Select all countries from where you do not want to receive e-mail messages

Click | OK |

  Tip

Only trusted countries
If you do not wish to receive messages from foreign countries at all, then click
| Select All | and only uncheck the boxes next to the countries you trust, for example GB and US. Domain names like .com, .org, or .edu will not be blocked.

Some spam messages from certain countries do not use the domain name of their country, but a more general name, like .com. It is not wise to block the .com senders, because many reliable companies also use the .com domain. Besides, it is not very useful to block these spam senders since they continually change addresses. At least, you can block messages from non-western languages, for example Cyrillic languages. This is how you do it:

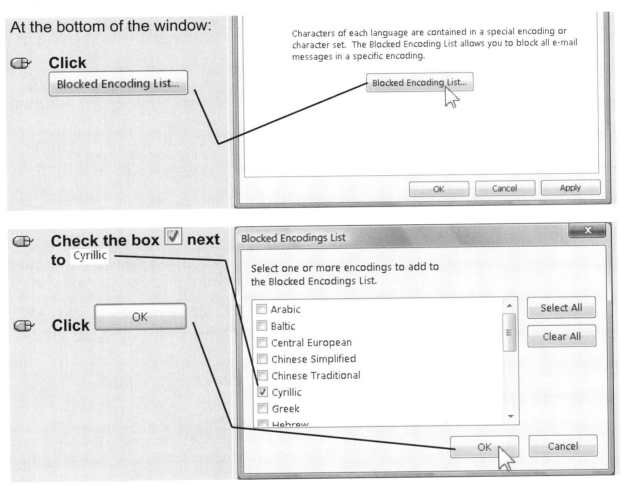

From now on, all messages which contain Cyrillic letters will be blocked.
Now you can take a look at the *Phishing* settings:

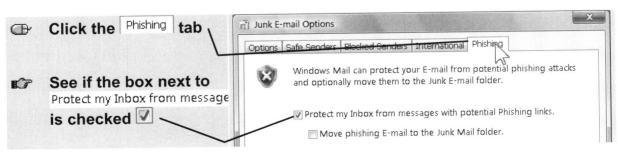

Phishing is a method of swindling people by sending e-mail messages from seemingly reliable addresses (like banks or large companies). In the message you are asked to click a link which will supposedly lead you to the website of that bank or company, but in reality will be a fake website. On this website you will be asked to fill in confidential information, such as passwords or codes. The information is then used by criminals who try to buy things using your bank account, or transfer money from your accounts. It is advisable to leave this protection enabled, even though this antiphishing protection method is not entirely foolproof. You always need to be on the lookout for this kind of fake message yourself.

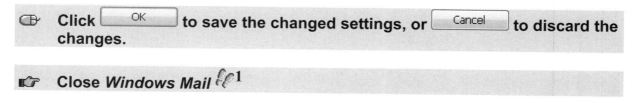

Close *Windows Mail* 𝕝𝕖¹

6.5 Cleaning Up the Internet Explorer History

While surfing the Internet with *Internet Explorer* a lot of data is temporarily stored on your computer. For example, the web pages you have visited, the *Browsing History*, *cookies,* and sometimes passwords and user names. By cleaning up this data you will be able to work faster and safer.

Open *Internet Explorer* 𝕝𝕖¹⁹

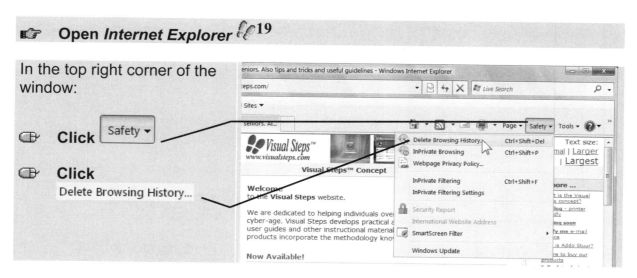

☞ **Choose the items you want to clean up by checking the boxes** ☑ **next to these items**

👆 **Click** Delete

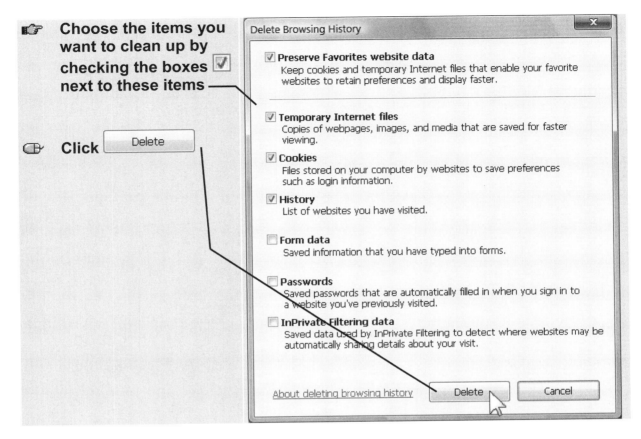

➡ **Please note:**

If you choose to delete all of the items, you will need to fill in your user name and password again when you visit websites where a login is required.

You will not be asked to confirm this action. *Internet Explorer* will start deleting the selected items right away.

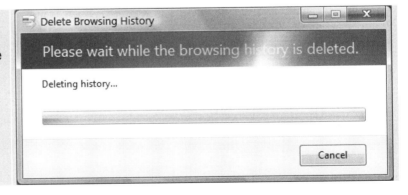

6.6 Add-ons

Add-ons are small programs that will add extra features or toolbars to programs like *Internet Explorer*. These add-ons might slow down your computer. Sometimes, add-ons will be installed without you knowing about it. It is wise to check which add-ons are installed in *Internet Explorer* once in a while:

In the top right corner of the window:

☞ **Click** Tools ▾

☞ **Click** Manage Add-ons

Now you will see all the installed add-ons

To disable an add-on:

☞ **Click the add-on**

At the bottom of the window:

☞ **Click** Disable

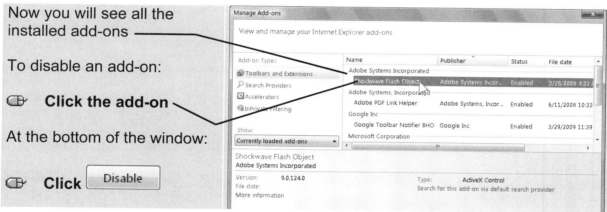

You will now see that this add-on has been Disabled :

☞ **If necessary, disable other add-ons as well**

At the bottom of the window:

☞ **Click** Close

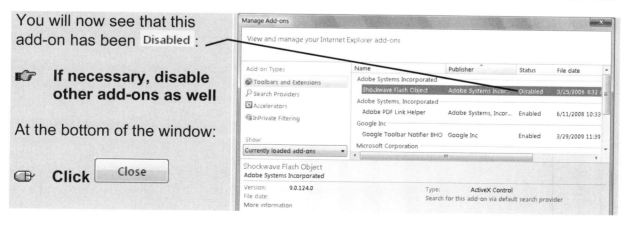

Tip

Which add-ons should you disable?
Do you see several add-ons you do not know? Disable them and see if it makes a difference. If you do not notice any changes, leave the add-on disabled. *Internet Explorer* might work faster this way.
Dou you miss a certain add-on? You can enable the add-on in the same window.
First click the add-on, then click `Enable` and `Close`.

Since add-ons are usually loaded when you open *Internet Explorer*, you might have to restart *Internet Explorer* for the changes to take effect.

☞ **Close *Internet Explorer*** 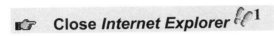[1]

☞ **Open *Internet Explorer*** 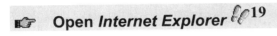[19]

If everything still works fine, you can leave the add-on(s) disabled.

☞ **Close *Internet Explorer*** 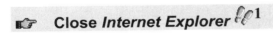[1]

6.7 Removing Spyware

Apart from installing add-ons, which are visible, some websites or viruses might install invisible *spyware* on your computer. Spyware is software that can run without you knowing about it, and without your permission. Spyware can start pop-up windows containing advertising messages, change settings (for example your default home page), or collect information about your surfing behavior on the Internet. This might slow down your computer and it is always a security threat.
Like other antispyware programs, *Windows Defender* can prevent the installation of spyware on your computer. However, it is possible that there still is spyware installed. To check for installed spyware, you can run a full scan with *Windows Defender* or some other antispyware program.
Windows Defender is a standard feature of *Windows Vista*.

 Please note:

Do you use another antispyware program, or does your antivirus program also check for spyware? Then run the check with that program. Most of these programs work in similar fashion.

This is how you run a scan with *Windows Defender*:

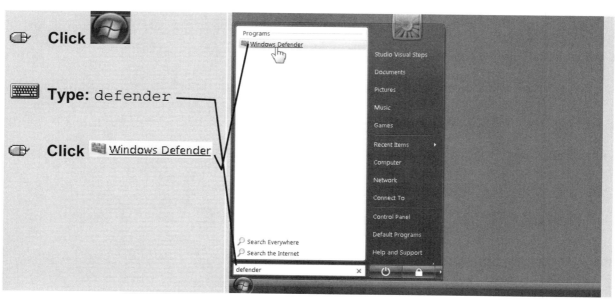

Click

Type: defender

Click Windows Defender

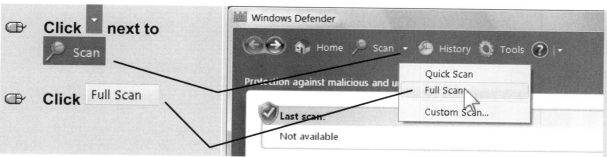

Click ▼ next to Scan

Click Full Scan

Now the scanning process will begin. This might take an hour or even longer, depending on the size of your hard drive and the amount of data it contains.

Meanwhile, you can continue working, although your computer might perform a bit slower.

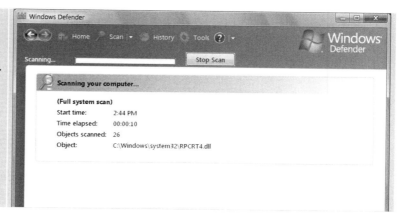

If no spyware is detected, you will see this window after the scan has been completed:

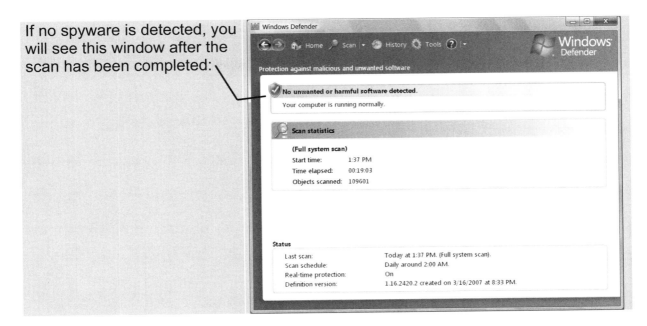

If *Windows Defender* does find something, you will see this window:

Windows Defender will indicate that it has found potentially unwanted or harmful items.

Also, the risk factor will be indicated. In this example it is Severe/High alert level: 1 :

Now you will see which items are potentially dangerous:

☞ **Click** Review items detected

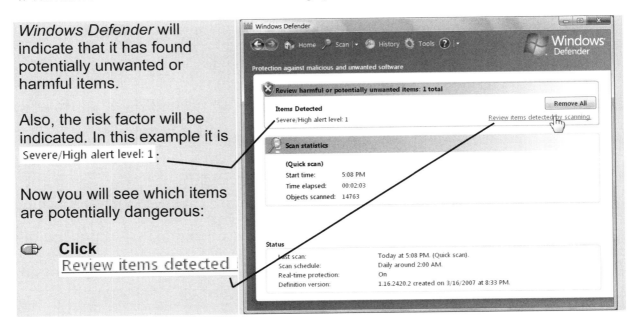

In this example, one item was found:

You will see extensive information on the selected item:

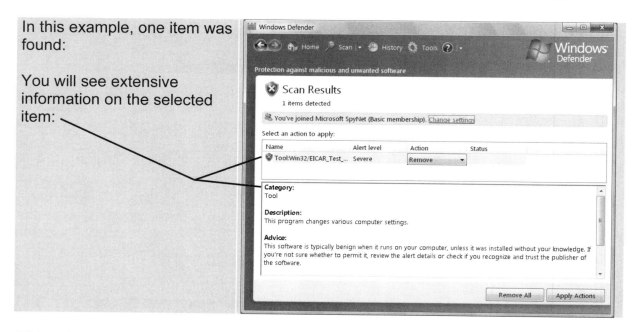

This information contains a description of the item and an advice by *Microsoft* on what to do with this item.

Below the description you will see the location of this item on your hard drive. Sometimes you might find a hyperlink at the bottom of the page, which will lead you to a *Microsoft* webpage where you can find additional information about this item.

If potentially dangerous items were found, you can choose what to do with them:

- Ignore : select this option if you are sure you want to save the item. Selecting this option will not affect the item.
- Quarantine : select this option if you have doubts about the item. The item will be set apart, but will not be removed. If you find out later on that you really need this file or program, you will always be able to restore it.
- Remove : select this option if you want to remove the item from your hard disk.
- Always allow : select this option if the item looks familiar and you are sure you always want to allow the item. The item will not be displayed any longer when running future scans.

If any suspicious items are detected on your computer, you can choose what to do with them yourself. If you have any doubts, check the information below the item and look for a hyperlink to the *Microsoft* website. There you will find additional information. If you do not see a hyperlink, you can always search the Internet for more information.

In this example the item is put in quarantine:

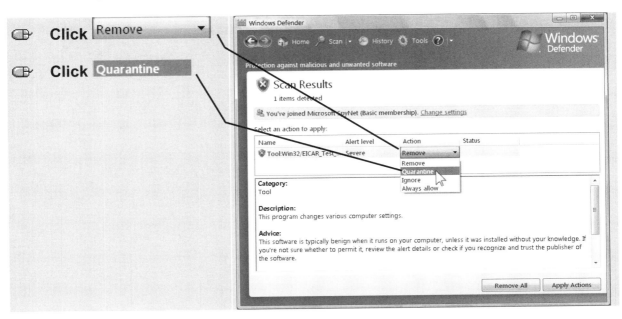

Of course you are free to choose one of the other suggested actions. If multiple items are found, you can choose a different action for each item.

☞ **View the detected items on your computer and select the desired actions**

This is how you execute the selected actions:

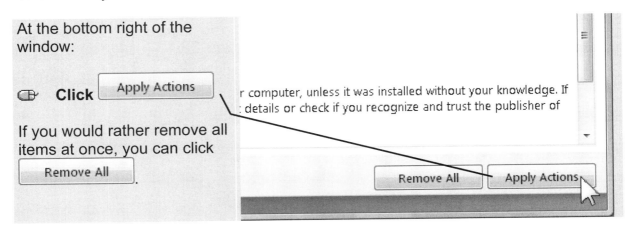

Windows Defender has executed your command. The status has now changed to:

Name	Alert level	Action	Status
🛡 Tool:Win32/EICAR_Test_...	Severe	Quarantine	Succeeded

Windows Defender allows you to set automatic scans as well:

Click Tools

Click Options

Adjust the scan settings for the frequency and type of scan

A quick scan will check only the most vulnerable and critical locations on your computer. An automatic scan will usually be a quick scan.

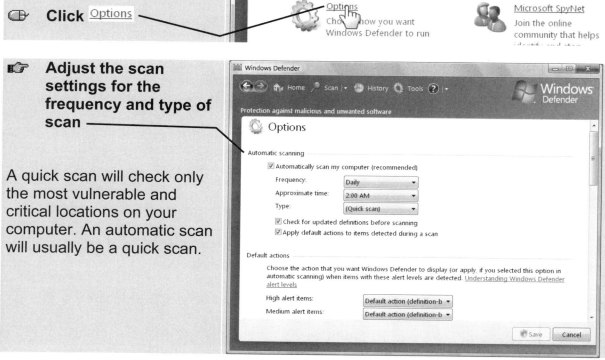

Drag the scroll bar down

Now you will see the items that will be checked by *Windows Defender*.

To save the changes:

Click Save

Click Continue

Or else:

Click Cancel

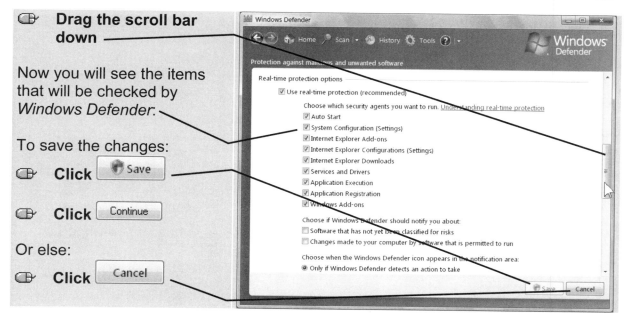

If you have clicked 🔲 Save , your screen goes dark and you will be asked for permission to continue.

☞ **Close all windows** ⁱ

Internet poses the biggest threat for your computer's safety, because an Internet connection keeps you connected to other computers all the time. If you keep your security measures up to date and automatically receive *Windows Vista* updates, you will reduce the chance of getting viruses, spyware and other unwanted software considerably. Your computer will work faster and you will experience fewer problems with your software programs.

In these Visual Steps books you will find extensive information on updating *Windows*, installing and setting up an antivirus program, and setting up a firewall:

Internet and E-mail for SENIORS with Windows Vista
Studio Visual Steps
ISBN 978 90 5905 284 0

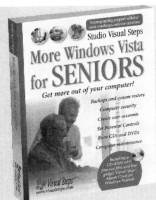

More Windows Vista for SENIORS

Studio Visual Steps
ISBN 978 90 5905 055 6

6.8 Background Information

Dictionary	
Add-on	A program that adds features to a web browser, for example *Internet Explorer*. Examples of add-ons include extra toolbars, animated mouse pointers, and interactive web content. Add-ons are also known as ActiveX controls, plug-ins, browser extensions, or Browser Helper Objects.
ActiveX	Technology for creating interactive web content such as animation sequences, credit card transactions, or spreadsheet calculations.
Cookies	Small text files that websites put on your computer to store information about you and your preferences. For example, cookies will be used when you book a trip via a website and you are asked to fill in personal information. When you click to continue onto the next page, your details are carried over by the information stored in the cookie.
Domain	The name that succeeds the last dot of an e-mail or Internet address. The domain name may indicate a country, such as .uk or .ca, or the kind of organization, such as .com of .org.
Export	Store data to a file, in order to use the data in another program.
History	*Internet Explorer* stores a history of all the websites you have visited. You can delete this information to save space on your hard disk or to protect your privacy.
Import	Read data from a file that is created by another program.
Message rule	A way to manage e-mail messages by checking to see if they meet certain conditions and deciding what to do with them based on those conditions. For example, you could create a rule to place messages from a particular person into a specific folder. Rules are also known as filters.
Spam	Unsolicited commercial e-mail (UCE). Also known as junk e-mail.
Spyware	Software that can display advertisements (such as pop-up ads), collect information about you, or change settings on your computer, generally without obtaining your consent.
Source: Windows Help and Support	

ActiveX add-ons

ActiveX controls add graphical features to web pages and can enhance these pages. Viewing these pages will become easier and much more attractive. However, Active X controls may become a security threat. Be very careful when installing ActiveX controls or add-ons onto your computer.

This is why it is advisable not to use ActiveX controls if you can also view a website without these controls. Some web pages or tasks really demand the use of Active X. In this case you will need to decide if installing the Active X control is really important to you.

You can remove ActiveX add-ons in the same way you remove other add-ons. But instead of disabling them, you need to remove them with a specific button you will find in the window for removing ActiveX add-ons.

Types of cookies

There are different types of cookies. Some types are necessary in order to be able to use a website, others will only affect your privacy. These are the different types:

- Temporary cookies (or session cookies) are removed from your computer after you close *Internet Explorer*. Websites use them to store temporary information, such as items in your shopping cart.
- Persistent cookies (or saved cookies) remain on your computer after you close *Internet Explorer*. Websites use them to store information, such as your sign-in name and password, so that you don't have to sign in each time you go to a particular site. Persistent cookies can remain on your computer for days, months, or even years.
- First-party cookies come from the website that you're viewing and can be either persistent or temporary. Websites might use these cookies to store information that they will re-use the next time you go to that site.
- Third-party cookies come from other websites' advertisements (such as pop-up or banner ads) on the website that you're viewing. Websites might use these cookies to track your web use for marketing purposes.

Read the *Tips* at the end of this chapter to find out how you can block or allow cookies for specific websites.

Source: Windows Help and Support

6.9 Tips

 Tip

Blocking or allowing cookies
Cookies can put your privacy at risk, but they may be essential for using certain websites. For example, to use Internet banking features you must allow cookies from your bank. Many travel and shopping sites also use cookies to keep track of the shopping cart. This is how you allow or block cookies in *Internet Explorer*:

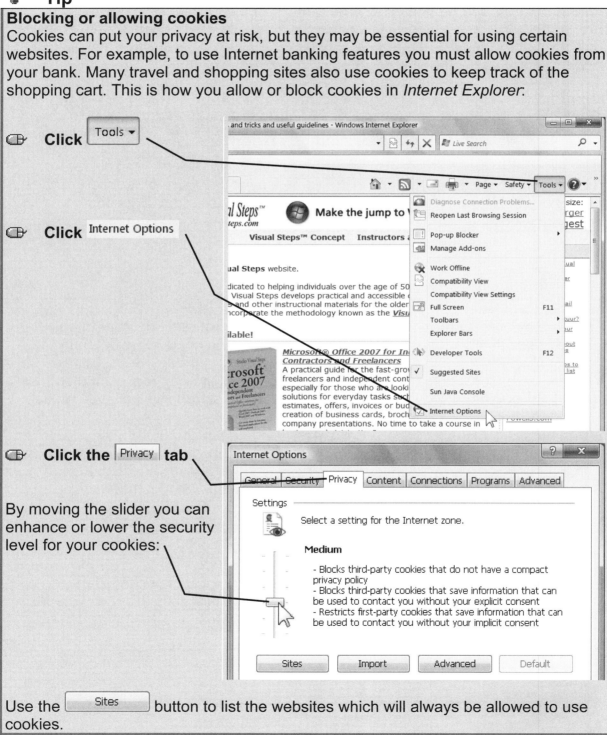

Use the [Sites] button to list the websites which will always be allowed to use cookies.

💡 Tip

Do not send automatic a read receipt

If you respond to a spam message, the sender will know that your e-mail address is a valid address, and you will receive even more spam messages. So never respond to these messages and do not use (fake) links that will supposedly allow you to sign off. Also, check the Returning Read receipts options:

☞ **Click** `Tools`

☞ **Click** `Options...`

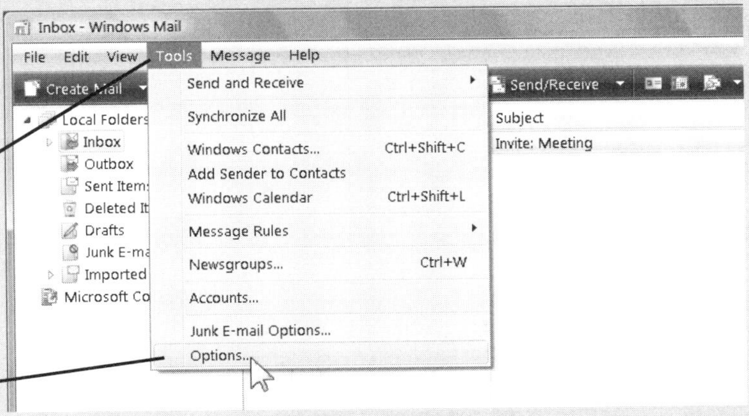

☞ **Click the** `Receipts` **tab**

☞ **Choose the Returning Read option**
`Never send a read receipt`

or

`Notify me for each read receipt rec`

☞ **Click** `OK`

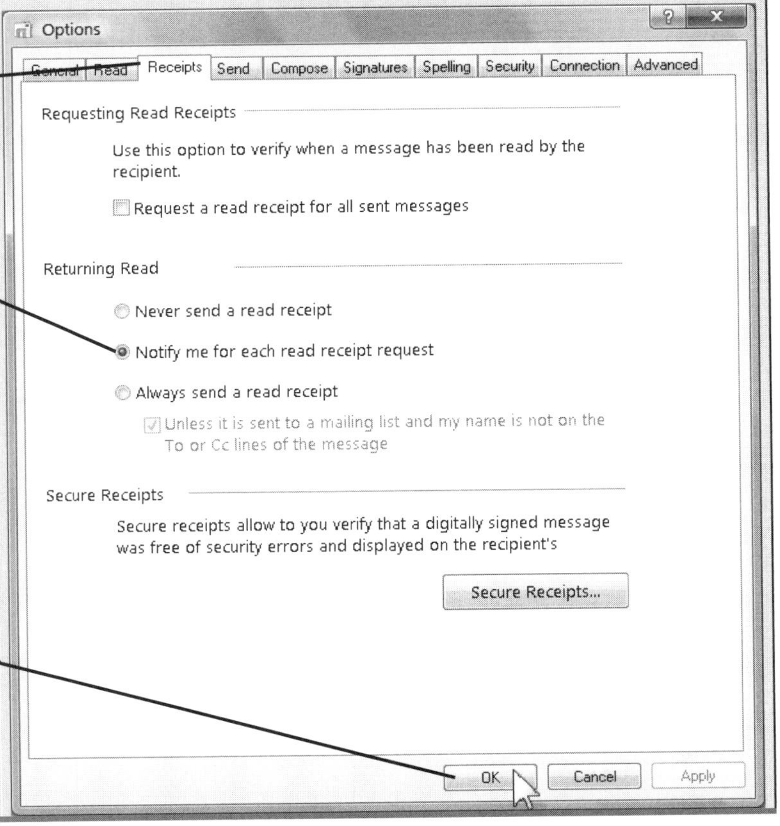

Notes

Write your notes down here.

Appendix A. How Do I Do That Again?

As you work through this book you may have noticed these footsteps 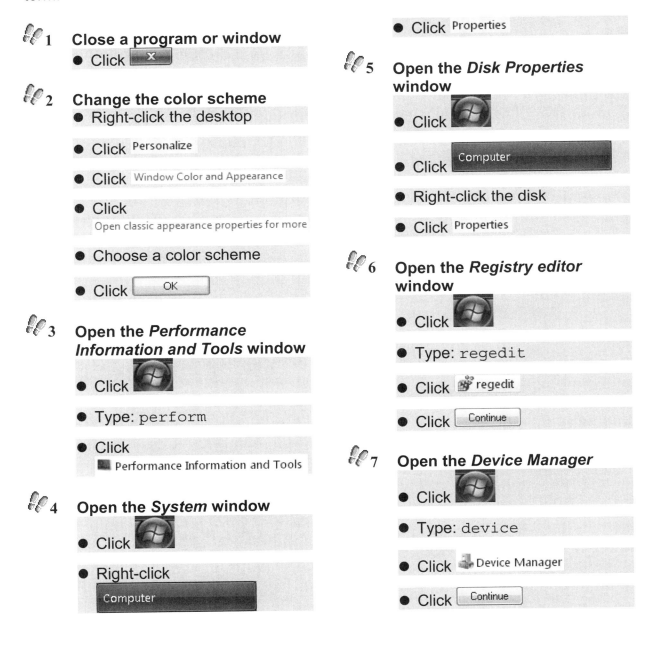ᵡ with a number beside them. This number indicates that there is a listing in the *Appendix A. How Do I Do That Again?*. Here you will find many short descriptions of how to perform specific tasks. Use the number to find the listing here in this appendix. This may come in handy when you have forgotten what is meant by a certain computer term.

1 Close a program or window
- Click [X]

2 Change the color scheme
- Right-click the desktop
- Click Personalize
- Click Window Color and Appearance
- Click
  Open classic appearance properties for more
- Choose a color scheme
- Click [OK]

3 Open the *Performance Information and Tools* window
- Click
- Type: perform
- Click
  Performance Information and Tools

4 Open the *System* window
- Click
- Right-click
  Computer

- Click Properties

5 Open the *Disk Properties* window
- Click
- Click Computer
- Right-click the disk
- Click Properties

6 Open the *Registry editor* window
- Click
- Type: regedit
- Click regedit
- Click [Continue]

7 Open the *Device Manager*
- Click
- Type: device
- Click Device Manager
- Click [Continue]

8 **Open the *Personalize* window**
- Right-click the desktop

- Click Personalize

9 **Delete a file, icon, or shortcut**
- Right-click the file, icon, or shortcut

- Click Delete

10 **Open a file or a folder**

- Click

- Click Computer

- Double-click the drive

- Double-click the folders until you have found the file

- If you want to open the file, double-click the file

11 **Minimize a window**
- Click

12 **Open the *Folder and Search Options* window**
- Click Organize

- Click Folder and Search Options

13 **Create a restore point**

- Click

- Click Control Panel

Under System and Maintenance, click Back up your computer

- Click Create a restore point or change settings

- Click Continue

14 **Open the *Control Panel***

- Click

- Click Control Panel

15 **Create a folder in the Inbox**
- Right-click Inbox

- Click New Folder...

- Type the folder name

- Click OK

16 **Move messages**
- Click a message or select multiple messages

- Drag the message(s) to the desired folder

17 **Delete messages or folders**
- Right-click the message or the folder

- Click Delete

18 **Open *Windows Mail***

- Click

- Click E-mail Windows Mail

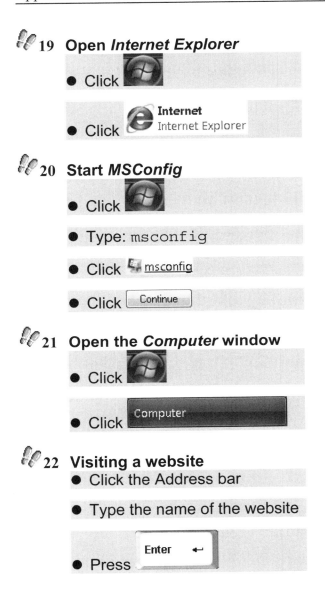

19 Open *Internet Explorer*

- Click

- Click **Internet** Internet Explorer

20 Start *MSConfig*

- Click

- Type: msconfig

- Click msconfig

- Click [Continue]

21 Open the *Computer* window

- Click

- Click [Computer]

22 Visiting a website
- Click the Address bar

- Type the name of the website

- Press [Enter ↵]

Appendix B. Index

Microsoft Office 2007 for Independent Contractors and Freelancers

Microsoft Office 2007 for Independent Contractors and Freelancers
Practical Office Solutions for the self-employed and freelancer

Author: Studio Visual Steps
ISBN: 978 90 5905 295 6
Book type: Paperback
Nr of pages: 408 pages
Accompanying website:
www.visualsteps.com/office2007freelance

A practical guide for the fast-growing segment of freelancers and independent contractors. Written especially for those who are looking for efficient solutions for everyday tasks such as creating estimates, offers, invoices or budgets and for the easy creation of business cards, brochures, newsletters and company presentations. No time to take a course in business administration? Work instead through this Visual Steps book at home and in your own tempo! Do the chapters that specifically apply to your business. As you follow each step, the results appear directly on your computer screen. In a few short hours you can complete an entire course. You will end up with a series of useful documents that can be directly applied to your business.

Characteristics of this book:
- practical, useful topics
- geared towards the needs of the self-employed, independent contractor or freelancer
- clear instructions that anyone can follow
- handy, ready-made templates available on this website

Topics covered in this book:
- **Excel 2007:** estimates, quotes, invoices, projects, schedules, mileage tracking
- **Word 2007:** letterhead, newsletters and mailing labels
- **Publisher 2007:** business cards, brochures, websites
- **PowerPoint 2007:** company presentations
- **Outlook 2007:** customer, vendor and contact information, organize and archive mail
- **Business Contact Manager 2007:** project administration, manage leads and prospects
- **Windows Vista and XP:** computer maintenance, back-ups and security

Windows Vista and Internet for CHILDREN

Windows Vista and Internet for children
For anyone 9 years old and up

Author: Studio Visual Steps
ISBN: 978 90 5905 056 3
Book type: Paperback
Nr of pages: 208 pages
Accompanying website:
www.studiovisualsteps.com/vista

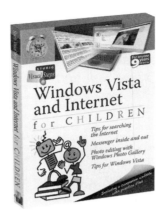

Do your (grand)children chat or mail with friends? Do they know how to use a chat program inside and out? This book will not only show them how to safely use Messenger but lots of other things too. Such as how to best find information on the Internet for their homework assignments. How to make their own e-mail address and do a video chat. How to organize files and folders and how to keep the desktop tidy. And what is really fun, is learning how to use Windows Photo Gallery to edit their own photos.
All of the exercises in this book can be done on their own computer. Everything is clearly explained step by step and each step includes a full color picture. You can get started right away!

In this book children will learn how to:
- mail with Windows Mail and Windows Live Hotmail
- chat with Windows Live Messenger
- do a video chat
- edit photos in Windows Photo Gallery
- search for information on the Internet
- create and open folders
- move, search and delete files
- customize your desktop
- change the color of your windows
- add a gadget to Windows Sidebar

For parents, teachers and caregivers
All Visual Steps books are written following a step by step method. They are designed as self-study guides for individual use. They are also well-suited for use in a group or classroom setting. More information for parent, teachers and caregivers can be found at the companion website for this book: www.studiovisualsteps.com/vista